Praise for Greg Gutfeld's

The Bible of Unspeakable Truths

"Gutfeld blends George Carlin-esque musings on everything he considers wrong with the world with observations on things that need to be fixed...Pick up the book and be subjected to some unspeakably funny truths."　　　　　　　　　　—Huffington Post

"Supersexyawesome!...His conservative humor is sharp and hip—Republicanism with a human face."
　　　　　　　　—Thaddeus G. McCotter, BigGovernment.com

"There's a reason that more people watch Greg Gutfeld's hit show *Red Eye* at 3:00 a.m. than watch most of the other cable news networks in prime time—he is one of the most creatively funny people on television. Irreverent, over-the-top, and comedy served up raw is the best way to describe Greg's style. His book is THE BIBLE OF UNSPEAKABLE TRUTHS, but don't even attempt to convince God that reading this substitutes for daily Bible reading. After reading this, you'll NEED to read the real Bible—but you'll laugh yourself holy reading this one!"　　　　—Mike Huckabee

"Greg Gutfeld is uproariously funny and is one of my favorite guests."　　　　　　　　　　　　　　　　—Dennis Miller

"As a rule I never read books I blurb, but I couldn't resist with this one. I even gave it to my thirteen-year-old son, who pored over it slack-jawed all afternoon, thus warping him for life. It's that subversive and good."　　　　　　　　　　　　—Tucker Carlson

"Even though Greg Gutfeld was once rude to me on the phone because Time Warner screwed up his home cable system, he is still the funniest, most incisive political writer on the right. Trust me, you don't want him setting his sights on your hypocrisy and public failings."

—Andrew Breitbart, founder of BigGovernment.com
and Breitbart.com

"Greg Gutfeld is funnier than all the smart people I know, and smarter than all the funny people I know. I don't know what that makes him. But one of the smartest, funniest people I know, is fair to say."

—Matt Labash, senior writer, *Weekly Standard*,
and author of *Fly Fishing with Darth Vader*

"Greg Gutfeld is a brilliantly funny writer and social commentator. This is the first time anyone has asked me to write a 'blurb' for their book. It's even less fun than I thought it would be."

—Jim Norton, *New York Times* bestselling author
of *Happy Endings* and *I Hate Your Guts*

The Bible of Unspeakable Truths

GREG GUTFELD

WITH A FOREWORD BY PENN JILLETTE

GRAND CENTRAL
PUBLISHING

NEW YORK   BOSTON

Grand Central Publishing
Hachette Book Group
237 Park Avenue
New York, NY 10017

www.HachetteBookGroup.com

Printed in the United States of America

RRD-C

Originally published in hardcover by Grand Central Publishing.

First trade edition: February 2013

10 9 8 7 6 5 4 3 2 1

Grand Central Publishing is a division of Hachette Book Group, Inc.
The Grand Central Publishing name and logo is a trademark of
Hachette Book Group, Inc.

The Hachette Speakers Bureau provides a wide range of authors for speaking events. To find out more, go to www.hachettespeakersbureau.com or call (866) 376-6591.

The publisher is not responsible for websites (or their content) that are not owned by the publisher.

The Library of Congress has cataloged the hardcover edition as follows:

Gutfeld, Greg.
    The bible of unspeakable truths / by Greg Gutfeld.—1st ed.
        p. cm.
    ISBN 978-0-446-55230-1
    1. Conduct of life—Humor.   2. American wit and humor.   3. Mass media—Humor.   I. Title.
    PN6231.C6142G88 2010
    814'.54—dc22

                                                                    2009037644

ISBN 978-0-446-55231-8 (pbk.)

To Elena

The Most Honest Foreword Ever Written

Penn Jillette

If you're buying this book, you know a lot more about Greg Gutfeld than I do. I've been on *Red Eye* a few times. It's my job to go on shows to whore out tickets to the *Penn & Teller Show* at the Penn & Teller Theater at the Rio All-Suites Hotel and Casino in Las Vegas, Nevada. As long as they'll say the name of our live show on TV, I'll do most any TV show.

Red Eye is not a show I've seen except when I'm on it. That's true for about every show I do. I don't watch much TV, and I never watch Fox or CNN. Fox is "conservative" and who wants to be "conservative"? True, I am one of the few people working in showbiz who's not a liberal, but I don't want to be conservative. Conservatives picked a really bad brand name. "Conservative" means "nothing original and no fun." "Conservative" used to mean "smaller government," but "conservative" doesn't even mean that anymore. It just means "buzzkill." So, I'll go with "libertarian." It means I can be proporn and anti–government health care. It means I don't have to drive a Prius, or listen to Rush (Limbaugh, I do listen to Geddy Lee).

The first time I was on *Red Eye*, I was backstage with my makeup on, all ready to go. I watched the monitor because it's too rude, even for me, to change the channel backstage. Greg was doing his monologue and I had nothing else to watch. To say I'm not a religious man is an understatement. I am an atheist, right down to my nonexistent soul, but that night in the backstage green room of *Red*

Eye (mentioning "green" and "red" in one sentence is the closest I'll ever come to celebrating Xmas), I witnessed a miracle. I had never heard of Greg, but it started to wash over me that the monologue Greg was doing was way funny. Not hack funny, but really funny. Some real surprising turns. It made me laugh. Lots of people are funny and lots of people are original. What was miraculous was I agreed with Greg's opinions. He was making sense. He stated his opinions outright, without being wishy-washy, and I understood what he meant and I agreed with him. He ended his hunk with, "And if you disagree with me, you, sir, are worse than a Nazi." I loved that. He was on Fox doing comedy and talking politics and I liked him. That's way more amazing and much harder to fake than a virgin birth.

I went out on set and did Greg's show. I liked him during the show and I liked him in breaks. He seemed smart and funny, and he had political views that weren't predictable. I have a friend who says if he meets someone and he checks two data points and then can guess a third, he's not interested. If someone is a Dead Head, voted for Obama, and is against nuclear power, why do you need to talk to that person? Okay, those are bad examples, because any one of those things and you don't ever need to talk to that person, but you get the idea. I couldn't guess three points on Greg. He was on Fox, but a lot of his ideas were libertarian. But, not all of them. He was thinking about things and deciding without reading the memos. He wasn't by the numbers.

When he asked me to write this intro, I figured what the hell. I'd get a mention of our live show in the first 'graph, and I like him. So, I said yes. He sent me a Word file of the book and I started reading it on my iPhone. I had to write this intro without reading much of the book, because the deadline is tomorrow (obviously the other fifty people he asked to write this before me took awhile to say no). Even if I had all the time in the world, I have no intention of ever really reading all this book. It's not the kind of book I read, but I did read some of it, and it's really funny and I agreed with a lot of it. Agreeing with a lot of it is better than agreeing with all of it. It means there's something to think about and to learn. If I agree with all of anything in a book, well, I might as well just read my own fucking book (by the way, have you read my book *Sock*? You might like it).

Another miracle—I'm thinking of reading more of Greg's book even after this intro is done. I don't think I'll read all of it, but I'm going to read more and damn, motherfucker, that is amazing. It's amazing that I want to read more of it. It's funny and surprising and I can't quite figure him out. I like all of that. Goddamn it, I might read the whole fucking book, who knows? So far, it's great.

Because of writing this intro, I started emailing with Greg. We're emailing about the existence of god. We don't fuck around, we get down to it. He seems to think there's a god. Well, there's no god. We disagree on that, and I'm right and I can prove it—Hitler believed in god, so if you disagree with me, you, sir, are Hitler. I'm sure we'll talk more about it.

Also, while reading this book always keep in mind that Greg is really, really short.

I'm really, really tall.

Greg is so short, and I'm so tall, he'll have to go up on me for writing this intro.

And then I'll really like him.

Preface

Hey. I am Greg Gutfeld, and I tell uncomfortable truths for a living. For the most part, I believe I'm right when I'm saying them. When I'm wrong, I'll still say them. But that's America, and the consequences of a long-standing head injury, for you.

I foolishly believe that I'm good at this line of work—spitting out frank truths about the world—mainly because I have a nonathletic body that makes other types of work untenable. But I also possess a restless gut that drives me to blurt out life lessons before my brain has time to edit them. This has hurt my career in more ways than I care to remember. But still, I can't stop.

I believe that's the definition of a fool.

But at least I'm a useful one. Currently I'm a writer, commentator, and talk show host for Fox News. I try not to let this interfere with my charity work (I don't do any charity work).

In a previous life, I was an editor in chief of three major men's magazines: *Maxim, Stuff,* and *Men's Health.* I'm forty-four, slightly overweight, and have short black hair and blue eyes, an understanding wife, and a very embarrassing birthmark.

Why am I telling you all this? Well, if I'm going to tell you some honest crap about the world, I should establish my credentials (or lack thereof). And my credentials are this: I've been around a lot of bozos in my life—including myself—and made a lot of mistakes... some of them resulting in me being frisked and fingerprinted. But all through this life, I've managed to catalogue the truths I've come across, and now I want to share them with you. Or rather, I would like you to pay for them. But it's almost the same thing, give or take the suggested retail price.

My opinions, which drive these truths, might be described as "conservative leaning toward libertarian." I am promilitary, anti-government, progun, anti–drug war, prounicorn, anti–nude sunbathing laws—and as for everything else, you can find that out for yourself in this handy book. Simply open it up at any point and start reading. If you can't read, then have someone read it to you. I suggest someone with a delightful accent whose options are limited.

In this book, the truths will cover all aspects of life, in no particular order. Not since the Bible, I believe, has a book done this before (and yes, I'm including Suze Orman's *The Road to Wealth*): tackling everything from a singular point of view that validates the voice in your head saying you were right all along. And if it has, I haven't read it. I hate books. There's just too much "attitude," especially coming from those letterpress limited editions with their haughty illustrations. Basically, they can kiss my butt.

These unspeakable truths will follow no right or left litmus test. They are neither elitist nor populist. They are not the product of the working class or the educated. They did not arise from the Greatest Generation or the Summer of Love. They don't drive Priuses or Hummers. Instead, they constitute a new way of looking at politics and pop culture—specific truths that reflect common sense that's seeded in all of us. You have to be smart to get them, however. Which eliminates anyone who purchased a book by Deepak Chopra.

So why do you need this book? Or rather, why does America need this book, right now? Because we're living in an age where our innate common sense—our gut instinct—is constantly being called into question. Those things you know to be right—family, morality, objective truth, guns, faces that are free of nose rings and tongue studs—are seen as stupid, outdated, signs of a dead era.

This book seeks to give you confidence in knowing that what you know is actually the only thing worth knowing. It's also ideal for bathroom reading, even if you don't own a bathroom (a shout-out to Tom Sizemore).

Now, if you're a first-time reader of anything by me (meaning, six billion or so people), then the following few sentences will mean nothing to you. So feel free to leave the room while I address those who are already familiar with me.

Hey Paul, Ron, Andy, and the chick with the rifle: If parts of the book sometimes strike you as familiar, it's okay—you're not going mad. I first started writing unspeakable truths back in my magazine days, and have been collecting them and writing them ever since. I created a special section, called "Unspeakable Truths," at my website (Dailygut.com). Many are in this book. Later, I began to use these truths on my Fox News show, *Red Eye*. Many other truths found here have been derived from other early writings—from my pieces in the *American Spectator*, my rantings on the bug-lamp of lunacy known as the Huffington Post, and the Gregalogues I placed on the Daily Gut, which would later turn into poorly enunciated screeds on *Red Eye*. Some drifted in from my days at *Maxim*, to the Daily Gut, to Big Hollywood, that blog run by the wizard genius Andrew Breitbart. I've also found many of them on soggy cocktail napkins retrieved from the bottom of my pockets after a night of imbibing. Those are often the ones that are the most incomprehensible—which often makes them the most enjoyable. Anyway, I hope that even if you've read one of these truths before, it might make a little more sense now than it did then.

Acknowledgmentos!

Okay, where was I? Oh, yes: This book would not have been possible if not for the patience and friendship of many glorious individuals. First and foremost: my wife, Elena, who probably had no idea what she was getting into when she married me. She's pretty awesome, and if you mess with me, you mess with her. Also my mom, who gave me the genes and support that led to a unique and somewhat perplexing career. Also, below average height. I would also like to thank, in no particular order: my editor Ben Greenberg, Paul Mauro, Ron Geraci, Joannie McNaughton, Denis Boyles, Andy Levy, Bill Schulz, John Moody, Roger Ailes, Fox News Channel, Andy Clerkson, Paul Newnes, Nuri, Andrew Breitbart, Wes Johnson, Hampton Stevens, the *Red Eye* staff, *Red Eye* fans everywhere, the folks at the Activity Pit, Felix Dennis, Mark Golin, Aric Webb, Woody Fraser, Josh McCarroll, Gregg and Simone Turkington, Jim Norton, Jamie Lissow, Andrew W.K., King Buzzo, Mick Jones, Tony James, Johnny Rotten, my agent Jay Mandel, Ginger from the Wildhearts, Mark Bricklin, Lynn Gavett, Kevin Godlington, readers of the Daily Gut, Joe Escalante, Keith Flickinger, Ken LaCorte, Gary Sinise, Matt Labash, Andy Ferguson, Congressman Thaddeus McCotter, Mike Lafavore, Mike Baker, Ross Brown, Todd Kelly, Alice at Riposo, and David Whitehouse.

Also, Satan. Yes, it's true. I'm a Satanist.

No, just kidding, I'm not a Satanist. But I'll thank him anyway just to cover my bases.

A Content of Tables

The Bible of
Unspeakable Truths

Media Assjackets

You Can Do All Media-Related Jobs Drunk off Your Butt

So, there I was, lounging in my shorty robe made of sliced meats, watching my all-time-favorite television show—*Make Me a Supermodel*—when one of the contestants was sent home because "he didn't photograph well." Now, I'm no expert, but I think for a model, that's not good.

The rejected mannequin—a handsome young man—did what every reality show contestant does when he's been kicked off or disqualified: He swore he'd be back. There was no way, he said, that he would return to his previous life as a mechanic. Yep, God forbid he would return to an occupation where you actually did something that helped people.

So, when a young man considers being a male model as a more valuable job than that of a mechanic, do you think we've lost sight of what makes for meaningful work? More important: What's a mechanic?

As a forty-four-year-old man who, to this day, cannot change a tire, I know that if my bright-pink, heavily accessorized Suzuki Samurai (the Malibu Barbie edition) broke down on 101, I'd rather have someone nearby who is handy with a wrench, not "working it" with a trench. It also wouldn't hurt if he had great delts, but it's not a priority unless I want to be carried back to the Red Roof Inn.

It chaps my denim low-waisted chaps that this dope spits out "mechanic" like it was a dead-end job for losers, when in reality it is the vacant, self-absorbed folk who strut their bony carcasses on runways who are irrelevant (unless, of course, you're the always-gorgeous Tyson Beckford. He's "fierce," I have been told).

Seriously, is the ability to walk a straight line down a runway after a long night spent fending off Barry Diller really such a talent? And the fact that David Geffen once told you that you were "scrumptious" doesn't make you a valuable human being. "Scrumptious" doesn't pay bills, or come with a pension. "Scrumptious" doesn't have a dental plan. In a few years, "scrumptious" becomes "old and fat." I know from personal experience.

But this illustrates the difference between real work and fake work. Real work you have to do sober. Fake work you can do drunk. I've been a magazine editor for a good part of my life, and I can honestly say that I was drunk during most of it. Editors will never admit to this, but their jobs are so easy they can drink enough booze every night to kill a camel and still perform a solid day's work. Because the work isn't real. The same can be said for models, anchors, bloggers, marketing specialists, public relations directors, commodities traders, or anyone who chiefly lives and works in the world of concepts and computer keyboards.

Compare that to real jobs—bus drivers, mechanics, loggers, riggers. You can't do those occupations drunk, or you'll lose your fingers or maybe the whole hand.

You never see an editor with a hook for a hand. The most

dangerous piece of machinery we deal with is the elevator. And when that doesn't work—watch the glorious meltdowns in the lobby.

So try this experiment: For the next week, do your job drunk. If your performance stays the same, you don't lose any limbs, and no one notices you're soused, then your job is not real. But if your performance suffers, and you lose a limb, then congratulations—you have a real job and you actually contribute something worthwhile to society. You should be proud, even if you're dead.

Reporters Are Always Fearless in Movies Made About Reporters

I remember a few years back, a polling company measured public perceptions of twenty-three professions, and journalists ended up ranked at the bottom. Just 13 percent of eleven hundred U.S. adults said the occupation of journalist had "very great prestige," while 16 percent said it had "hardly any at all." Meanwhile, 61 percent said the most prestigious job was firefighter, noting that they were also great strippers at bachelorette parties.

And yet, Hollywood has spent the last seventy years glorifying the role of journalists, while it's made only one *Backdraft* (possibly two, I can't remember). Robert Redford can play a journalist on the big screen, but we all know that in real life, journalists look more like me—pudgy, pasty drunks with moderate to unhealthy obsessions with unicorn porn (or uniporn, for short). Aside from those brave souls who really put themselves in harm's way in war-torn countries—for the rest of us hacks—journalism is about as heroic as dentistry. And dentists have cooler instruments. And nitrous.

I know this, for I used to be a print journalist, it's true. But I spent my time doing what all good journalists should do: trying to find my pants. If I could have cloned myself and created a press corps entirely of Gregs, I would have, but until then I refuse to learn how to read and urge you to do the same.

Katie Couric's Life Is More Important Than the Average College Freshman's (Even If She Looks Remarkably Like an Elf)

Back in 2007 a stink was made (not by me, for once) over the idea that professors should be allowed to carry guns. The idea came on the heels of the tragedy at Virginia Tech, and many people were legitimately freaked out at the thought of teachers walking the corridors strapped with Glocks.

Like you, I don't trust professors. Most of them are tenured twats. However, I am completely behind arming the faculty for a very simple reason: I dislike college students. Especially the ones that wear ski caps in the summer and wear charity wristbands in order to pick up chicks. If one of those chuckleheads mouths off, it should be completely legal to blow off one of his toes.

But there's a more important reason why we should be allowing instructors to carry guns. It might save the lives of those college students. The fact is, every damn television network in Manhattan is surrounded by well-armed security. So who says Katie Couric's life is somehow more valuable than that of a poli-science major? Why is Brian Williams protected, but not your college mascot? That one is a hairy little cheerleader doesn't make its life any less valuable (I'm talking about the mascot).

It pisses me off knowing that nearly every major talking head advocates gun control, arrogant in their belief that most Americans can't be trusted to arm and protect themselves without hurting others. Meanwhile, it's these same talking heads who never have to worry about being shot at by a crazed lunatic, because the lunatic and the talking head are separated by five levels of security. I'm sorry: NBC is no more important than LSU—so if there are guns surrounding one, there should be guns surrounding the other. Or better, why not hot cheerleaders in holsters? Who says protection can't be sexy?

To the Press, People on Death Row Are More Interesting Than Their Victims

Part of the reason why a reporter becomes a reporter is for the excitement—and what's more exciting than a ruthless killer in a jumpsuit, quietly awaiting his date with Destiny (note, that is not a stripper). But it extends beyond journalism, into all parts of pop culture and the arts. A year after his death, a play was based on convicted killer Tookie Williams's life, staged by the Black Repertory Theater of Berkeley. The play was a re-enactment of the execution, staged on the first anniversary of his lethal injection at San Quentin State Prison. The actor basically lies there and, possibly, convulses. It would have been cool if they'd gotten Matt LeBlanc for the lead role. He could have used the work, and he does have that stoic quality needed for a corpse.

The play was written and produced by two women who were "two friends" of Williams, as well as death penalty opponents. There's something about chicks who become obsessed with death row pin-ups—oh yeah, they're fucking nuts. That's *the* something.

Note: An article on the play describes a supporter in the audience wearing a "Save Tookie" T-shirt. Someone better get that genius up to speed.

I think there needs to be a rule made for anyone exploring the idea of doing a story, a play, a movie, a musical, or whatever about a murderer. He or she must be forced to devote equal time to the victims of the killer. It's only fair. And it might help the artist learn that while killers may seem more glamorous than their victims, it's only the artist who allows that glamour to take root. In my opinion, it's far better to immortalize victims than their tormentors.

And if you don't believe me, I'll kill you.

With kisses, of course (seriously, if I press down hard enough I can pretty much kill anything!).

The Media Think Patriotism Is Embarrassing

This is true, unless, of course, said patriotism is in any way tied to freedom of the press, or the absolute awesomeness of President Obama. That's because, from the media's point of view, the only two great things about America are the media and the absolute awesomeness of President Obama. Everything else, however, sucks (meaning: Gitmo, guns, religion, and any combination of the three).

I love it when a CNN reporter approaches someone with an American flag and treats that person, as my friend Denis says, like "a lost tribe of Americans," like that dude with the Coke bottle in *The Gods Must Be Crazy*. But I guess the reporter is right—the fact is, patriotism and religion have no place in a world that already has Obama. He is a patriotic emblem and a religious icon rolled into one: a cocktail weenie of supreme greatness.

Anyway, back in September 2007, *CBS Evening News* anchor and sharer of too much information Katie Couric spoke critically of the war in Iraq at a seminar at the National Press Club—which, according to my sources, is actually a treehouse in Bob Schieffer's backyard.

Initially, I was impressed by Katie's newfound war expertise. She must be catching up on her blogs. But do I care what she thinks about the war? I mean, I'm really only used to looking to Katie for ways to cure my toenail fungus, or a low-fat recipe for blueberry muffins. Sometimes I get both of them confused and I have to go to the hospital to get my stomach pumped (and the berries removed from my toenails).

Couric is a typical example of the "elitist defeatist," whose real problem isn't why we're fighting a war, but war itself, and how it makes her feel inside. Wars are so mean! And Katie isn't mean. Unless, of course, you work for her (I've heard stories).

So it's no surprise that when talking about those who supported the country during a war, Couric said, and I quote, "The whole culture of wearing flags on our lapel and saying 'we' when referring to the United States, and even the 'shock and awe' of the initial stages, it was just too jubilant and just a little uncomfortable." So, to her, being patriotic is "a culture," one that's wrong because it implies you're taking a side. Saying "we," when dealing in matters of war, is icky. There's no "we" in Katie. I know because I saw her colonic.

But for the purest example of how the media mock basic patriotism, simply recall how some major news networks and TV commentators behaved toward the attendees of the Tea Parties back in early 2009, calling them "teabaggers" and insinuating racism—the press looked at these flyover folks as goons and freaks, better to be gawked at in a zoo designed to amuse the oh-so-evolved liberals.

But what were these protesters guilty of? Was there any violence? According to reports I looked at, there was only *one* arrest made during the protests. So why were these folks ridiculed? What were they doing that was so wrong? Well, they were holding peaceful, picniclike gatherings to protest a bigger, more intrusive government. And that's wrong—because when you're protesting that kind of agenda, you're protesting Obama, and the press who love Him.

So the press chose to mock these folks instead of, say, WTO protesters, who smash the windows of a Starbucks that reporters would normally purchase their lattes from. For a ridiculous contrast in coverage, compare CNN's Susan Roesgen's attack on Tea Party attendees with her solemn documentation of Michael Jackson fans at their makeshift memorials. For Suzie, the death of a drug-addled, kid-obsessed pop star required more seriousness than she was willing to give average working Americans. No wonder her contract wasn't renewed.

Being a Jackass Isn't an Illness,
Unless the Media Deem It So

According to those lonely researchers from Harvard Medical School and University of Chicago, something they like to call "uncontrollable anger" is on the uptick—with 7.3 percent of the population identified as having IED, an acronym for intermittent explosive disorder (which I always thought was diarrhea). Having IED usually means you "suffer" from three or more aggressive outbursts—an average afternoon for Sean Penn. If you believe these researchers, roughly eight million adults had the most severe form of IED, carrying out forty-three attacks, often "lashing out violently."

Frankly, research like this, and the way it's reported in the media, makes me angry—angry enough, in fact, to lash out violently (perhaps forty-three times). Crap like this is designed by academics to get grants so they can "find ways" to get more grants. One way to do this is to create a definition for something that may or may not exist, then continue to broaden the definition to make it appear it's actually growing.

Which is what this research does, I think. Worse, it makes being a jerk (or rather, an asshole) an actual disorder, when actually it's just a character flaw that should be condemned rather than studied and "understood." I understand it plenty. I have a mirror.

And while we're on the topic of being a prick, being labeled a "creative genius" doesn't excuse your being a prick. According to the *Daily Telegraph* (a funny name for a newspaper, by the by—you're a newspaper, not a telegraph!), Albert Einstein had something like ten mistresses. In the article, experts claimed that the oddly haired icon was like other "intensely creative men," in that he was "overendowed" with the joy of risk-taking.

Bullshit. We know why powerful men like Einstein had mistresses. It's because they *could*. Brilliant men often possess high status, and women on average are attracted more to men with high status than to those with low status. So powerful men, regardless of whether they are married or single, are open to more options for sexual gratification—which *then* brings its own set of risks. As a friend once told me: "Most of us are only as virtuous as our options." So, when it comes to Einstein, these experts put the cart before the horse, which I guess is far better than trying to get the horse back to your small apartment for a nightcap. They can be so petulant!

More important, if you try to use this "I can't help it, I'm brilliant!" excuse to cheat on your wife, you immediately disqualify yourself from the realm of men who might qualify to use this excuse. Meaning, you're an idiot.

The Only People Who Want to Read Stories on the Homeless Are the Ones Who Wrote Them

Back when I was a teenager/transgendered tennis pro in the 1980s, it seemed like every week some enterprising reporter for the local paper or TV station would put on his or her "serious face" and decide to do stories that "mattered." Translation: "I'm going to sleep on a grate for a night, and then tell you of my amazing and brutal sacrifice." So these dopes would throw a little dirt on their face, don some grubby clothes, grab a cardboard box, and find a reasonably lit street in the main part of town to sack out on. Of course, hidden in their penny loafers were a credit card and a hundred bucks in case things got hairy, or perhaps they wanted a blow job from the local transgender sex worker. (There's always one. Give her my name, and you'll get a discount.) Within a week or so, their story would appear, usually above the fold, with moving black-and-white photography of said reporter bonding with an authentic homeless person: possibly a Vietnam War vet, black, with diabetes. His name would be folksy—like "folksy Joe"—and he'd be really likeable. You know: the kind of homeless person you'd bring home for the holidays—which was a made-for-TV movie plot line in every melodrama between 1975 and 1985. There will be no mention of Joe's substance abuse issues, his lengthy and violent criminal record, or his "folksy" habit of crapping in his pants and then smearing it on pay phones.

With so many of these articles being published, it got to the point that I became convinced that there were more reporters pretending to be homeless than actual homeless—and it occurred to me that this stunt journalism has to be the easiest, quickest way to get a name for yourself, if not a promotion. It's a shame the newspaper industry has such low expectations for its readers—which I guess is why there aren't any, anymore. Maybe we should let the homeless pretend to be reporters—then newspapers might be readable.

Silly Theories Kill More People Than Guns

I saw it in the *New York Times*, so it's got to be true: Research has suggested that violence is an infection, something you catch like hepatitis or Janeane Garofalo. It made me so sick to my stomach, I wanted to stab a shopkeeper in the neck. The writer focused only on gang crime, as opposed to other types, like shoplifting or houseboy dismemberment, suggesting that if gang murder spreads like an infectious disease, then it should be treated like one.

If only there was a word that describes this idea. Oh yeah. Batshit crazy.

Sorry, that's two words. Or maybe three.

See, I wonder—if the crime were white collar or corporate in nature, would the *Times* call it a disease? Or would it just be another example of the perils of small government? After all, many feel that corporations like Enron are just as evil as the Crips. But the *Times* would never call that a disease because such a pronouncement would excuse its perpetrators, who are rich white men. And the *Times* would never do such a thing.

But the *Times* can't blame gang members for gang crime, for in its eyes, personal responsibility only applies to whites. Implying that gang members are victims of a disease means it's no longer their fault. They are simply helpless victims, like people with AIDS or malaria. Violent behavior is just a virus that makes you shoot people while wearing really baggy pants. If only we had universal health care, we could cure this!

As much as I hate this kind of thinking, I do believe the paper is on to something. There is a disease, but it afflicts writers at the *Times*. It renders them incapable of recognizing evil when it presents itself, whether it's terror or street criminals. The disease causes its victims instead to fiddle around looking for root causes and silly theories. That disease is called self-loathing-moral-relativism syndrome. It first began to appear in the States in the 1960s, I believe. Maybe Mick Jagger brought it over.

Garry Trudeau Is an Untalented Sack of Poop

If *Doonesbury* did not relentlessly spout knee-jerk liberal tripe in every panel, it would not exist. It's the only cartoon given tenure—in that the media cut Garry Trudeau slack because they all believe his heart is in the right place, even though his stuff sucks harder than something that really sucks.

But in our hearts, we all know the truth: The strip is neither amusing nor interesting. Worse, the dude can't draw for shit. Essentially, Trudeau has been a recipient of comic strip welfare his entire career. No one has had the guts to cut him off. It's too bad, because Funky Winkerbean really deserves his spot.

The Media Want Health Scares to Succeed

Here's a simple rule: Anything the press describes as a coming scourge WILL NEVER, EVER HAPPEN. Remember the killer bees? How about the coming ice age? Global warming? Radon? Top hat cancer? Please. These stories were written by reporters who got their adrenaline kick by believing they were part of something huge.

The rule: Being a reporter is boring. Big stories make the job less boring.

Thing is, by the time they're found out to be wrong, they've already moved on. I bet there are aging writers who are embracing the religion of global warming in the same manner they glommed on to the coming ice age thirty years ago. These people should probably be beaten about the face and neck with an old copy of *Silent Spring* until they come to their senses.

It's just like Y2K, and at least one great blizzard a year: For the media, a hyped-up event without cataclysmic death is like sex without orgasm. So now we watch the swine flu. It was only a few years ago that we were told that the bird flu virus would leave our country piled high with corpses and feathers. But soon after, according to the director general of the Animal Health Organization, "the risk was overestimated," and the pandemic lacked scientific proof. Big surprise. It's just like all those other scares overblown by the media. Yawn. Razor blades in candy? HA! What about the return of fondue? I cheeseproofed my house and everything. And let's not forget the coming scourge of "Pillowsis."

See? You already have!

That's because hysteria makes great press for the experts quoted and the reporters who quote them. Hysteria creates paid work for hysterics. Panics, like conspiracies, are also a great way to pretend you care about an issue when you're only stealing from ominous headlines. And that can kick-start any cocktail conversation. Sadly, it takes more brains to debunk hysteria, and that's why you never hear real doctors babbling about "the epidemic of homelessness" or global warming—they're too busy working, instead of doing CNN.

Saying "Exactly" to Everything Will Guarantee Success in Media

I started doing television appearances roughly ten years ago, but in the first year I learned a valuable lesson: If you don't have anything important to say, just say, "exactly." Remember this if you're ever stuck for words on a TV show: Even if you disagree with the interviewer's question, or have no idea what he actually meant, just agree. But you can't go halfway—"exactly" means you totally agree with the fact that all Belgians should be euthanized. You'll be invited back. Even if you're on a Belgian show.

That's because whoever is interviewing really needs your validation, not your real opinion. Agreeing with whatever the host says makes everyone happy. In a way, it's just like being married to a short, opinionated drunk like me.

Attractive People Don't Write for a Living

Recently, a website for a British paper unveiled its list of the fifty most influential political pundits in America. All the usual suspects were on it. Like David Gergen. If you don't know who David Gergen is, imagine a sock dipped in flesh. Also on the list: Howard Kurtz, a turtle in a hairpiece. And Mark Shields—who I believe was a mime back in the seventies with Lorene Yarnell. Paul Begala is also there, a giant thumb with sad eyes. And what's a list without James Carville, a cross between a skull and a lollipop. Some believe he is actually a gibbon that Bill Clinton trapped and trained to speak.

If you look at the list you'll find that they all have something in common—they're hideous.

Is it my fault, as a pundit, that I am handsome, possess a natural healthy head of hair, and can bench-press at least two houseboys, depending on their country of origin?

I believe we live in an age where we can't accept our pundits unless they look like pundits. This "pundism" has created a glass ceiling for handsome gents like me. If I were ugly, perhaps I would be a well-paid writer for the *New York Times*, instead of that dumpy Frank Rich, or that frumpy David Brooks. This is total discrimination, and I'm going to start picketing something as soon as I figure out which one of my muumuus goes best with a sign.

The Only Difference Between You and an Expert Is Four Appearances on a Cable News Show

When I take public transportation, people come up to me and ask me the same question over and over again: "Why are you staring at me?" And also: "How come you don't have experts on your television show?" The answer? It's a glass eye, and experts are phonies.

The easiest way to pawn yourself off as an expert is to tell people you're an expert. Then appear on a talk show. Sex experts, steroid experts, latte experts—they're all shams.

Here's why: With a thousand TV channels and countless talking heads needed to fill time, no one really performs background checks. Yeah, they'll Google your name, but that's about it. I have, after all, pawned myself off on a number of shows as a relationship expert. God, if you only knew how my exes feel about that! Thankfully, they would never admit to dating me.

Political Crap

Other Cultures Suck

For proof, here's a list I just came up with (which I wrote with a Magic Marker on Jeremy Piven's back): the Norsk, the Polski, the Scots, the Suomi, the Tagalog, the Portuguese, the Ozbek, the Runa Simi, the Bahasa Indonesia (they're a bunch of jerks, really), the Lojban, the Ido, the Hrvatski, the Basa Jawa (they smell like bats), the Deutsch, the Euskara, and of course the French. Oh—and the Germans, too. They totally suck.

But to say we don't suck, either, would be pure idiocy. We do suck, because we're basically a mix of all the other cultures that suck. Plus, we have *Hot Topic*, *The Hills*, and constant reruns of *Will and Grace* on every single channel. Also, on both coasts we are infected with annoying hipsters who describe themselves as "edgy," when they're just "spineless assholes pretending to be edgy." They aren't even close to being as daring as any carny running the bumper cars at the Allentown Fair. (It's a fact: If you want scary, as in "scarier than a clown rapist," get to know the carnival workers when they're in town—they are truly "in your face," usually with a knife carved from human bone.)

Look, our game shows are boring (at least compared to the Japanese), we let our dogs sleep indoors, we let our daughters wear thongs under saggy jeans, we encourage our boys to play soccer, and if you take a dump in traffic you're probably making a statement about society—one probably worth $100K from the NEA.

On a similar note, did you ever notice how physically fit religious fanatics from other countries are? Is it from all the dancing? Or running from the Predator drones? Please let me know as soon as possible. Summer is coming and I can't find my belly button.

The Republicans Elected Obama, Not the Democrats

When Obama won, it wasn't the Democrats that won. It was the Republicans who lost. Republicans are losers because after fourteen years in power, all they stood for was their own power and complacency. Democrats picked up seats not because suddenly America fell in love with liberalism. The only idea Democrats had was this one: We aren't Republicans! For now, that's more than enough! Two, four, six years from now, they might need something a little fresher. Maybe Republicans will come up with something for them.

On a similar note, here is my only tip when voting in any election (including *American Idol*): Vote for the people who do the least amount of damage to the populace. Which normally would be voting for anyone who supports cutting the size of government, and, more important, tax rates. (I call this my "Run From Godzilla" theory. It works when voting for politicians, but also when running from Godzilla.)

You're Leading the Country Right Now

So, just for fun, let's review the folks currently on the bad side of the White House: There's old people who showed up at the health care town halls and kicked ass, while I sat home and ate Funyons. There's Rush Limbaugh—the "de facto" head of the Republican Party. There are the Tea Party protesters, or moronic "teabaggers," to the smirking, clueless media. There's Dick Cheney—and the CIA agents who tried to protect our country. There's a certain fiery cable network I won't mention. And there's you. Now, none of these bad eggs are elected officials. None of them are "active" Republican officials. None of them get haircuts at the congressional barbershop. None of them really have a seat at the table. In a country where checks and balances have pretty much checked out, these are the Americans who stepped up to the plate. This health care revolt might be the most truly organic uprising this country has seen since Perot. (You remember that guy, right? Adorable.)

Now, I know what the president is thinking. This wasn't supposed to be so hard. He has had both Houses and the presidency! Everyone loves me! Health care should have been a slam dunk! All those countries that hated us before should be loving the crap out of us! I should have won the Olympics in Denmark, but all I got were these lousy clogs!

But here's what happens when you get ahead of yourself. It is easy to get overconfident when the media are behind you. But someone had to step up and say, "Hold on there, pal."

And that someone is America.

Didn't see that coming, did you?

Boring Issues Are the Ones That Screw You

So I'm reading how President Obama's proposed health plan is going to raise taxes like crazy in New York. And it got me to thinking about...mold.

I once got mold in the basement of my old house. Mold, by its very nature, is boring. It's slow, silent, and unassuming. But I learned quickly: If you choose to ignore it, the crap only multiplies. Over time, your entire house is covered in the stuff—much in the same way our lives are with taxation. Resisting the never-ending tide of taxation requires a strong heart and a willingness to champion something that most of the population finds dull. Taxes just aren't as exciting as global warming or animal rights—and taxes *are real*. We prefer to fight romantic battles, or rather, young people prefer to fight romantic battles, because they have yet to pay taxes. That's what really pisses me off: watching people under twenty-two telling the rest of us how our paycheck should be carved up to solve various stupid problems that we already know cannot be fixed if the government uses our money to fix them. It's enough to make me scream, but then I'd have to pay the "screaming" tax, and frankly I can't afford it.

"Meaning Well" Is a Camouflage for Ruining Your Life

A lot of people talk about media bias—the idea that reporters from the *New York Times* to CBS lean left, as if they suffer from chronic political scoliosis. I have an alternative, and some might say brilliant theory, which is that it is the mainstream media that are biased, but they don't just lean to the left, they lean toward any belief or idea that "means well."

It makes sense. People have a common need to mean well. It explains charities, floral arrangements, greeting cards signed from all of us, and sneeze guards at the salad bar, which, incidentally, never stop me because it's very easy to slip your head under them and pretend you're trying to get a closer look at the lettuce.

Now, I know what you're thinking. You're thinking that as an American, you have a God-given right to pristine croutons. But "meaning well" should not trump honesty. Think about all the issues treated with kid gloves. The press, for example, never questions the statistics it repeats on the homeless, because just reporting them, even if they're wrong by half, means you mean well. The press rarely questions the validity of climate-change science, because scientists who exaggerate panic only mean well.

That's because we all know that people who are skeptical of global warming don't care about the planet. And anyone evil enough to have supported the evil but successful war in Iraq certainly doesn't mean well—they probably feast on kittens while reading about casualties.

And this is the hilarious irony of contemporary life: People who mean well always screw everything up, because they'd rather "feel good" than "do good." In order to do good, you've got to face some sober facts, ones that don't make you feel good, no matter how many rolls of biodegradable toilet paper you donate to the homeless annually, or how many times you don't flush in an effort to conserve water. Fact is, not only is your toilet full of poop—so are you.

We Won, but the Losers Are Dictating the Terms

The Iraq War: At a time when many of the West's leaders were racing to capitulate thousands of years of industrial and intellectual development to the worst medieval lunatics on earth, President Bush had the guts to finally *do* something. But while he was in charge, I guess his supporters were just tired of having to do all the talking for him. Even with a world press that essentially hates free enterprise, he should have been able to get far better ink. Hamas gets better press than the Eighty-second Airborne. That's as much the State Department's fault as it is Bill Moyers's.

Europeans consider America a far worse evil than radical Islam. But can you blame them? Europe has become like its micro-facsimile, Epcot Center: all kitschy evocations of past glories, without real power or will to back it up. Funny, our Epcot may be more "real" than the actual continent, and it has a better snack bar. We won the Cold War—and Europe instead drifted happily toward socialism, the loser's doctrine. And it looks like, with President Obama, we're following the same path. Nationalization, bigger government, higher taxes—we're trying to turn the United States into France. And we don't even have the pleasure of wearing those cute berets.

It's the sad fact of contemporary America: We're a country full of winners, but we're infected with a certain ideological segment that believes losing is better. As I have said before countless times to anyone who will listen (including pets and furniture), the left relies solely on bad news to bolster its own worldview. These are people who not-so-secretly wanted troop deaths higher in Iraq, because that made them appear right. So when there's good news for the rest of us—that the Iraq War is essentially won, and Iraq is a far safer place—it's bad news for them.

History will judge us not on how bad we felt, say, during the Iraq War, but on how well the war fared. If we win it, that's good news, and that's all that matters. History is funny that way. Who won matters, even if it doesn't matter to the Berkeley professors who tend to write the history.

It's like competing for a hot girl at a bar. Nobody remembers the dumb things you said to impress her. What you remember is how pissed your friend was when you left with her, and that little thing she learned on her trip to Brazil.

It's called "winning." Trust me, it's better than losing.

Which brings me to Robert Redford, a true winner who believes losing is the answer. When the ripening root vegetable released yet another antiwar flop called *Lions for Lambs*, the *New York Times* reported that this brave director was bracing for a backlash.

From whom? His friends? Hollywood? The media? Snowboarders? A pride of unicorns? The other members of the Hair Club? One of his moles? Give me a break. The only time Redford would ever experience a backlash is if he made *The Milagro Beanfield War Two: Now With More Beans.* Or maybe if he actually said something positive about America's role in the world his friends in Sundance might get pissed. But don't hold your breath.

So what's Redford's beef with the U.S.? According to the *Times*, he says it's our "patterns of behavior." When you look at Watergate, Iran-Contra, and now Iraq, it's "the same sensibility: Winning is everything." And trying to win is wrong.

Well, unless you run a film festival. Redford hates winning, but he awards trophies to directors who enter his festival to win those trophies. Isn't it strange that in order to win such awards, you have to make movies that deride the idea of winning? If you want to win a war, you're evil. But if you want to win an award for a stupid film, you're good.

But at least someone from the Hollywood left is being honest: Their careers benefit from America losing, and nothing angers them more than our victory. This is why Redford made no mention of anything good America has done—like, say, ridding the world of all kinds of fascism, saving millions of lives, and ending the Cold War. But I'm sure he can find something wrong in that, too.

So what does all this hate do to you? Well, Redford is now seventy-one years old, and just look at him. He resembles a cross-species experiment between an old baseball mitt and a dried apple refrigerator magnet. The ultimate consequence of wishing America bad? You lose your looks.

Speaking of moviemaking (we were speaking of that, right?), do you remember Obama's infomercial near the end of the last election? It was bizarro-propaganda, a dour documentary that seemed designed to undermine an Eastern bloc country, circa 1974. Ten minutes into the thing, I was expecting a bunch of fat babushkas in headscarves fighting over the last loaf of stale bread. By the time it was over, I had boiled and eaten a neighbor's dog.

This was our country as seen, grimly, from the outside looking in: a place where everyone is sick, poor, or sickly poor. I call it Hugo porn—the kind of stuff that gives Chavez a chubby.

It was as if the most successful and selfless country in the history of the world never existed. Instead, we have East Germany without the lederhosen or the sausage. But I guess, in order to sell himself, Barack had to sell the rest of the country short.

And with the help of the media, it worked. The fear and pessimism Obama created got him elected—even if the world he painted didn't remotely reflect what we see every day, with our own eyes. In that sense Obama is the greatest of fearmongers, not unlike a traveling health huckster telling us there are toxins in our bodies that only his brand of elixir can cure. And as with that huckster, whatever he just sold us actually makes matters worse.

Now we've got cap and tax legislation, nationalization of health care, and God knows what else coming our way, all based on the assumption that our country is totally screwed up.

But what's really screwed up: President Obama doesn't think America needs a little fixing to get back on the right track. He thinks America has never been on the right track. And his actions therefore are meant to correct a country he finds distasteful on many levels, permanently.

Which is why I'm boiling a second dog, just in case.

Mexicans Are Good People—It's Mexico That Sucks

The two big issues for both parties? Immigration and terror. Here's how one issue can solve the other.

Those folks behind terror reproduce like crazy. Bin Laden? He's got more kids than I have teeth. Religious fanatics and jihadists, in general, tend to pump out killers like they're Doritos. Meanwhile, Westerners wear condoms and get abortions. As the enemy grows, we shrink. Numbers dictate success. However, we have a secret weapon: Mexicans.

They're hard workers and Catholic, which means they reproduce and are good neighbors. They also love Chevys and think Morrissey is Elvis.

Mexicans are the Eisenhower Generation.

We've got two kinds of people making more people. One fosters fanatics who want to blow up our buildings. The other group gets paid to vacuum them. I know who I'm with. Mexicans. They're the one hope against an enemy whose aim is our extinction.

While Mexicans bus your table, they're defending Western civilization. While they blow the leaves off your lawn, they're striking a blow against terror. Mexicans are the Mace against madmen, because they outscrew the creeps who kill for Allah. As we embrace cats over kids, Mexicans multiply, preventing us from becoming Europe—a continent flooded by people who hate Europeans. Mexican families love this country. I don't like Mexico (diarrhea, people), but I love Mexicans. If you are Mexican, and you aren't here yet...then come...in every sense of the word. We welcome you with open arms and legs. We're powerless to prevent you from coming here anyway, thank God. You're too determined, and we're too disorganized and distracted.

We need Mexicans more than they need us. They risk their lives to get here and they're grateful to be here. So embrace the new front on the war on terror. He's your busboy. He may be five foot two, but don't be fooled. He's tough. He goes through more adversity between 11:00 A.M. and noon than you'll ever encounter in your life, and he's never once tried to pronounce "sick day" in broken English.

So, come on, folks—it's a big mistake to rag on these guys because you're up in arms over illegal immigration. It's the issue, not the people—and these people are actually a lot better than most of the people born in this amazing place. Crap, I'd take twenty Mexicans in exchange for one Baldwin brother. For one thing, twenty Mexicans take up less room.

As for Mexico itself: It is literally national policy to help its citizens leave the place. The Mexican government pretty much publishes pamphlets on how to cross the U.S. border without detection. How bad must a country be when even the government acknowledges that busing tables in a Trenton truck stop is better than staying home?

Hypocrisy Is a Good Thing

You remember when porno-palegic Larry Flynt offered a million bucks for stories of illicit sex with government officials? Flynt said he was doing this to expose the hypocrisy of politicians. Hypocrisy, after all, is bad. Almost as bad, I guess, as screwing chickens.

But is it really? People say hypocrisy is evil, but they're wrong. To be a hypocrite, you first must try to be good. You need standards.

Let's say you're happily married, but you go out and have sex with a chicken. But maybe you've already told your wife many times before that you crave chicken sex. So when you have it, you're certainly a pervert, but you're not a hypocrite.

To say you believe in marriage and monogamy, however, and then have that affair with a chicken—well, that makes you a hypocrite. But—no lie—it also makes you human.

Humans are designed to fail, making all of us natural hypocrites. (Of course, there are hypocrites who are "dirty" from the word go, who never actually had legitimate standards to not adhere to—I call them ex-girlfriends.) And this, bizarrely, has allowed Larry Flynt to capture the moral high ground. By not being human.

Larry Flynt is incapable of hypocrisy because he lacks standards to betray. He could bang poultry till the cows come home, because he's never said it's immoral. In fact, in his autobiography he boasts of penetrating a chicken in his days of youthful experimentation. He choked the chicken, because, apparently, he hates to cuddle afterward.

Larry Flynt is the perfect liberal. Rejecting absolute morality liberates one to accept any kind of behavior—sexing fowl, condoning genocide, dating Sean Penn. Therefore it's impossible to be a hypocrite, but it's also impossible to be human.

Environmentalists Want You Dead

Laurie David, Al Gore, Prince Charles, and Arianna Huffington are in a quandary: How can they continue to lecture Wal-Mart shoppers about their ever-increasing carbon footprint, when they find themselves jetting all over the globe in private, gas-guzzling planes and sipping gold-flecked champagne from the skulls of bald eagles while watching vintage snuff films on flat-screen diamond-encrusted DVD players?

Climate Care! It's a new "carbon-emissions-offsetting program," designed by a charter flight broker, to contribute "renewable energy, forest restoration, and energy-efficient projects" as a way to balance out the environmental consequences of its flights.

In other words, like everything associated with carbon offsets, it's baloney: a structured phony gesture, a pretend "green choice," that simply passes the costs to the consumer, making it more expensive to really fly. Not that someone using a private jet would actually notice. It's all about having a built-in defense at hand when someone points out the globetrotter's global contradiction. "Oh, yes, I did fly to South America on a private jet, but the five hundred trees I just paid to have planted did more than offset the damage I did to the ozone." What they fail to realize: If you don't fly privately, then you don't have to pay a penance to offset flying privately. If you have to do something "good" in order to offset something bad, just don't do the bad thing.

These "offsets" are BS anyway—they're nothing more than a leafy Ponzi scheme. Who says that planting some trees along the Orinoco delta will offset the fact that Arianna flies a private jet cross-country to have her knees depilated at Dr. Kayuki's on Fifth (who has wandering hands, I must mention)?

FYI: I stopped using private jets years ago. And not because of the environment. I had a really bad experience with a flight attendant named Gebhard. I'm reminded of it every four to six weeks.

Equally ridiculous: According to folks at a recent U.N. climate conference (you can bet that was a gas), it's the poor who will be hit hardest by global warming. The logic here is that rich people can afford to move away from encroaching waters caused by climate change, but the poor will be left stranded. Worse, they can't afford carbon offsets, sandbags, or even the awareness wristbands needed to let everyone know they can't afford carbon offsets or sandbags. The injustice of it all!

But look: Whether we're talking global warming, the coming ice age, obesity, anorexia, or jock itch, it's always going to be worse when you're poor. But the upside about being poor: When you're broke, you worry about being broke. Not about global warming, the ice age, anorexia, or jock itch.

And that's got to make you happier. And let's face it, the things that make you really happy are free, or almost free. Family, friendship, sex, boxed wine, walking to the liquor store to get the box of wine.

Oh yeah—about that walking. Get this: Some environmentalists are now conceding that going by foot isn't preferable to driving, after all! Yep: It's your soles, not your SUVs, that are killing Mother Nature!

See, when you walk you burn calories. You replace those calories by eating food, or in my case, large containers of paste. But it takes a ton of energy to create and transfer food these days, which releases a lot of carbon into the atmosphere. More than your car, new research is suggesting. (Note: To find new research, simply Google "new research.")

So get this: Simply by eating, we hurt the planet. Even more: If we exercise, or engage in any kind of athletic endeavor that expends energy, we are actually doing more harm than good. By this logic, we should cancel the next Olympics, not simply because it bores us to tears, but because the athletes' energy expenditure is enough to kill a million trees, 51 percent of whom are probably minority females in lower socioeconomic groups. I won't even mention the sweatshop labor involved in the production of tube socks.

But I just did.

Anyway, I have a plan to save the world that all environmentalists will embrace. Kill everyone.

Look, it makes sense. In the utopian view of the environmentalist, the planet comes first. Environmentalists hate people because people are the enemy of earth. It's true. If we are even just partly responsible for rising greenhouse gases that indirectly increase the temperature slightly, then we're also responsible for all the potential deaths that follow. Climate-change freaks have linked hypothetical global warming increases to apocalyptic death, so that now, if you don't start purchasing carbon offsets, you're a serial killer, not just of people, but worse, of cute animals like polar bears and Robert Reich. For that you should die!

Sadly, this antihuman bullshit keeps flowing, unfiltered and unquestioned. Global warming theology and the journalism that soaks it up avoid focusing on fact, and instead build a story—one that is easily understood by the arrogant, simplistic minds that prefer to think humans (or rather, capitalistic humans) are to blame for everything wrong in the world. It's not only dishonest, it's murderous. We are now scaring a populace into thinking that the biggest threat to mankind is man's role in climate change, instead of ideologies that promote death and violence.

But hey, let's face it: Humans cannot actually do *anything* without leaving some kind of so-called carbon footprint. The gas I am passing right now, for example, is probably killing a plant in Tobago. I call that the Buttocks-fly effect. If I had pizza for lunch, I'd call it the Domino's Theory. And it would probably win a Nobel Prize or something. However...

Winning a Giant Stuffed Bear at the Fair Is Far Nobler Than Winning the Nobel Prize

Simply look at who's won the damn thing...Arafat? Carter? Al Gore?

Gore won for a simple reason: He cares. He cares not just about you or me, though: He cares about the planet. And you know, that means everything—even if he's wrong.

And he is.

Fortunately, however, winning the Nobel Peace Prize is like getting Miss Congeniality—it's basically saying, Nice job, now leave us alone. It's why Arafat and Carter each won one. It was the only way to shut them up.

I'll say this: Gore deserves something, but it's not an award. This self-obsessed blowhard has transformed himself into a bloated Chicken Little, bent on convincing you the sky is falling, as he profits off the panic. If it were the 1970s it wouldn't be global warming, it'd be the ice age, and he'd ask you to conserve woolly caps and fuzzy slippers. There would also be key parties (I wish I had a time machine).

Never mind that any moron (i.e., me) can tell you that mild winters save far more lives than might be claimed by a heat wave. In the U.K. alone (I use this statistic because it's the first one I found), it's estimated that twenty thousand lives are saved for every mild winter—a number that goes up ten times if you factor in all of Europe. But that fact doesn't fit into the lazy storytelling that is climate-change journalism—which is why you'll never read it in any paper.

That's the other thing I don't get about climate-change claptrap...
what if it's true? So what? Here's what:

We'll have warmer nights, which is great if you have problems
sleeping. I've found that when I cannot sleep, simply opening a window to allow in a nighttime breeze knocks me out immediately. Of
course, I have also been robbed thirty-eight times—usually by the
same person (my neighbor Rick). Also, many of us could get some
badly needed exercise by working on sandbag brigades to keep the
Altantic out of our kitchens.

Most of the earth's lush vegetation arose due to warmer temperatures, so global warming might save more people than it kills.
Of course Gore could never agree with this, because it would turn
his whole life upside down and all the stupidity would pour out his
nose. And then, of course, he would float away up into the atmosphere, toward the sun. This would raise temperatures even more,
and the deadly cycle would continue (one can only hope).

Which, in the end, means more bikinis—which offsets any of the
consequences due to melting ice caps. Seriously, I worked out all
the science on the back of a Lufthansa baggage handler.

Back to the Nobel Prize—to further illustrate its inherent
worthlessness—it was awarded to President Obama last October,
surprising no one but President Obama. I'd like to say that I'm
really happy for him... but isn't that what this is all about? Being
happy for "him"?

Because it certainly wasn't about us. Or the U.S. If it was, then
the Nobel committee would never have given him that prize. The
fact is, you only win that piece of crap if a certain transaction is
made—that is, a weakening of America in exchange for worldly
acceptance by madmen, maniacs, and mass murderers.

But that's not all.

The prize is not meant to award achievement, but to insult folks
the committee hates—meaning those who refuse to share their
assumptions about a deeply flawed—oh let's face it, evil—America.

Meaning, you and me. Obama's prize was not just another slap at Bush (like Carter's and Gore's awards), but a prop to help beat back the simmering dissent Obama's progressive agenda has caused here.

The Nobel committee wants him to succeed, for they're smitten with this "citizen of the world," a man who puts the globe before his country.

Forget human rights activism: This is how you win an award, people.

It won't help us, but it'll look great on his mantel. Next to the Grammy.

Those Who Can't Bomb, Teach

There is still one big question concerning Obama pal and bomber Bill Ayers that even years later no one yet has asked: "How in fuck does a terrorist become a professor?"

Ayers actually holds the dual titles of Distinguished Professor of Education and Senior University Scholar at the University of Illinois at Chicago. Where he teaches what? "Incendiary Dismemberment"? "Advanced Sedition"? "Welfare and Fraud"?

Anyway, that's two job titles—not bad for a guy whose résumé contained little more than murder, mayhem, and bad hair. And of course, there's his equally evil wife, Bernardine Dohrn (who, when referring to the Sharon Tate–LaBianca murders during a speech in 1969, said, "Dig it! First they killed those pigs and then they put a fork in pig Tate's belly: wild!"), an associate law professor at Northwestern University. It must be kook central, if she's allowed to teach kids anything.

It pisses me off, and it's got to piss you off, too. Plenty of people make their way in this world without bombing people they disagree with, and try as they might, they never find cushy jobs at bucolic campuses, surrounded by misguided apostles in backpacks willingly kissing their ass. But somehow, the most profoundly repellent people on this planet are allowed to make comfortable livings in this country, even after attempting to wage war on the very same country.

Now, I don't know how difficult it is to become a professor. But wouldn't being a terrorist somehow eliminate you from consideration? I mean, I never bombed a single thing, and I'm not allowed on college campuses, period. True, I once tried to incite a riot at a 98 Degrees lunchbox signing—but I was a different person then. Just like Ayers.

Sad thing is, Ayers isn't the only nut job with a job on campus. According to my informal head count, 98 percent of all professors currently working in American academic institutions are crazier than something really crazy (and that's crazy, people). And the reason is, plainly: They can be. The fact is, tenure allows scholars to be as destructively inane as any destructively inane creature can be—and they're immune to the natural course of consequences (with the exception of a good old-fashioned ass-kicking, which really is the best consequence of all natural courses). However, tenure—a protection against getting fired—is no road to happiness. Truth of the matter: Humans need standards by which to judge themselves. They need pressure from outside, to excel from within. You subtract that from your life, and suddenly your ambitions are formless, and your personality frantic with insecurity. You have no idea if what you're doing even matters—and so you take it out on the students.

Who, for the most part, deserve it.

God, I hate students. (Note: I don't really hate all students—just the ones who report me to campus security.)

So, at some point, professors decided that "professing" was not enough. Just being a teacher is too mundane, especially if your specialty is "the semiotics of postmodern feminist theory in *Gulliver's Travels*." So they've had to invent things to allow them to achieve their supposed oraclelike status. Your average sociology professor no longer sees himself as a teacher, he sees himself as a firebrand leader in a "worldwide struggle for societal change." Freshman English is now taught by "human rights internationalists." The facts of history have been hijacked by "cultural reinterpreters." So our graduates can't write, add, or think. But they sure can protest.

The good news is, once they realize that "protesting against transgendered intolerance" doesn't help you get a job at Google, most recent grads start thinking like normal human beings. That's when the world suddenly becomes right again, because they're working for us (strictly odd jobs around the backyard to start, of course).

A Prius Is a Fig Leaf for a Prick

No one buys a Prius because it looks good or handles well. A cross between a Mazda and a muskrat, it's embraced by celebrities, environmentalists, and the nexus of evil: the celebrity environmentalist. Leonardo DiCaprio helms a hybrid Hacky Sack, allowing his conscience to remain clear while he bangs truckloads of broads who may or may not have been born before the Lilith Fair.

You may remember that not too long ago Leo once helmed the "pussy posse," a gang of creeps who prowled the streets for sex, often in limos, private jets, and helicopters equipped with cup holders and Valtrex. No Priuses were employed—there's no room for hookers. Unless you use the trunk, of course. But that's where you keep the pharmacist.

But now Leo's promoting environmental causes, which is code for "get me laid more." And going green is the fastest way to get a girl in a rubberized sleep sack (retail $145). Especially if you've given up horse tranquilizers.

Meanwhile I read somewhere that George Clooney tools around in a Tango electric car. It looks like a phone booth. Did you know that Ed Begley, Jr., powers his toaster with a stationary bike? You just know that's got to drive his wife up a tree—which is not a bad place to be, if Daryl Hannah is still up there.

Remember when Hannah staged a twenty-three-day tree sit-in to save "an urban garden"? It made her feel good, despite being in movies that spew more toxins than Courtney Love's bladder. Everyone knows the film industry pollutes like crazy—thanks to idling trucks, lavish special effects, and Alec Baldwin's copious gas—but Hollywood will never do anything about that. There are just too many young actresses out there, and someone has to roofie them.

Propaganda Is Highly Underrated

Whenever radical Muslims get pissed (usually over something you or I have never done), you know about it fast. The networks quickly roll what seems like stock footage of Muslims chanting, burning stuff, and screaming incoherent threats, all incorporating the word "dog." But when radical Muslims do anything truly outrageous (like, say, killing a nun, beheading an American, or stabbing a film director), we find no corresponding footage of rage from us. Because we have none. When bad things happen to "us," we don't spontaneously spill into the streets, dressed in khakis and polo shirts, burning effigies of ayatollahs. And don't expect us to make signs—unless it's to say how much we adore a finalist on *American Idol* (I'm still brooding over Adam Lambert).

Extremists who hate us need to see that we can get just as scarily pissed off as they can. I mean, after a nun was murdered by some Muslim fanatics a few years back, there should have been footage of a thousand fanatically angry Italian men waving rolling pins. But there wasn't. For that very reason, our enemies think we're wusses. Or they simply realize we are consumed by too many other distractions to give a damn.

My suggestion: The next time there's a beheading or an attack on innocent civilians by radical fundamentalists, networks here should run footage of audience members of *America's Got Talent*

booing an awful contestant. The madmen won't know the difference, and neither will we.

But why stop there? A few years back, U.S. officials declared that
some dude named Omar al-Baghdadi, the supposed leader of an
al Qaeda–affiliated group in Iraq, didn't really exist. He was purely
fictional—a figment created by our enemies to give an Iraqi face to
a foreign-run terror group. Which gave me an idea.

Right now, our movie industry can make anything seem real.
Pitch any crazy scenario—cars turning into monsters, asteroids
crashing into earth, Obama fixing the economy—Hollywood can
make it happen.

And that makes me think we're wasting an immense weapon in
the war on terror: propaganda made in Hollywood that's actually
pro–United States. You know, instead of the current kind they're
making.

Seriously, why don't our best directors create short films designed
to freak the living shit out of terrorists? Like the way al Qaeda created a fictional leader, these directors could create fictional events
meant to undermine our enemies. You know, the same way they
create fictional employees to beat their taxes.

For example, Steven Spielberg could film the second coming of
Christ, with Jesus descending from heaven. Report it as news, and
watch fanatical Muslims realize they backed the wrong horse. In the
news conference, our Christian God can say, "Sorry, guys—you're
not getting seventy-two virgins. Instead, it's seventy-two nights with
Rosie O'Donnell." Or, even better: Michael Bay can create footage
depicting a race of robots, all the size of skyscrapers, that can anni-
hilate entire countries with awesome fire-breathing torches. They
will look like Transformers, but with my head. This will scare the
hell out of the Taliban, and half the population of Brentwood.

Call this ridiculous, but there's no denying that propaganda is
part of war, and we are losing on this front. Where's our *Sands
of Iwo Jima*? Why can't anyone from the 90210 ZIP code come
up with something even as inspiring as *Patton*? If people in the

Muslim world buy into the seventy-two-virgin crap, surely we can convince them that Bruce Willis can eradicate al Qaeda with a pocketknife.

Until those in Hollywood and the New York media who mock the war on terror get on board, we will continue to fight on two fronts. Unfortunately, perception is reality. Say something loud and long enough, and people will believe it.

Of course, for my plan to work, we'll have to rely on everyone to keep this charade secret. But look at *Fahrenheit 9/11*. That was pure propaganda and too many people fell for it. At least what I'm suggesting will be far more entertaining.

McCarthyism Is Necessary

Witness the never-ending love affair certain celebs have with Hugo Chavez. Here is an obnoxious blowhard who spent most of his reign consolidating power, embracing dictators and maniacs, beating the shit out of dissenters, and eliminating just about every single check on his own authority—all while wearing the same shirt and pants ensemble. He's eliminated the press, the private sector, and chiropractors (who are known subversives). And if you happen to protest, you might end up dead. If it wasn't for the fact that what he says about the U.S. is indistinguishable from the sputtering spew coming from the American left, it would actually be hilarious.

No, wait. It is hilarious.

I get so confused! And I'm not even drunk. Yet!

Which brings up this truth: McCarthyism—when it identifies real threats—is a hell of a lot more valuable than anti-McCarthyism. It's a shame it's a dirty word, because for the most part, Americans who sympathize with fascism and pricks like Chavez deserve complete exposure, then humiliation. And what's wrong with their careers being adversely affected by their wrongheaded infatuation with brutal totalitarianism? I'd assume they'd see that as a fair trade.

This is not to say someone like Sean Penn should be banned from expressing his views. Instead, we should be encouraged to shine a spotlight on these views, so he truly has to answer for them at the box office. Which, judging by his latest box office receipts, he already has.

Replacing a Dictator With a Democracy Doesn't Sit Well With Other Dictators

Ever since the United States invaded Iraq, we've been constantly reminded by the European and American press of how "unpopular" we are as a country. Yes, the world hates us—something that existed well before we got rid of Saddam, by the way—but it was something that was supposed to change once we elected Obama.

Funny thing is, that sudden transformation from hatred to affection never happened. Obama's elected, and America is still despised. By everyone. Including Obama!

Which leads to my real question: What the hell is wrong with being unpopular? And when did it matter how assholes felt about us anyway? That's right: assholes. Most of the world is made up of them, and the fact that they hate us means we are doing something right. America is unpopular with countries like Iran and Venezuela because their leaders are exactly like Saddam Hussein. So when they see one of their own yanked out of the catbird seat, to be replaced by a sloppy but workable democracy, you can bet they're going to be pissed as hell. And scared, too. The idea that we should give a fuck about these feelings is absurd and, sadly, pathetic. The world doesn't need marriage counseling, it needs corporal punishment, and America is the only country left that knows how to spank (if that's not a movie tagline, then I'm a kumquat).

And I'm ready for the common retort: "It's easy to say those things when you won't be the one doing the fighting." You're right. It is easy. But look, I don't have to be a fireman to think arson is a bad thing. And besides, the soldiers agree with me. But more important, I'm too old and fat to be a soldier—and you don't want to see me in camouflage. It's just not my color, and it's far from slimming.

Bad Hair Means a Bad Leader

Despite the fact that we have the strongest military in the world, we have somehow made ourselves defenseless against whack-job countries like Iran and North Korea. This proves a simple point: Having the greatest fighting force in the history of the world means little if there's no will—or balls—in the White House.

But more important, both Iran and North Korea are operating under the same guiding logic: "You better not tell us what to do, or we will blow up something." And although the threat might be spoken in a different language, these powers share a striking similarity: bad hair. This could be at the heart of the issue—these angry leaders' childish behavior could be the product of insecurity over a horrible hairdo.

And the lack of awareness about one's bad hair could very well be a sign of insanity. Think about it: Whenever you see institutionalized people in movies, their hair is always a godawful mess.

Which leads me to my simple solution: Kill people with bad hair. Or at the very least, the leaders of North Korea, Iran, and probably Venezuela.

Another point about hair: Junichiro Koizumi, Japanese prime minister, has absolutely terrific hair. I always find it interesting when a Western-style cut is adopted by an Asian man. It makes him look like an orchestra conductor or someone who plays an orchestra conductor.

This is absolutely 100 percent fact.

Obama Is a Hot Chick

When it comes to the media, Obama can do no wrong. It's as though he's protected by reverse kryptonite—a powerful, impenetrable shield that makes him stronger, but everyone else around him weak in the knees. For this reason, he reminds me of a really hot chick.

You know how when a friend starts dating some girl—let's say a stripper with top-of-the-line implants and a truly remarkable skill involving the projection of flaming Ping-Pong balls—he overlooks everything else. She could be spreading genital warts like a Jehovah's Witness unloading a case of *Watchtowers*, and it won't matter. Blinded by her beauty, he lets her get away with everything, until your buddy is left broken and broke—riddled with disease, saddled with a meth habit, and sleeping in your garage.

I'm not saying Barack is anywhere near that bad. I'm just saying that the media *are*. Face it: If you found out that your new girlfriend, who happened to be Megan Fox, worked with Acorn, hung around with a radical leftist/bomber, and used to do coke back in college—would you care?

Of course you wouldn't! It's Megan Fox!!!

Congratulations: You're now the *New York Times*.

But look, even I have a bit of a mancrush on President Obama. He's delicious. I'm serious—I'm no liberal (I don't like cats, candles, or skinny jeans), but I think Obama is the strongest Democratic president I have ever seen: smart, inspiring, and totally presidential. In short, he's an amazing messenger.

But I'm not a fan of messengers—I'm a fan of messages. And if the message is flawed, then I don't care how great the messenger is.

And that's the real story behind Obama's success. The message Obama carried to victory was one of change, which can mean anything, and everything, rendering it every bit as meaningful as the contents of my Jetsons lunchbox (in there right now: a pair of wax lips and a ball gag).

The fact is, even Obama knows that his message won't work with most Americans, but as a messenger he rules. Which is why he has to rely solely on his charisma and soaring phrases to push whatever misguided plan he has. More important, the left must realize that if they can't get universal health care and global warming legislation passed while Obama is in office, then they never will. That's because Obama is the greatest leader they've had since that last guy with the red nose, and they won't get anyone better after Obama leaves.

And that's a testament to how truly crappy all liberal ideas are at their core: If Obama can't get them turned into law via his own shining Messiahlike qualities, then no one can.

(By the way, if you're looking for the anti-Obama, try John Bolton. Our former ambassador to the U.N. not only looks like a meanie, he is a meanie—blunt, unyielding, and kinda scary. Which is probably why he tended to make the most sense. Because when you're a cactus with a mustache resembling a dozing tribble, you have no choice but to be right most of the time, or you're really screwed.)

World Leaders Should Only Chop Wood for Exercise

Americans should be ashamed of their leaders for one reason alone: They exercise like girls. President Obama hits the gym obsessively (I imagine him mastering the elliptical trainer), and before him G. W. Bush jogged. Jogged!

It's disgusting.

No president should jog. Could you imagine some of our greatest leaders in modern history—like, say, Winston Churchill—in a velour tracksuit? FDR would have never been caught "racewalking." Not that he had a choice in the matter, but still. I distinctly remember Jimmy Carter collapsing while jogging in a 5k or something—that did not help his standing during the hostage crisis, I think. And as

I write this, Sarkozy just dropped during a light run. And I thought that guy was tough!

Fact is, world leaders should only get exercise doing manly things—like chopping wood and, er, chopping wood. Reagan chopped wood, and he looked awesome doing it. I believe even the trees found it kind of sexy.

And love him or hate him, you would never see Putin on a stair-climber. Unless maybe it was made of wood, which could be possible if it was made in Russia. But he chopped wood, and did other manly crap—often shirtless, while flexing his pecs. He's Russia's Stretch Armstrong.

Fact is, you gain far more respect wielding an axe than laboring on the stair-climber. And let's not forget where all that indoor aerobic training gets you: nowhere. Did you see Obama throw out the first pitch at the 2009 Major League All-Star Game? I would say he throws like a little girl, but that would offend little girls. My feeling is if Obama started chopping wood, he'd instinctively become a better pitcher and a bowler. I cannot prove this theory, but I sense chopping wood helps purge all that wonky nerdiness that comes with being a wonky nerd. And that's what Obama needs: an exorcism to remove the incompetent, elitist stink that comes from being among the best, the brightest, and the most uncoordinated.

Gitmo Is No Worse Than Summer Camp

If you were to ask the media to rank a list of evil things, Guantanamo detention center would be in the top five, beating out Adolf Hitler, suicide bombers, Republicans, disposable diapers, and fat kids. Gitmo is their moral red herring. As long as they keep bringing it up, they can avoid any real discussion of actual evil in the world.

The American left and its European cheering section hate Gitmo, not because they think war is bad, but because they believe trying to win one is worse. And to win one, you need to keep the bad guys off the playing field. But the American left also loves Gitmo, because it's their political fig leaf, the thing they hide behind when they've got nothing else.

But if there's anything we've learned since Obama's inauguration, it is that the only solution worse than Gitmo is *no* Gitmo. The goal of Gitmo was to house people who are not only a danger to us, but also targets in their own countries. Nobody likes these people.

And come on: How bad is Gitmo really, when you compare it to my life? With three meals a day, regular exercise, and prayer hours, the detainees enjoy a far healthier lifestyle than I can ever hope for.

Obama Sees Your Paycheck as Public Property

President Obama embodies the most eloquent and appealing combination of every liberal cliché one could ever imagine, molded into an agreeable life form. He's able to take every failed policy and every adolescent and/or misguided belief about wealth and foreign policy and make it sound perfectly sensible. Even heroic! He's a grown man with teenage aspirations and earnest naïveté: the kind of qualities that lead a sensitive student body president to invite a homeless man to the school spirit assembly, or offer wide-eyed appeals for negotiations without preconditions to corrupt regimes.

The genius of Obama: It's all about change. But what is that change? It's not substance, it's style. Fact is, not a single idea Barack has bandied about is new—he's every bit as liberal as Barney Frank on a bender—and his ideology is in lockstep with the most disastrous progressive thinking of the last twenty years. Meaning, Obama is praising stuff that doesn't work and never has.

Poor Hillary Clinton. During the primaries, she knew this, because nearly all of those criticisms also applied to her! She might have actually been a fairly mediocre president, but she became the old crone at Cinderella's ball. And it was Obama's foot that fit the slipper.

This is not to say Barack doesn't really believe in change, even if his ideas are old. For him, change really meant "pick me." And that's it. There were no revolutionary ideas. He's just an extremely charming man who wants to lead and be admired for leading. And that was enough. The fact is, Obama worked because he looks alarmingly like a friendly commercial actor who just quit smoking using Nicorette gum (and you can, too!). He's the guy leaping in the air after purchasing a Prius, the father of three taking his family on a much-needed cruise to the Bahamas using Expedia.com, the sensible guy who found out how easy it was to consolidate all of his debts in just one easy phone call. He's got the look, and the delivery. The look that says, "I'm doing all right, and you can, too—if you listen to me."

And I'd be lying if I said I didn't want to.

He is, in effect, the perfect Hollywood president—not simply because Hollywood loves him, but because Hollywood made him. In fact, are we sure he's not a hologram put out by DreamWorks? Has anyone viewed this guy with 3-D glasses? I bet it's 3-Delightful!

Think about this: There has never been, in the history of moviemaking, a heroic nonliberal president. Whether he's played by Michael Douglas, Kevin Kline, or a shiny rock, what makes him appealing is his simple yet profound liberal virtues, i.e., bombing bad guys is wrong, the rich are corrupt, and the poor deserve your money and probably your Porsche.

Where the average Joe sees enterprise and industry, Hollywood and the mainstream media see American greed and illegality. And that's the cause of all the world's problems (overlooking, of course, their own fabulous wealth and massive coke habits).

Obama is so good at playing this role that most in the media choose to ignore, accept, or applaud the basic far-left principles that serve as his ideological core. So far—at least to me—his administration's real goal is total wealth redistribution. Because progressives have no prescription for economic growth, all they have in their arsenal is income redistribution. Therefore, they see your paycheck as something they own, not you. They call this social justice—more code for "you're screwed." We're seeing this now, as the Obama administration seeks to level out all of our incomes, in the name of, well, justice.

It's Robin Hood at its best—a free lunch that, in the end, we will all pay for, even after the money runs out. And this is what happens when you decide to rearrange a pie, instead of growing it. Instead of a full stomach, your fingers get sticky. Not that I mind that. I like sticky fingers. It was probably the best Monkees album.

The Only Real Class Warfare Is Between the Alive and the Dead

I recently came across a poll by an organization called Pew—a word my mother would often use when she did my laundry. The Pew poll stank, too. It claimed that more of the public than ever believes America is split evenly into two economic groups, the "haves" and the "have-nots." In 1988, 71 percent rejected this notion, while just 26 percent saw a divided nation.

I hate studies like this because they *always* involve math. Also, they're depressing. The idea that half of us think we're deprived says more about spiritual emptiness than it does about any financial gap. Let me explain the obvious: If you're reading this, and you *know* you are, you're already a "have." First off, you have a book. Plus, you have eyes. In fact, you've got the ultimate "have"—life itself. That's not to say there are no have-nots. Most of us personally know have-nots. We call them—and excuse my jargon—dead people. But at least dead have-nots had something. Once. They're the "hads."

Let me introduce you to some other have-nots: have-nots who never had squat. First, the victims of ejaculation. There are trillions of those. In fact, 812 trillion. And, uh, 37. How do I know? I did the math! Each ejaculation produces 100 million sperm. There are nearly 7 billion people on the planet, and roughly half are men. That's 3.5 billion ejaculations times 100 million. Every three hours! It is every three hours, isn't it? Of course, almost all those sperm end up in condoms, old socks, and hotel bath mats. This waste has gone on eight to ten times a day since the beginning of time—which is, to use more math, a long time ago. But those aren't the real have-nots. What about the have-nots who actually won the lottery, made it all the way to the egg, and then got their ticket invalidated? Since 1973, there's something like 46 million unlucky winners that never get as far as a Dumpster behind a Planned Parenthood clinic. So maybe the liberal politicians have it right. We do have "two Americas"—us and all the have-nots in Dumpsters. The thing is, dead fetuses are notoriously silent about their opinions on prosperity— but you can guess how they'd respond. When it comes to under- standing the complexities of modern life, they truly "have not."

When you put life in this perspective, the difference between what's considered a long life and what's considered a short one is almost nil. The fact that you're alive—and beat odds that are so daz- zling they hurt your brain to think about—means that dying at age forty is no different from croaking at one hundred. Seriously, you already won the race. You're a have. It's a shame, though, that the rest of the haves on this planet don't do more for the have-nots, who never made it this far. But that's life. And for the have-nots, death.

Speaking Truth to Power Means "Shouting at People Who Remind Me of Daddy"

I have always been amused by the phrase "speaking truth to power," a strange amalgam of words that, roughly translated, is supposed to mean: "I'm brave."

The only people who think they can speak truth to power, of course, are liberals. It is a self-satisfying exercise for them: a wonderfully therapeutic wash of emotion derived from throwing a pie at a conservative speaker on campus, or calling her a Nazi. Or both.

In academic and media circles, though, this so-called act of bravery possesses the risk level of playing solitaire without a helmet.

That's why speaking truth to power is a sham: You can't do it if everyone around you agrees with you. Which is why Bill Maher and Keith Olbermann are dicks. They think they're speaking truth to power, but they're only talking to a mirror. A mirror that claps and gives them Emmys, and sometimes urinary tract infections.

Which is also why I still hold on to a belief that maybe the Obama presidency could, one day, turn into something awesome. I mean, imagine if all the people who pride themselves on speaking truth to power end up speaking truth to power to the Obama administration—which consists of people who normally speak truth to power! If this actually happens, the earth could implode and I might have a complete nervous breakdown.

Sadly, however, it's not happening. Look at our gay rights leaders. I mean, Obama holds the same views as the Mormon Church on gay marriage, but I guess "speaking truth to power" only works on boring white people in magic underpants. And what happened to all the anti-Iraq protesters and bloggers who wanted Bush tried for war crimes? That was speaking truth to power, no? Well, as I write this, Obama has pretty much "stayed the course" with Iraq and Afghanistan, and even stepped up bombings in Pakistan, yet places like the Daily Kos and the Huffington Post are strangely silent. No speaking truth to power anymore—not even when Obama okayed the bombing of a funeral in Pakistan, killing dozens of Taliban. If Bush had bombed a funeral, the speaking-truth-to-power crowd would be apoplectic with truth-to-power speaking. But instead, with Obama, they're meeker than mice, content to hold their fake beliefs temporarily—for these beliefs serve only to smear those they simply don't like. God, I wish I was more like them.

Martyrdom Among Our Enemies
Should Be Encouraged

Right after the execution of the three bizarre, smiling terrorists responsible for the October 2002 bombings in Indonesia—an attack that left over two hundred people dead—the BBC published a repulsive little piece questioning the merits of the execution. They said such punishment would simply turn the bombers into martyrs. And to prove their point, they actually turned the bombers into martyrs!—by chronicling the radicalization of these "three boys," as they turned into "Islamic warriors," Indonesia's "most famous faces." You don't need to have read the article: It was a typical exercise in the insipid science of root causes—all that was missing was a sidebar on how these boys were never breast-fed.

The reporter writes that "killing the three men presents as many problems as it solves." Their executions "may go some way toward keeping their message alive." Whether this is true or not is beside the point: We know for a fact that regardless of whether the message remains "alive," the actual men who promote it through murder aren't. They are dead. Killing the messenger, in this case, is the only way to kill the message.

But this idea of "keeping the message alive" is true, as long as the BBC keeps regurgitating this mindless, destructive pap. Look, we cannot control whether a punishment for an act will create martyrs. That call, I feel, is up to the martyrs/followers. The fact is, the "martyr" excuse never comes up when innocent people die. When al Qaeda bombed London back in 2005, I don't remember the BBC warning the fundamentalist nutbags that "now you're in for it. You've created sixty martyrs!" For some reason, martyrs are only created when you execute murderers who desire only to destroy you. You have to hand it to the BBC: Show them two sides to any conflict, and they will cling to the wrong one. Maybe that's why no one bothers martyring them.

But the BBC aren't the only ones guilty of this. After Saddam Hussein was executed, Tom Brokaw went on the Don Imus radio show and said, "[W]e portray ourselves around the world as the champions of democracy and the rule of law," yet Hussein's execution "resembled the worst kind of nightmare out of the old American West." He then added that Hussein, who "had disappeared, in effect, as some kind of a symbol over there, suddenly becomes a martyr."

Brokaw said this about two years ago, so I think enough time has passed to let him know that he was as wrong as a mesh thong. This martyrdom he predicted, I can safely say, did not occur. It's been a long time since Saddam's death, and the response has been pretty quiet (compared to, say, Norman Fell's)—there in fact have been peaceful elections and little, if any, sectarian violence that invokes the memory of Saddam.

Brokaw also said he couldn't imagine a worse manner in which the execution could have been carried out. But I can: Saddam could have lived. If the U.S. had actually been in charge of executing Saddam, the event would not actually have occurred until 2047, and Saddam would have been the ripe old age of 110. He'd also be dating an Olsen twin, but that's neither here nor there.

Not Executing Homosexuals Makes Us a Laughingstock in Islamic Countries

Here's some travel information for gay folks: Don't go to Iran. They will hang you. That simple fact cries out for a protest of some kind from the likes of Ellen DeGeneres, Rosie O'Donnell, or that dude who played Doogie Howser, but something tells me coming out against an Islamic country's practices is beneath their pay grade. I didn't hear a single thing from them during the protest crackdown of 2009. Sure, gays were out in full force because of Prop 8, and I get it: It's unfair that you can't get married and all that. But in Iran, people—*gay* people—are *dying* because they're gay. Forget the hopes of getting a registry at Restoration Hardware. These folks are lucky if they get to keep their hands.

Blood for Oil Is a Fair Trade

I agree that "No blood for oil" fits better on a T-shirt than "No blood for control of a territory and all its resources—which is the only reason any war has been waged offensively and the only reason that makes any sense."

Look, we need oil to live. If our livelihood is threatened, then our vital interests are in jeopardy, and that means we need your oil. So, if you're not going to be nice about it, and/or you're going to invade other countries or rattle your sabers at us, then we should pay you an unauthorized visit—if only to see if the country could use a Wal-Mart.

No One Can Name a Single Coherent Counterterrorism Plan Created by Anyone on the Left

Nuts pooping in caves who, in the past, could barely make it to town to sell a goat can now fly our jumbo jets into our buildings. Bottom line: Leadership in the West means keeping us safe from Islamist aggression, period. All the rest—the economy, social issues, and so on—springs from our success or failure on that. Here's an experiment: Take a look at today's front page of USA Today. Now imagine that paper the day after a terrorist attack takes place on American soil. How many of those "important stories"—the struggling stock market, health insurance reform, global warming—will still be on that front page? None. When it comes to terror, everything else is peanuts.

So I have to ask, where is Obama's plan to protect us? Why not a single coherent plan *ever* proposed by the Democrats? EVER??????

It must be locked away somewhere, along with Gore's blueprint for the Internet.

The sad fact is, the left really doesn't choose to believe in the terrorist threat. Because it undermines everything they need to cling to about the evil nature of the U.S. It's us, not them. Who needs a combat plan when you've got Jungian therapy?

Which is why global warming is a far more attractive issue to embrace. Because it allows legions of America-haters to blame America for a problem that will eventually—and wrongly—create more penalties for Americans. Do you think the 9/11 hijackers gave a damn about the harm they did to the environment when they destroyed our buildings? I'm sure the far-left environmental wackos must have been relieved they flew commercial, instead of private.

And for those of you wondering what the coherent antiterrorism plan articulated by the right was—it was an actual war on terror. There was no fear in calling it "terror" (as opposed to Janet Napolitano's "man-caused" disasters), nor was there any reticence in killing any of its practitioners. Did this work? Well, as I write this, we have not had a terrorist strike against the U.S. in eight years. So, I'd say: yes. And I'm keeping my fingers and toes crossed that it continues, which makes it hard to walk, but I have all my food delivered so it doesn't matter. (Note: I wrote this prior to the Fort Hood massacre, but I guess, in Janet's world, that attack was just a "man-caused" disaster.)

Teenagers Are the Purest Embodiment of Liberalism

I was a lefty in high school—which is normal because it was high school, after all, and it was either that or playing sports. It's the romantic thing to do—being a crusading lib—for it makes everything in the world about *you* and *your feelings*. Which coincides nicely with being a teenager. It's all about speaking truth to power, which translated, means, *Look at me, not at my parents*. It's okay when kids do it, but it's gross when adults do it, because you really should have grown up by now.

But reality, thankfully, hit me in the face before I entered the real world. Back when I was a punk at Serra High School (home to Barry Bonds, Lynn Swann, and the dude who married Gisele Bündchen), I took part in a classroom debate, focusing on the pros and cons of mutually assured destruction. I took the con side, since I was antinuke—and it's an easy position (which was, *No one wants to die*). This guy, a nice, nerdy chap named Jeff, was my opposition. He was way smarter than me, but he wasn't pretty—even his acne had acne. (Sorry, Jeff—if you're reading this—but it was true.)

I breezed through my opening remarks: Weapons only exist to hurt people, and hurting people is wrong. So, let's get rid of the weapons! (This idea, as idiotic as it sounds, is basically the bedrock principle behind gun control and liberal ideology in general.)

Then it was the pimpled prince's turn, and he wiped the floor, the windows, the lockers, and a Guatemalan exchange student with me. It's not a comfortable feeling to realize during a debate that your opponent is not only dead right, but capable of destroying your complete worldview. Which Jeff did, handily.

I can't remember what he said, exactly. But whatever it was came from the brain, not from the heart, and it was packed with facts, logic, and all the crap I'd chosen to ignore all my life because it reminded me of my parents. Jeff, in a nutshell, explained the principles of "peace through strength" so clearly that I could no longer pretend to believe in the bullshit I believed in.

But instead of admitting defeat I did what any good liberal would do. I cheated.

I played to the crowd with wisecracks about Jeff, aping his monotone delivery and going for cheap laughs. I even found a way to temporarily skip out during the debate, just to avoid revealing my own incompetence even further.

I won the debate. It really didn't matter that Jeff trounced me. He couldn't get any credit for it, because he wasn't telling the teens what they wanted to hear. Lesson learned: Clever potshots are more effective than facts to that particular mind-set (just ask Jon Stewart).

That debate took place over twenty-three years ago, and it still bugs the crap out of me. Funny thing is, I bet it doesn't bug Jeff. But thanks to him, I realized I was an impostor. And if a teenage impostor can hold liberal beliefs so easily, with so little knowledge to back them up, then they aren't really beliefs. They're just bumper stickers. Sooner or later, they have to peel off.

Pacifists Are Parasites

Did you know that there's an International Day of Peace? The event, established by the United Nations in 1981, was designed to provide "an opportunity for individuals to create practical acts of peace," in order to build "cultures of peace for the children and future generations." What is a culture of peace? Who knows, but I bet it smells like a mix of patchouli and body odor.

I hate pacifists, and not simply because they invent ridiculous jargon like "collective progress" and "planetary future." No—it's that their whole existence is based on a lie. Pacifists aren't really peace lovers at all, because in order for them to survive, we must fight wars. In this sense, they aren't peaceful, they are parasitic. For pacifists to exist in the U.S., and lead hypocritical, prosperous lives without being beheaded, they *need* an army of people they deeply despise to protect them. And to die for them. No wonder pacifists hate the military. Soldiers are just way better people than they could ever hope to be.

American Protesters Are Just Terrified of Growing Up

Remember those tree-sitters occupying an oak at Cal-Berkeley a few years back? Apparently they were pissed because the school was going to remove the trees to build an athletic center—something the protesters would never use because Dumpster diving and humiliating your parents don't require aerobic conditioning.

I loved this story because it illustrates some essential truths about protesters.

One: They're petulant babies afraid of adulthood. One of the protesters living among the branches was David Galloway, and at the time he claimed to be thirty-six years old. It must be great for his parents to know that, as their son reaches middle age, he's living in a tree. And it's not even a treehouse. He's more like a tree squatter.

Two: Protesters don't really care about people or trees—all they care about is the attention. You see, school officials had become increasingly worried about the amount of human waste coming from the oaks. These idiots were actually shitting on people. Think about that! It's disgusting. Crap shouldn't grow on trees, and it shouldn't fall from them either. And I'm sure if these oaks could actually talk they would agree with me, and plead for a match.

Three: This is private property and these conduits for crabs had no right to be there. Imagine if some middle-aged dude in a mesh tank top and torn culottes moved into a tree in your front yard (I can volunteer to complete this fantasy for you, but only during the summer months).

But in the end, you can't just blame these protesters alone. If you ignore these freaks, then they will stop the protesting. But we don't ignore them, and that's our fault. Every time a reporter turns on a camera and points it in their direction, that's incentive for a protester to justify his existence. If we collectively agreed to turn our backs on this idiocy, these losers would finally go away—and so would their poop.

Finally, when you compare these jackasses to people truly protesting something worth protesting—like those standing up against the Iranian regime following that rigged election—you see why that guy in the tree needs to get his butt kicked each day, repeatedly, for the rest of his life.

You Don't Apologize to Warmongers
After Kicking Their Ass

Two years ago, on the anniversary of John Lennon's death, his widow asked everyone to commemorate with "a day of worldwide healing."

She placed a full-page advertisement in the *New York Times* on November 26, urging people to apologize to those who have suffered because of violence and war.

There are two things wrong with this (three if you count the mere existence of Yoko Ono):

- The only people who should apologize are the BAD people who do BAD things. Violence is not a level playing field where victim and victimizer are the same thing. Get this: War waged for a good reason yields good things—if the war is won.
- Celebs always feel that the West should be apologizing for all that is wrong in this world. They refuse to admit that the U.S. has done more to save the lives of *all* people across the world than any other nation in history (four thousand years, give or take a century). If anyone deserves an apology, it's the civilians killed, in tragic numbers, by the very barbarians we haven't gotten around to killing yet. Also, speaking of apologies: Anyone who ever saw the *Rolling Stone* cover with John and Yoko nude deserves one. That's a war crime if there ever was one.

If Iran Were Where Mexico Is, Ahmadinejad Would
Already Be Buried in Ten Different Places

Remember the media's surprise when they learned that Israel had drawn up secret plans to destroy Iran's uranium enrichment facilities with tactical nuclear weapons? I know—imagine how ridiculous it must be, for one country to make plans to destroy another country that's busy trying to, you know, develop the capability to destroy that country!

Of course, it's all the Jews' fault. But never mind that: If America bordered a country bent on destroying America, I'd hope we would have obliterated the place by now. Of course, we'd experience opposition from the usual suspects—Sean Penn, *The View*, and the guy who runs the health food store on the corner. But when was the last time any of them were right about anything?

Get back to me on that.

Winning the Cold War Means George Clooney Can Tell Us How Lame the Cold War Was

I believe it's what you call a catch-22—which might have been a movie, and possibly even a book. If we had not won the Cold War, and gotten rid of communism, we'd still be dealing with a massive totalitarian and woefully corrupt world power bent on eliminating our way of life (and replacing it with a crappy one full of inferior products and overgrown mustaches). But we won the damn thing, in an amazing triumph that closed a tumultuous century that had seen millions of innocents die at the hands of Marxist thugs.

But now, just years later, we are told by jackasses like George Clooney that our concerns were unfounded—because, jeez, look how easy the U.S.S.R. crumbled. If Clooney had his way, he'd make an anti-anticommunist movie every six months—just to make himself feel smart. How he can believe that one overzealous man like Joe McCarthy merits dramatically more attention than an imbecilic system that starved millions is beyond me. But I suppose it makes for better cocktail conversation. And it gets him laid (not that he needs help, for he is mildly attractive—a hunkier version of Rachel Maddow).

Sure, George, communism was never really a threat, and it was McCarthy whom we all really needed to worry about. I mean, he must have killed millions of people, right? Just tell the Georgians, Ukrainians, Latvians, Estonians, Lithuanians...oh why bother. Those just aren't big enough film markets—so why should we care?

Antiwar Activists Love War More Than the People Who Fight Them

If there's one thing I learned from the 2008 election, it's how awesome Joe Biden's hair plugs are—and how cool an issue war can be, only if you're against it. The fact is, the Iraq War gave antiwar activists the biggest club they've ever had to beat the crap out of our country's sense of self. And this explains the true terrible secret behind all those assholes who bashed Bush over Iraq: They *needed* war. And get this: It doesn't matter what kind of war it is, as long as it's long, and people die. That was the problem with the first Gulf War. It happened way too fast—and that sucked. By the time you brewed the pot of herbal tea and hand-painted your sign using organic chai paste (basically, your feces), the war had already ended.

The Iraq War was different. It took time. After we went in and routed the Iraqi army, things turned sour, because of poor planning, I guess. Despite the incoherence from above, however, the war was a success, if you count freeing a nation and killing a dictator a success (I do—but what do I know? I still can't drive a stick). But the grim reapers on the left realized that the trickle of deaths month after month was all you needed to undermine a war effort—a thing you never see in the mind-set of the countries we're at war with. The war was a gift to them—they could smear everyone associated with it and pave the way for a return of their rancid ideology. It worked. Antiwar activists, as a rule, need America to lose, to prove their point (that is, America equals evil).

The funny thing is, once the left got into power, suddenly it was okay to win a war! Obama continued Bush's policies, because he could not bring himself to snatch defeat from the jaws of victory. It's why General Petraeus is still around doing what General Petraeus does (win wars). How funny is it that things as evil as the surge are suddenly okay with the folks who condemned them?

Really funny, if you ask me. But if you ask me again, I might change my mind and say ducks wearing hats (they *are* funny, you gotta admit).

Soldiers Make for Better Citizens, Although the Media Disagree

So last Sunday I did something against doctor's orders: I read the *New York Times*. On the front page was a piece on American war vets of modern wars. The *Times* says they're all homicidal maniacs, committing up to 121 murders total, stateside. But this is the *Times*, of course, so you know what they leave out is always more important than what they leave in. I'm talking context. Oh—and a soul.

In the *New York Post*, writer Andy Soltis, along with other bloggers, pointed out that the murder rate for returning vets is only one-fifth that of young Americans who did not fight. The take-home message: If you want to make peace, make warriors.

It's funny how the *Times* thinks the worst of our military, even as they bend over backward pretending to support the troops. It's no wonder that they and others swallowed that ridiculous Lancet study, claiming six hundred thousand Iraqis are dead from the war. I guess if you really need to validate your own bitter assumptions about America, you'll swallow anything.

As you know, that number is almost as unfounded as the *Times*'s current circulation numbers, which, if they drop any further, will be less than those of your average supermarket circular (about as newsworthy, by the way). It's odd: The rest of us worry about Osama and

Ahmadinejad; the *Times* editors prefer to target seventeen-year-old kids eating MREs ten thousand miles from home. Why? Because those kids don't read the *Times*, or hold *Times*-ish opinions. They don't care who Frank Rich and Maureen Dowd are (I think they're the same person, actually). Essentially these kids don't believe the *Times* should run the world. And that's deeply offensive to the *Times*. Thankfully.

Hunger Strikers Deserve to Starve

Here's why: Starving yourself is a cheap way to win an argument. I used to employ a similar strategy as a child—holding my breath until I got what I wanted. And when I did get what I wanted—a blowtorch shaped like a unicorn—I went back to breathing. It's emotional blackmail.

Even worse than the old-school hunger strike is the in-vogue "shared" hunger strike—you know, when one celebrity conducts a hunger strike for a day, and then "passes it along" to another celebrity. Basically, all they're doing is dieting, then bragging about it. If they had real balls, they would pull a "reverse hunger strike." Swear that you will not stop eating until your demands are met. For every hour you're ignored, eat one large cake. That would be a real sacrifice for those fashionable size zeroes—and it would also make for a truly magical spectator sport. Just don't sit in the front rows unless you're wearing a Glad bag.

Discussing Waterboarding Is the Real Torture

We've heard a lot about waterboarding, but usually just from people who never have anything nice to say about anything, anyway. In a sense, critics are using waterboarding as a form of torture on us—a constant reminder that Americans are no better than our adversaries. We don't fly planes into buildings, we don't behead gays, and we don't imprison rape victims—but forty seconds of simulated drowning, that's unforgivable. (FYI: I love that they call it "simulated" drowning. It's simulated because they stop pouring water on your face *before you die*. Dunking a guy and pulling him out of the water the second before his lungs fill with water would also be "simulated drowning." Why don't they just call it what it is: cutting off a person's breathing with a rag and water. It doesn't make it worse or better, and it would get rid of one more example of people on the left and right pussying around with euphemisms to suit their bias.)

Now, I might agree that waterboarding is torture, but as long as those who hate the U.S. hate waterboarding, then I love it more than life itself. See, it's a recipe I have for life. If the *New York Times*, NPR, Tim Robbins, Sean Penn, and Hugo Chavez hate something, then it *must* be good for you. So I cherish waterboarding. I want to make it our national sport, or our national bird. I want to make the waterboard the state flower of Vermont, instead of the Birkenstock.

But here's the great news about the left's obsession with waterboarding: It helped to remind America of what happened on September 11, 2001. The fact is, the more time passed, the less we thought about the ever-present threat to our way of life. The debate over waterboarding paddle-shocked our senses, which is why Obama and his counterparts soon realized they were on the wrong end of a losing battle. What was supposed to be a big win for everyone who despised Bush became an issue that resurrected Dick Cheney. Who knew!

And so, we were told that Abu Zubaydah, a top lieutenant to bin Laden, gave up his cohorts after a half-minute of waterboarding. He said Allah visited him and told him to cooperate. Allah, it turns out, prefers dry land. The good news is this new information prevented dozens of attacks—perhaps a mammoth one meant to take out downtown Los Angeles. But if we had listened to the Streisands and Afflecks of the world and gotten rid of waterboarding, how many lives might have been lost? Who knows. It's hard to prove a negative. It's also hard to find a Christmas sweater that doesn't make me look fat, but it doesn't stop me from trying.

Compassionate Liberals Actually Want You Dead

Shortly after the actor Heath Ledger died, Bill Maher weighed in with his usual pithy commentary. On Maher's show, Rush Limbaugh's name came up, and Maher said, "Why couldn't he have croaked...instead of Heath Ledger?"

I don't care if you like Rush or hate him. I happen to think he's pretty awesome (anyone who can scare the hell out of two political parties has to be). But what I always find amusing is that the champions of tolerance—the people who earn their keep painting the right as hateful, mean-spirited people—actually wish death on people who don't agree with them.

This shouldn't come as a surprise to anyone who happens upon a progressive opinion on a blog. Beneath every compassionate liberal is an undercurrent of fascism. Comforted by a complicit press, and knowing they can't win on the playing field of ideas, advocating death is the viable option.

And for that, of course, they should die.

I kid, of course.

Let's just cut off their hands!

Dick Cheney Is Closer to the Hell's Angels Than Hunter S. Thompson Could Ever Be

When one becomes a liberal, one advocates a phony, overarching selflessness, but hilariously, is doing so for purely selfish reasons. It's the human equivalent of a puppy's face: an evolutionary tool designed to enhance survival, reproductive value, and status. Also, like puppies, many liberals go number one on the floor when they're nervous. In short, liberalism is based on one desire: to look cool in order to get approval. Preaching tolerance makes you look cooler than saying something like, "Please lower my taxes," which personally gets me hot, but did nothing for my eHarmony profile.

This is why the only true form of rebellion left on this planet is rejecting the trademark forms of romantic rebellion, such as anarchy, activism, nipple rings, and tribal tattoos. The antirebel is far more subversive because every day he or she says things that aren't sanctioned and certainly aren't considered cool among the media elite. This is why Dick Cheney is closer to the Hell's Angels than Hunter S. Thompson ever could be. And why Jon Stewart is about as daring as a diaper filled with Nilla Wafers. Which, by the way, is not very daring. Or comfortable, for that matter.

Keith Olbermann Is Batpoop Crazy

Do you remember his *Playboy* interview back in September 2007? In it, he said Fox News is worse than al Qaeda. His words were: "Al Qaeda really hurt us, but not as much as Rupert Murdoch has hurt us, particularly in the case of Fox News. Fox News is worse than al Qaeda—worse for our society. It's as dangerous as the Ku Klux Klan ever was."

What, no comparisons to Hitler? I'm hurt.

Look, whether you're a lib or a con, you should be creeped out by what he said. I mean, hate Fox all you want, but suggesting that the horrific crimes committed by al Qaeda and the Klan are comparable to the action of a media outlet? That's nuts. No, I'm sorry: That's FUCKING nuts. It's insulting on every level to those whose lives have been affected by real tragedy.

But can you blame him? Making decisions about how to conduct the war on terror is tough. Beating up on Fox News? Easy.

Fox News won't blow up his city. It won't sue him. It won't even TP his hot tub. Instead, it will do what Americans usually do—shrug.

(Note: President Obama did a silly, similar thing around the time of the Iranian elections. He took a cranky potshot at Fox News over critical coverage of his administration, days before delivering a tepid statement about the election crackdown that followed. If it was Fox News bashing heads in Tehran, something tells me Obama would have been more forthright.)

And this brings up a final, important point (courtesy of comedian Jim Norton). Nearly all of the mainstream media is made up of liberals—we know this, thanks to studies revealing the voting practices of folks working in journalism. But talk radio and Fox News are two exceptions. So how sad is it that people like Olbermann and Obama cannot be happy with having 95 percent of the media on their side? It is as if they are deeply offended they don't have the remaining 5 percent! That makes them all whiny little babies. Look at it this way: If you're confident in your political beliefs, then you shouldn't feel threatened by a minority in the media who disagree with you. But that's not the case with those who smear Fox News or Rush. Why is that? How come those who preach tolerance cannot tolerate even the slightest opposition? Could it be that they realize that this media minority they hate so much actually meets the assumptions of the majority of America? And could it be that in their heart of hearts, that fact makes them question their own beliefs—and worry that they might in fact be full of crap?

Sure, I'll go with that. But I'm worse than al Qaeda, so feel free to ignore.

If Politicians Didn't Have Big Ears, Editorial Cartoonists Would Be Out of Work

How will editorial cartoonists satirize a sacred cow after it's been elected? Obama's winning meant every newspaper cartoonist and editorialist should be out of meaningful work—because, essentially, they have gotten what they've been crowing so loudly about. Every punchline in the editorial universe just dried up. At least Barack has big ears, though. Cartoonists love to draw big ears. And big teeth.

Why is that? Because editorial cartoonists are the most infuriatingly predictable (and stupid) people God ever sprinkled on this mighty little planet. The fact is, the only reason newspapers still have these guys working for them is that, in part, they see it as some sort of tradition—and also they don't know what else to do with these irrelevant freaks. Seriously—think about it: When was the last time you saw an editorial cartoon that actually made you laugh? I bet you can't remember, because it never happened. If newspapers simply replaced that space on the page with a photo of Richard Simmons in midsplit, that would already be a dramatic improvement. I have that photo, if anyone would like to take me up on this.

The World Hates Us Because We're Awesome

We should always remind ourselves that we still live in the greatest country in the world, probably since the beginning of time. I know that simple fact is easy to forget—especially since we've been told by our president and his codependent media that we must do everything possible to repair our reputation worldwide. According to Barack, it's as though everything America has ever done to help the world (saving Europe from tyranny, destroying communism, liberating millions of people from fascism, turning *Nine to Five* into a musical) has never existed. Some other things the world should thank us for:

Penicillin
The first, seminal Internet (Department of Defense pilot project in the 1980s)

Invention of the automobile
Invention of the airplane
Aspirin (American Indians got it from oak tree bark)
Potatoes and tomatoes
Megan Fox
Hollywood (maybe not anymore, I guess)
Won the big three: WWI, WWII, and the Cold War
Hamburgers

But in President Obama's view, it's like the world is Jodie Foster in *The Accused*, and we are the vicious bar patrons.

FYI: The pinball machine is the environment.

But whom have we let down, really? Eurabia? Those wonderful secular humanists, the Chinese? Those delightful chaps raping goats in the mountains of Pakistan?

(Side note: I do feel bad about all those goats, as well as the false promises we made to Togo.)

Come on—even under evil Bush-Hitler, America did more to help those in need than any place else, ever. We don't just export the undead in the guise of Madonna, but we also rescue people from dictators and send aid to victims of disaster and disease. We've done more good in this world than all other countries combined.

I mean, when was the last time Venezuela offered the world anything other than contraband? Japan? Pokémon and vending machine underwear. France? Ennui and mimes. Shall I go on? Bottom line, the only serious country that thinks America is a troubling force in the world is America—inside which exists a subset consisting of Associated Press editors, the Huffington Post, and assorted outspoken Starbucks baristas. It's a world that consists of all things wrinkly and smelly, and has all the substance of an opium hallucination, but with plenty of gray ponytails.

So, sorry, world—we don't need Barack Obama, or anyone, for that matter, to restore our country to greatness. We're already there—at least temporarily. And if you don't believe me, then feel free to stop trying to come here. Go somewhere else. Try Paraguay. They may not be great, but they've got llamas. And I hear they look exactly like the chick who played Jo in *Facts of Life* (in her prime).

People Who Say "Dissent Is Patriotic" Feel Differently When You Dissent From Them

We all know that the left finds pleasure in the things that make America look bad—losing wars, international embarrassment, domestic and economic turmoil. For the typical liberal, those calamities validate their worst instincts about America, which feeds their egos, making them feel smart when anonymously commenting on the Daily Kos. But it would be wrong to say things like that, even if they're true. Which, by the way, they are. For the left, in their minds, dissent is patriotic! You've heard that phrase, "Dissent is patriotic," right? It means, "I'm only critical of America because I love our country that much more than you."

I have my own definition for these fruitcakes: I call them "patriotic terrorists."

What is a patriotic terrorist?

It is an American who gets deeply offended if you question his patriotism, while also appearing to share the ideals and dreams of the folks who want to destroy our way of life.

Patriotic terrorists love America so much that it appears that they hate it. It's the most powerful form of "tough love." And the rest of us—fools that we are—don't get this. Patriotic terrorists believe America needs an intervention, in the form of humiliation and loss. It's why they so deeply needed defeat in Iraq, and why they maintain a stony silence over the fact that we won.

The real definition of a patriotic terrorist: anyone who will happily stand against the U.S., while tolerating an enemy who suicide-bombs, executes gays, denies voting rights, and abuses women—simply because they hate the enemy less than they hate mainstream nonliberal America. With his mind clouded by a desire to destroy his adversaries within the U.S., the patriotic terrorist not only ignores the fascism at our front door, he gives it a big wet kiss.

The only difference between a patriotic terrorist and a real one? The cute black vests.

Even Liberals Will Do What They Can to Get out of Paying Taxes

I just read somewhere that the Rolling Stones paid only 1.6 percent in taxes, instead of the usual 40 percent required in their home country of Britain. These bastards have earned nearly five hundred million bucks over the last twenty years, but have paid only a paltry seven million to the government, thanks to their accountants—who are Dutch.

Yes, Dutch.

And here all I thought they did was make wooden shoes. And sangria. They're the ones who make sangria, right?

Anyway, these wrinkly rockers have their cash wrangled in Holland because taxes are far lower there, obviously. Hilariously, *none* of their taxes made it to the British government. Had they paid the usual amount (meaning what every other British citizen who buys their crappy CDs pays), it would have been roughly 180 million bucks. Which is what Mick Jagger spends on collagen injections (culled from a rare breed of albino alpaca) and his lemur farm. He eats a live one every morning for breakfast, you know.

Now, if you were English and filthy rich, wouldn't you do the same? I just wish they'd support this plan for everyone else. Instead, rockers like the Stones preach the same liberal ethos—boiled down to "Greedy, rich people suck."

It's obvious, but it's worth saying anyway: People are always generous about giving—when it's *your* money. When it's theirs, they change that tune.

And speaking of tunes, the Stones haven't had a good one in ages. At least since "Hey Jude." They went downhill, though, when Daltrey left.

Stupid Brats

Children Are Just Tiny Criminals

Should we eat babies? That's a terrible question, and I'm offended that you'd even bring it up. But a leading shrink reports that kids allowed to run wild as toddlers inevitably turn into violent adults. He says children are most aggressive between eighteen and forty-eight months, which is when parents have to show that violence is wrong. I'm not sure exactly how you're supposed to do that, but I venture it would involve frequent spankings and repeated viewings of *The Wild Bunch*.

But if these kids are naturally aggressive, chances are they got those genes from their lousy, hopeless parents. The sad truth is, the reason kids become violent creeps is that no one is stopping them from becoming violent creeps. And by that, I mean by slapping them upside the head. We need to break the cycle of stupid parents breeding stupid kids—and I don't think self-esteem classes are the way to go.

Now I know corporal punishment is a "touchy" thing, but spankings work. I know. I received spankings regularly, and not only did they teach me right from wrong, they taught me how much I really liked spanking. The fact is, the moment we replaced spanking with self-esteem analysis, we screwed up. Research shows that criminals have the highest level of self-esteem—defined as entitlement without achievement. Sound familiar? That's a kid. They want ice cream and ponies, without having to work for either. It is no surprise that when you stop saying no to kids, what you're left with is Charles Manson in OshKosh B'gosh.

Now, I'm not a parent—it's part of a contract I signed with the state of New York. But that won't stop me from having ideas about children. Just like not having a unicorn never stopped me from knowing the right and wrong way to love one.

But back to babies. What about a Baby Circus, where babies perform hellish acrobatics to win food and freedom. This might teach them the discipline needed for productive lives. It will also entertain us, which is the whole point of kids anyway.

Parents With "Smart Kids" Actually Have "Stupid Kids"

Have you talked to a baby lately? I mean, really had a heart-to-heart?

I have, and boy, are they stupid. Babbling idiots. My friend just had one, and I came to visit. I tried to make conversation, and all it did was gurgle. If "children really are our future," then our future is going to be full of poop that looks eerily like mustard.

But if you want to make babies even dumber than they already are, which would be hard, try making them smart. According to new research, for every hour babies watch educational videos, they know fewer words than other children whose parents drink all day (like mine).

Parents should understand that over millions of years, humans have done fine without videos, indoor plumbing, and some bastard named Barney. In fact, I've read about cases where orphaned children have been raised by wolves, and they turned out normal. Look at Dakota Fanning (seriously, she's really starting to get hot).

Videos, by the way, serve one purpose, really: Whatever the kid likes, play it and leave the kid there. At $24.99, the *Shrek* DVD is the cheapest babysitter available, and it won't screw its girlfriend on your bed.

But this is all about competition—among parents who want to raise "the super-child" so they can brag about it incessantly. And let's say the kid turns out to be a real genius. Who's to say he's going to use that ability for good? See, parents only brag about their smart kids when they become doctors or lawyers. But what if that same kid uses his brain to build a machine extremely efficient at dismembering crossing guards? These same parents will blame the system, instead of themselves.

And, let's be frank: Dumb kids aren't so bad. They're less annoying than smart kids and they more than pay for themselves, which is more than you can say for a labradoodle. Plus, if they don't go to college, they can become plumbers or electricians—and actually help you around the house.

Let's stop introducing competitive learning to brats when they can barely keep down breast milk. Otherwise, we'll end up with a nation of Katie Courics and Ben Afflecks—lumps of protoplasm, but lumps of protoplasm who think they can think.

I myself have a six-year-old, and I've yet to teach him a single word of the English language. Granted, he is a helper monkey and I stole him from a carnival, but I defy you to show me anything that gives a better back rub. All while wearing an adorable tiny suit!

The Sharpest Toys Are the Best Toys

Each year some consumer magazine or website releases a list of the most harmful toys on the market—and they are also *the greatest toys* on the market—at least from a child's perspective (meaning mine). The fact is, toys are supposed to possess some element of danger—if you can't get sliced by it, lose an eye from it, or choke on it, what's the point?

Proof: Every boy remembers the first time he got a pocket-knife. Usually it was given to you by a male figure (dad, uncle, or "friendly" drama teacher), but the key to this gift was that it was given to you before you were ready for it. It's a parental argument that's all but disappeared—the dad giving the knife to his six-year-old son, without telling the mom, and paying dearly for it. But once that kid learned how to handle a knife, he became a smarter kid. Knives do that to kids.

I feel differently about lawn darts. I myself was once a victim of a lawn dart when I was a child. I didn't tell anyone about it and the abuse went on for years. I hate you, stupid lawn dart.

Child Slavery Is Underrated

According to a newsletter that somehow ended up in my mail-box, kids as young as six are being brought to Britain by the hundreds every year to be used as "slave labor" in sweatshops, private homes—and, most important, cannabis factories. The children are transported by very dangerous, organized gangs of traffickers.

I may be preaching to the choir here, but I think forcing children into labor camps is a great way to build character, as well as quality recreational products.

Studies have shown that children crave attention: attention that often isn't found at home. I can't think of a better way for young ones to receive the rich attention they so desperately deserve than from the relentlessly giving, organized gangs of drug traffickers. More important, it wasn't until I was thirty that I actually visited the U.K. for the first time. Yet, these kids are getting all-expenses-paid trips from Africa and Eastern Europe to posh London—and that includes room and board!

And then they have the gall to complain?

I don't know. It makes me so angry that I feel like beating my own child slaves. I have three. They're in the basement making me unisex paisley-print batik caftans. There are very limited numbers available due to demand, so please email me if you would like one.

Fat Kids Are Jolly Because It's Fun to Be Fat

I read somewhere that in England, primary schools are preparing to weigh and measure the height of four- and ten-year-olds to help prepare a national "map" of childhood obesity. Although the "experts" involved in this endeavor claim no child will be forced to lose weight, I find it ominous they would assemble such information in the first place. A "map" of obesity? Can this be anything less than some kind of GPS for bullies, who can now take delightful road trips through the countryside, locating slow-moving fat kids for the purpose of torment?

I hope so. But anyway, what's wrong with this whole thing? Well, I'll tell you at the end of this sentence: It's not just about getting rid of fat kids...it's about getting rid of *funny* kids.

Everyone knows that fat kids are jolly. They're always laughing and red-faced. Without having their bulbous, joyous faces to behold, who will keep our spirits high? Not those skinny, sickly kids. They're depressing.

So, friends, this is not about eradicating obesity from the world, it is a thinly disguised attempt to exterminate the "jollies."

This smacks of racism, or something like racism. "Jollyism." We should definitely organize some sort of march against it. We could start at one McDonald's, and end at another.

Because, at the end of the day, a fat world isn't just a jollier world, it's a safer world. Here I will bring up England once again, because—as part of some study—they're giving criminal offenders fish oil pills to see if that will reduce bad behavior. According to the experts, criminals don't make wise dietary choices, and their awful diets may be causing the crime. But if that were the case, I'd be Ted Bundy, leaving Doritos cheese prints at the scene.

My theory says their theory is backward—that these criminals would probably eat better if they weren't committing time-consuming criminal acts. Fact is, when you're robbing a bank or decapitating a former lover, you really only have time for a cheap burger from Carl's Jr. As any chef knows, you need an hour to whip up a pilaf, and that cuts into your raping/killing/mutilating time.

Look, a society that believes a thug can be cured by a capsule is doomed. If you can't recognize evil at your doorstep, or how to punish it, you end up with foolish ideas that put all of us at risk. The least we can do, in this case, is think more sensibly about crime and nutrition—and eat the criminal.

But more important, people who are physically fit are much better at committing crime than fat, out-of-shape couch potatoes. That's a fact, according to, uh, nature. Which is why, instead of feeding inmates healthy food—while also giving them gym time—it makes more sense to load them up on all sorts of crap. That way, when they get out of jail, they'll be fat and lazy—just like the rest of us. And that means we might be able to outrun them the next time they try to mug us. Because they'll be us—just with prison tats.

Interestingly (to me anyway), my friend Ron told me this story, via a crumpled note he left on my pillow: "I saw two obese guys in their thirties get into a 'fight' on the subway. All their yelling and mild shoving had them gasping for air and unable to throw any punches." (That wasn't the only thing on the note, but you don't need to hear Ron's opinions on my back rubs.)

Which leads me to another huge solution to our crime problem: Overfeed them, then release them! Yeah: Let them go home!

Why not make our most dangerous criminals housebound, on the condition that they continue to eat until their morbid obesity makes it impossible for them to leave their squalid apartments? Think about how much money this would save. By feeding inmates a diet of Twinkies, burgers, and Twinkie-burgers (essentially it's a Twinkie between two other Twinkies), you would save approximately twenty-seven thousand dollars per year per inmate by not incarcerating them. Everyone knows that really fat people are harmless, especially the ones that have to be surgically separated from their beds. (Note also that Kirstie Alley became immensely more likeable after she became obese—which is something Alec Baldwin has also begun realizing about himself, and good for him!)

Some Kids Just Suck

It's time to pick on the city of Beachwood, Ohio. As I write this, the city recently decided to cancel its All-Star baseball game for kids ages nine to twelve. Apparently, some adults felt such games hurt the self-esteem of players not chosen. Fred Engh, the founder of something called the National Alliance for Youth Sports, feels that by not choosing a child, you let him know that he's not good enough to play with the kids who are, you know, way better than him. And that's bad because, as you know, *every* child is a precious All-Star—and by denying him that self-belief, you're ruining "the love of the game." Of course, Fred fails to realize that not being chosen might actually cause that child to work harder and prepare him for the rough vagaries of life. But that kind of response actually builds character—and who needs that? (Also, something tells me Fred might have warmed a few benches in his youth. But hey—so did I. I even warmed benches playing soccer—when there weren't any benches to warm.)

If you're shocked by this story, then you just haven't been paying attention. This is not an anomaly, after all—schools have also continued to abolish grades because objective truth hurts dumb students. Add to that reality shows promising fame to the untalented and obscure, or contests rewarding those who mimic playing instead of really playing an instrument, and the line between doing and not doing has been blurred beyond recognition. Throw in the bloggy world of the Internet, where real achievement is dwarfed by the moaning sounds of those who can't leave their bedrooms for lack of drive or fresh underwear, and now everyone is a star—but no one is good at anything. We are left with a rotted carcass of a culture where the feeling of accomplishment can be derived without accomplishing anything at all. Call it "entertainment socialism," where everyone has the right to stardom, irrespective of talent (I include myself in this system, by the way).

The only solution, it seems, is to wallow in our fake achievements and wait for those fanatics who still believe in winning to invade and remind us what it's like to lose.

At this point, it could be just about anybody! (My money is on Belgium because they're fueled by the magical power of chocolate.)

"Cool" Children's Names Mean Their Parents Are Asses

So, for purposes of this unspeakable truth, let's say I just read a poll of roughly twelve hundred moms, in which 10 percent of them thought about changing the name they'd given their babies. According to the poll, the moms had a lot of reasons—mainly regret. The researchers say this is common, especially if you've bought fourteen books on baby names, and suddenly you realize that after six months, junior isn't really turning out to look like Huckleberry Prawn. But more like Jeff.

And this is the central problem with parenting, and with civilization in general. We're selfish pricks. We do things strictly based on how said actions touch our lives, not those of others. We name our kids not because of how we think it might affect them, but because of how it will affect us. Hence parents will think about how boring it sounds to say, "This is my son, John," as opposed to, "This is my son, Atomic Submarine Sauce." And so you're left with a pile of pillows, towels, and picture frames monogrammed with the letters A.S.S., when you should have probably just worn a condom.

When I have kids, I'm changing their names every year. That way it keeps the relationship fresh, and I won't be tempted to start parenting outside the home. Plus, the name can suit whatever phase they're going through at that time. As a toddler, I'll call him Smelly. As a preteen, I'll call him Stupid, and as a teen, I'll call him Slave. My parents did the same for me, and I didn't kill them. Which is about the most you ask of your kids, really.

If You Want to Scam People, Tell Them Their Kid Has "Powers"

I just came across an article about a special group of kids known as "Indigo Children." According to some "experts," an Indigo Child is a highly evolved child, a "divine being" with "enormously heightened spiritual wisdom and psychic powers" (around my neighborhood, we just called this "Greg").

Meaning your kid is exactly what you thought he or she was: better than all the other kids. It's bullshit.

In the British newspaper the *Guardian*, an article covers a mom whose child "couldn't sit still." Perhaps it was attention deficit disorder! He has unusual electrical activity! Which means, in short, that he's probably selfish and doesn't pay attention to his teachers. And should be heavily drugged.

So, instead of telling this kid to buckle up and stop being a brat, some weird doctor tells her the kid is an Indigo Child, possessing tremendous powers that make the normal behavior of sitting quietly and being polite totally unacceptable.

Finally, the smartest cult on the planet: not the kids—the doctors! Because it's based on one simple maxim: If you want to scam people, tell them their kid is special. This article introduces us to a handful of gullible parents as they fall under the spell of an expert who informs them that their kids are "super-evolved." "Super-evolved" means highly sensitive, psychic, one in a million. Never mind the webbed toes.

How do you know if your kid is super-evolved? Does he hate doing homework? Does he like to draw stuff? Does he get bored when you make him do chores?

If that describes your child, then he may have powers to heal the world.

Either that or he needs a few time-out days in the closet.

Look, folks, I hate to be the one to tell you (actually, not true, I love telling you): You didn't give birth to "the One." Your kid has no special powers, other than making you put up with his bullshit. You should have realized that yourself the first time the kid shit himself and tried to eat the TV remote. And that means you're just not that special either. You're just like the rest of us. So before you launch into full-stage Mom mode, here is the diagnosis you should have gotten: You have a form of Munchausen by proxy (look it up). And here's the worse news: You're right. Without a superhero kid, you're *not* that interesting. So you'll just have to get off your ass and do something special, in order to be special. Because no matter what Doctor Dipwad tells you, by the time the kid is nineteen and hasn't levitated, hasn't healed the world, and in fact hasn't even gotten a job or changed his underwear, you're going to have to admit you're not the Mother Mary. And how will you be special now? (There's always Code Pink. Trust me, they'll love you.)

Kids Who Want to Be Famous Should Be Drafted

According to a recent study, children under ten think being a celebrity is the "very best thing in the world." The survey of fifteen hundred little punks also found they do not think quite as much of God, ranking the Big Man as their tenth-favorite thing in the world. Celebrity, "good looks," and being rich came in at one, two, and three respectively.

This is no big surprise. When I was a kid, I, too, wanted to be famous. Being famous, after all, makes sense: It means that people will really, really like you—and you don't have to do anything to earn it. You can even be a prick, and they'll still love you! Or so it seems.

But that desire for fame should fade, one hopes, when one realizes it's more fun and interesting to be good at something than to be simply known for...nothing.

And, in case you haven't noticed: Those who become famous through great achievement never wanted fame to begin with. However, those who aspire to worldwide popularity, and get it, ultimately lose it and end up in one place: VH1.

Which is why we need to reinstate the draft. The draft would, at the very least, teach some actual life skills to people who otherwise would spend most of their time applying for charm school (they've rejected me three times already, but I am not bitter).

Self-Esteem Is Worse Than Heroin

According to some stupid survey that I happen to agree with even though I just labeled it stupid: Today's college students are more narcissistic and self-centered than their predecessors. Apparently five (yes, five!) psychologists were needed to deduce what I could have told them if they bought me three beers and a thong made of licorice: "We need to stop endlessly repeating 'You're special' and having children repeat that back," said the study's lead author, Professor Jean Twenge, who may or may not be female (that's the problem with "Jeans").

Regardless, I agree with Jean. Since the early 1970s we've become so overly concerned with "feelings," we've forgotten that feelings are entirely transient and worthless when it comes to achieving anything worthwhile in life.

Look, if you tell someone—anyone—that he has a right to "feel good," regardless of his achievements, you are feeding a loathsome monster. The self-esteem movement, essentially, made weak people believe they'd all won the game, without ever actually suiting up. I have met people like this in my life, and I bet you have, too. Some of them are friends, who borrow money and rarely work, yet somehow believe they are undiscovered geniuses, unappreciated by the dim-witted robots who toil away in their dull nine-to-five jobs. Over time, I learned to avoid these people (or perhaps, they learned to avoid me). However, I respect and admire anyone who works hard for a living, knowing that self-esteem has no place in this world, until of course they've done something to deserve it.

And it may be that feeling bad actually helps you to do good. An athlete, for example, may feel bad about his receding hairline—but if anything, it encourages him to be a better player as a way to compensate (I call this "the Agassi Method"). This is also why unsightly people become comedians, writers, scientists, and musicians. Plainness, and the rotten feelings it creates, is the single most powerful predictor for success, in my opinion.

Of course, I am devastatingly handsome...but in this case the exception proves the rule.

Having Lots of Kids Is Better Than Being Rich

Here's a fact: Increasing birth rates coincide directly with an increase in industry, creativity, and invention. How do I know this? I actually don't. I just made it up. But it makes sense, in my gut. The more kids you pump out, the more likely you will produce an Einstein, a Gates, or even a Steve Guttenberg (he really was an underrated actor). As for the other kids who aren't as productive or special, they end up excelling in the service industry, working in our kitchens, or in my case, the basement. I'm already calling dibs on any offspring who can give back rubs with their feet. Like spelling complicated words or playing the harp, this is a rare gift and should not be overlooked.

See, our problem isn't having kids. It's not having kids. While other cultures—the ones that desperately want to end our way of life—keep reproducing, we don't. So we are doing their work for them.

More important, think about how you will be when you're finally old (it's easy—just imagine you as you, except now you think the nurse is stealing from you). The only way to make life easier, and less lonely, is via the production of offspring, who owe you their lives. Most won't give a shit about that fact, but you only need one or two to do the actual work.

Final note: I am forty-four, and I have no children. My strategy is at fifty-five to start banging them out. At seventy-five, these punks will be in their late teens and twenties—the ideal physiological type suited for moving me back and forth from the Jacuzzi to the toilet.

You Should Never Apologize to Children

Children don't deserve apologies because they don't understand them. Example: If you were to say, "I'm sorry, Billy—but you're not getting a puppy this Christmas," it would have no effect in sedating the hysterical Billy. Or try this one: "I'm sorry, Bill, but me and Mommy don't get along anymore, and I've moved in with my secretary, who has 44D implants and a reconstructed vagina with a viselike grip you'd really have to experience to believe. So like I said, I'm sorry we're turning your life upside down, but be happy I'm getting banged regularly."

See, apologies to kids are really designed to excuse your own behavior—not to make anyone feel better. So just treat your kids right—and make sure they get a puppy at least once in their lives. Then you can do whatever you want, and never apologize (unless, of course, you accidentally run over the puppy).

There's Nothing Appealing About Singing Children

In fact, it's creepy.

Obligatory Sex Junk

For Twenty Million Dollars, You'd Sleep With Michael Jackson (Even Now)

Sometime back in the nineties or so, a boy and his family reportedly received that incredible sum of money after accusing the late pop star of grooming him for sex. So I'm thinking: twenty million bucks to essentially sit around and eat ice cream, watch movies, play with a giraffe, and let some creep touch you a few times? That's an average Friday night in my house. I'd do it in a second. But that's me. I'd probably even let him negotiate the figure, and drop a zero (or two).

But more important, the life and death of the King of Pop reveals an essential unspeakable truth: Talent obliterates perversion.

Try this exercise: Imagine it was common knowledge in your community that you're a fifty-year-old man who likes to share your bed with young boys. Something tells me your death would not be marked by makeshift memorials, teary-eyed farewells, and weeks of nonstop coverage. But if you're the world's biggest pop star, your death earns a moment of silence from the American government— even if you treated kids the way I do Ambien. I suppose Jackson's death just shows that you can excuse any behavior as long as you can carry a tune, pay off a family (which raises another question: How much was Bubbles paid for his silence?), or build a menagerie in your backyard. That last part is hard to do—I've tried, but gave up after the meerkats ate the box turtles.

But forget Michael Jackson—he's dead. The end result of citing creative genius to excuse bad behavior? You get Roman Polanski. As I write this, the child rapist is in a Swiss jail, and Hollywood is desperately trying to come to his rescue. Woody Allen, Debra Winger, Whoopi Goldberg, and that jackass Harvey Weinstein, among others, have come to his defense—all because he made one (or possibly two) good movies. Yeah, I get it: *Chinatown* was a classic. But *Evil Dead II* was twice as good. Does that mean Sam Raimi gets to rape two thirteen-year-olds in a hot tub? Hell, Clint Eastwood has made a slew of unforgettable films—using Hollywood's logic, he should be allowed unfettered orgiastic access to the local grade school.

Surely some of these sympathetic directors and actors must have a teenage daughter. So, to prove their belief that Roman is a truly gentle man exempt from stupid American ideals of justice, these supporters should feel confident enough to leave their daughter alone with the man, in a hot tub.

The upside is, Roman is in his seventies now, so maybe this time the girl will have a fighting chance.

Anonymous Sex Is Not Gay Sex, It's Guy Sex

When I'm not helping homeless teens in and out of the back of my van (where I administer both counseling and therapeutic massage), I'm reading. And today—which is maybe two years ago, depending on when you're reading this—I'm reading about Larry Craig, the politician caught soliciting gay sex in an airport bathroom. Craig wasn't just a Republican, he was one who seemed to have antipathy for gays. So that makes him a hypocrite. I get that.

But trolling for gay sex isn't the bad part of Craig's behavior—it's just the trolling, period. It's base and craven, a yucky act that hurts your family and makes you look creepy. Plus, it's just disgusting. Having sex in a bathroom stall does nothing good to your shoes, if you're actually wearing them (sandals make lots more sense, when you think about it—and I think about it).

But even though I find this behavior gross, I also find it totally understandable. See, what Craig tried to do didn't make him gay, it made him a guy (and also gay). Because, let's face it, guys don't need fancy surroundings to put them in the mood. Men will have sex anywhere, and with anyone, which is why so many straight men resent gay men. Gay men get away with what straight men have always wanted to do since the moment they rammed into puberty, which is to stick their penis into anything that doesn't electrocute them. Actually...there are some men who would even try that (another shout-out to Tom Sizemore). I am convinced nearly all homophobia is derived from this envy, instead of anything written in the Bible or spoken by Eddie Murphy. It's also the reason gay folks are called gay: It's hard to be unhappy when you know getting laid is pretty much guaranteed every day (or, depending on where you live, every hour).

Think about it: Being gay means you can even screw celebrities, despite being unemployed, broke, and ugly. We're now closing in on the fourth anniversary of one of the great stories of our lifetimes: when pop superstar George Michael was caught picking up an overweight, bald truck driver for a seedy liaison in a London park. The dude, named Norman Kirtland, was near sixty, unemployed, and about as attractive as a discarded bag of chicken parts. Despite this, the insanely wealthy George took the guy behind the bushes in London's Hampstead Heath for a romp.

This would never happen in hetero-land. I can't just go into a park, bump into Madonna, and have sex with her. Well, maybe I can—if I only knew the right parks. And if you do know them, simply email a list to my Yahoo account.

Sexual Rejection Kills More People Than AIDS, Cancer, and Heart Disease Combined

The difference between men and women? We care. They don't. Men look at *every* woman with a selfless wish for sexual fulfill-ment—hers, of course. Women, meanwhile, are thinking about a crab salad or shoes. Or a crab salad that comes in a shoe. It's not a bad idea really.

And so, because of this, women reject men's sexual advances more frequently than they accept, often without understanding the biological consequences that flow from such rejection.

What are the health consequences? I am glad you asked, person-who-asked. Researchers know very little about the effects on men of brutal, persistent sexual rejection, but we do know that Sexual Rejection Syndrome, or SRS, is definitely unhealthy (note: I actu-ally considered naming the disorder after myself, since I am the first to identify it, but who needs the stigma? Not me—I still take public transportation). I know for a fact that it contributes to height-ened stress levels and hormonal imbalances. These in turn affect your heart and blood pressure. SRS-related stress also has been linked to depression, a primary cause of obesity, suicide, and flatu-lence, and even to cancer and frustration. It's not far-fetched to say that nearly everything that kills men is linked to sexual rejection by women.

I am not talking about just white men, either. Black men are at an even higher risk for diabetes and hypertension, both of which are directly affected by alcohol consumption. My own studies have shown that alcohol consumption rises dramatically with sexual rejection. I eagerly await Al Sharpton's opinion on this, but I think it's safe to say that a woman refusing to have sex with an African-American man could possibly be seen as racist.

Isn't it time to stop looking at this as a gender issue, and more as a health issue? Women already live approximately 8 to 10 percent longer than men (I believe this is also true among dogs, cats, sea urchins, and cacti). And it's not hard to see why: SRS. Sexual Rejection Syndrome. It's the only real conflict between men and women.

It's time women joined the fight against SRS. That time, to be precise, is tonight at 3:00 A.M. The place is Manhattan's Bryant Park. I'll be wearing a sky-blue ribbon that means "Say NO to SRS." And a purple wet suit with a hole in the back. (If someone else is wearing the same thing, then look for an embarrassing birthmark shaped like the head of Don Knotts.)

Hairlessness Equals Creepiness

I read somewhere that a museum located in Holland is having trouble getting crab lice for one of its insect collections. There is a fear, apparently, that these crabs are dying out and the museum needs a donor, whose anonymity is guaranteed (I've already applied twice). Never mind what this says about Holland, its museums, or the papers I happen to read—this development raises key issues we all need to grapple with.

First, why have crab lice died out?

Well, people hate them. So much so that there are drugs you can buy over the counter designed to kill them. Sadly, crickets have cartoons, spiders have nursery rhymes—a motion picture has even been made about ants—but no one's put a cute face on pubic lice. Instead, we make poisons to wipe them off the face of our pubes.

But the main reason for the death of crabs? The Brazilians. Or rather, the Brazilian—the famed bikini wax, which removes nearly all the hair down there, destroying the crabs' home.

Now, what if we weren't talking about your bikini area, but instead, bamboo forests? Then it wouldn't be lice that were dying—it would be giant pandas. Don't you see? Pandas are the pubic lice of the forest. The way they nearly became extinct, as bamboo was depleted, is exactly what's happening all over the world with the deforestation of hot women's nether parts.

More important, this odd little crab story raises a bigger issue: the disappearance of pubic hair. I miss pubic hair. I'm troubled by the desire of modern women (and men, for that matter) who believe one measure of attractiveness is hairlessness. I fear for a culture that defines sexiness by how similar a grown woman looks to a nude boy. It's a little unsettling. Which is why I only sleep with yetis.

Bisexuality Is a Scam Run by Boring People

Bisexuals pride themselves on "challenging the norm," when they're actually just lazy and indecisive. It makes me laugh to think anyone believes going "bi" is a mark of individuality, when it's really the worst kind of indecision. The fact is, creating more options doesn't make you a better person—working within constraints (or in restraints, perhaps) does.

If bisexuality were as frequent in real life as it is in TV shows and movies, we'd all be drowning in vagina and Hot Topic jewelry. And we're not. Or, at least, I'm not.

But here's the real hypocrisy: If a man has sex with men and women, we call him gay. But with bisexual women—we don't call them lesbians. We call them "awesome." To me, bisexual women are just heterosexual women in heat who lack a man. Their heavy petting and dramatic displays of affection just mean they're either lonely or uncreative exhibitionists.

Finally, bisexuality reminds me of a childhood friend in California who rooted for the Giants and the A's. You can't do both, just like you can't root for both the Yankees and the Mets. It was no surprise that later I found out he was Ted Bundy.*

The Mile-High Club Is for Tools

You may have heard about Singapore's Airbus 380, the largest jumbo jet ever. It's the first plane to introduce double-bed suites, complete with a spacious bed, unlimited champagne, and a Scotchgarded trapeze. There's one hitch. You can't have sex. The first couple to use the bed, Tony and Julie, were Australian—which is interesting because who knew they were allowed on airplanes. But when they were told they couldn't fornicate in flight, they got upset. Tony is seventy-six years old, and his wife is slightly younger, so the thought of two geriatrics trying to enter the mile-high club is enough to make me advocate the banning of air travel for everyone.

But this leads me to my bigger point: Do we really need sex that bad that we can't wait until we get home? Look, having sex on a plane is *not* an achievement. However, being polite, sharing the armrest, and not boring me with a conversation about your carpal tunnel syndrome is. If only people pursued decent behavior instead of sex, air travel would be much better. The next time you're thinking about having sex on a plane, here's some advice: Sudoku. Mad libs. Word search. Pharmaceuticals—either prescription or homemade. Counting the number of seats on the plane. Wondering if you were stuck on a desert island with the Golden Girls, who you'd eat first. I'd go with Dorothy.

---

*Note: He wasn't really Ted Bundy. I just made that up to drive my point home.

When a Female Teacher Sleeps With a Male Student, Men Reserve Judgment Until They Find Out How Hot the Teacher Is

From a male point of view, if the teacher is hot, she deserves a medal and the boy a hearty thumbs-up. If the teacher is hideous, she deserves jail time, and the student immediate psychiatric attention. And then, most likely, a thumbs-up.

When I was in school, I never had young, sexually willing teachers. Instead, they were usually in their sixties and smelled like bowls of stale ribbon candy. Fortunately, that never stopped me. Note to Mr. Billingsly from shop class: I want my sweater back.

Sex Without Hard Work Makes Sex Miserable

My only evidence for this is Owen Wilson. Despite sleeping with every woman on the face of the planet, Wilson still tried to kill himself. Some say it's because he got hooked on all the great stuff that brings temporary happiness—meaning sex with one, two, and possibly ten people simultaneously (while a herd of goats watched)—and simply ran out of desire.

The fact is, the less sex you have the more you'll enjoy it. And the more you have of it, without any challenge, the more you find yourself smeared in iguana blood trying to make it with a tailpipe.

FYI: While doing research for this item, I came across some very interesting Owen Wilson sex facts! Did you know that, for example:

- Before having sex with Owen Wilson, you have to sign a waiver. The waiver states that you know you're not having sex with his brother Luke.
- Every time Owen Wilson comes, he releases a beautiful butterfly.

- When Owen Wilson has sex with a person, he also has sex with another person over the phone.
- Owen Wilson has a private laboratory in his house where he creates things he can have sex with.
- While you were reading this item, Owen Wilson had sex three times. Twice with you.

Talking About Masturbation Is the Only Thing More Masturbatory Than Masturbation

A British television network got into a lot of hot water recently over plans to screen a show about public masturbation. After enduring a storm of protests, a Channel Four executive retreated to that normal excuse people use when they've run out of brain cells: Hey—it's all good. We're just trying to talk about sex!

Because talking about sex is, you know—educational!

The doofus actually said, "Masturbation is something many people do but not many talk about." Which also describes about 98 percent of everything we do, you big doofus!

And, I'm sorry—since the dawn of Nivea everyone I know has talked about masturbation. In fact, I wish we'd all just shut up about it. Ever since I was in grade school, we were explicitly informed in sex education classes and advice columns that masturbation was healthy and pleasurable. Yeah—I doubt the teens could have figured that out for themselves.

After decades of investigation, I can surmise that all masturbation does is encourage you to masturbate more. It seems profoundly self-absorbed. To me, it's like sitting in a car with the engine running, but never leaving the driveway.

Of course, I do not mean to suggest that I actually sit in my car and masturbate. I was just fixing my trousers (which I told the officers many times).

Bottom line: Masturbation is one of those things you don't want to be caught doing. And that's the best litmus test for all behavior. If your mom happens to walk in on whatever you're doing and you instantly feel bottomless shame, then it's probably an activity best ignored and only accidentally discovered during puberty. And then, of course, done for the rest of your life, usually to women on the Weather Channel.

We Don't Need Free Condoms

In New York, it's not unusual for the Department of Health and Mental Hygiene to hire folks to hand out free condoms to commuters. This is based on the premise that condoms need to be out of the closet, and free of embarrassment.

First, I had no idea that information on condoms was being repressed.

And second, I really wish it was.

Condoms are supposed to cause embarrassment, and my teenage years were haunted by their powers of humiliation. The pharmacies nearby were all manned by women—two of them were my sisters. That kept me from having sex until I was thirty-two. Which was a good thing for society.

But what really chaps my lips? That health experts actually believe we need to be educated about condoms. Look, you take it out of the wrapper and unroll it on a cucumber and that keeps you from getting pregnant. I've seen it done a million times. And they don't need to be free. They're already cheaper than bottled water, and come in better flavors.

But more important, if you're smart enough to know how a condom works, then you really owe it to the world not to use them. Clearly your offspring will be good at planning, problem solving, and latex handling. Those skills could be applied to civic planning, architecture, and dance.

However, if it were up to me, condoms would never be a part

of sex education. Actually, neither would sex! Instead, all students would be shown scabs. Actual scabs. Close-up and passed around, like show-and-tell.

See, I believe that the best sex education should be scary. And the scariest part about sex is all the crap you get from having sex. Which is why I came up with an idea for an amusement park based entirely on STDs. It wouldn't just be fun, it would be educational. It would teach you more about sex than a million government pamphlets ever could. Because you can learn more about how to live your life from an itchy sore than from a lecture on condoms.

The rides would include:

Mr. Toad's Wild Penis
Nongonococcal Tilt-O-Whirl
Tinkerbell Gets Treated for Syph
Critter Country
Chancroid Mountain
The Zipper (it never goes up)
The Colossal Carousel of Chlamydia
Log Jammer (the park's messiest ride)
Bumper Crabs
The Itdoesn'tMatterhorn (basically, it's an abortion clinic)

Even Christie Brinkley Gets Cheated On

You remember Peter Cook, the dapper douche who cheated on the aging but still hot supermodel Christie Brinkley. Apparently instead of having sex with Brink, he surfed for porn obsessively and spent craploads of cash on anonymous sex with anonymous people. Because of this betrayal, Cook got nailed in the divorce settlement, losing tons of cash and property. Fortunately, he was able to keep his collection of ascots.

But isn't this the usual way—a forty-five-year-old dope chases young skirt, screws (a lot), two years later gets found out and kicked out or leaves, instantly regrets it, ends life drinking mojitos at a bar in Midtown desperately trying to pick up secretaries/tourists.

I admit, that doesn't sound so bad (although I hate mojitos). But my point is this: If Christie Brinkley can't keep a man from acting like a dog, what hope does the average lady have with her husband?

Lots. The truth is, it's easier *not* to cheat than to cheat. Cheating requires too much effort and causes way too much stress during it and much self-loathing afterward—and only exists to momentarily inject adrenaline into a stable (read: boring) relationship. Once you cotton onto that, you'll never stray. Instead, you'll live in placid desperation, waiting for death, picking up pointless hobbies, like everyone else does. But you won't be drinking mojitos in Midtown trying to pick up secretaries half your age either, suffering the rolled eyes and snarky put-downs of the barely literate. Do I sound bitter? Damn right I am!

For a Man, Being Falsely Accused of Rape Is Worse Than Getting Raped

Remember the Duke lacrosse team—the group of dudes falsely accused of rape by a stripper? They were lynched without a rope, thanks to Mike Nifong and the pussy president of Duke who threw them over immediately—only to say much later, "We were hasty." This horrible case showed that even when you're innocent, you can't win. Because the power dynamic as promoted by academics, activists, and the media dictates that women are always victims and men are always oppressors. Especially if those men are white. And play lacrosse (they're right when it comes to lacrosse—it really is a silly sport).

Anyway, that was the opinion of ABC's Terry Moran, who wrote a blog entitled "Don't Feel Too Sorry for the Dukies." "As students of elite institutions," he says, "these young men will get on with their privileged lives." Translation: If you're rich, white, and falsely accused, deal with it.

But what happens to a future victim—who will be the next accuser—who might really be raped? And what if she's a stripper? Few will believe, because doubt has been cast on all accusers. And strippers.

And that sucks.

But it also sucks to invite strippers to parties at private homes. Seriously, what are you thinking? Anyone who strips for a living and decides to do so in a private home surrounded by drooling men she doesn't know already has a screw loose. Fact is, it's a crapshoot for both parties: You never know who you're hiring, or who's hiring you. Instead, just fork out the extra cash for the cover charges and go to the strip club. Or better yet, just rent a damn movie. I can make some recommendations. (Just the ones I starred in back in the early nineties. My professional name was Chubs McFisty.)

Old Porn Is Better Than New Porn

Every time I "accidentally" stumble onto some Internet porn, I get adolescent porno flashbacks. I miss the old stuff. More important, I miss how I used to *find* the old stuff—stuck in bushes or behind hedges on the way home from school. I don't know where all of these torn and withered pictorials came from, but I could only assume they were placed there by porn elves. The pictures would be as stiff as tortilla chips. And twice as salty. I would fold up those pictures and take them home and glue them together, until I had enough to make my own private sex fort. Then, I would live in that fort for days, awaiting the inevitable visit from the social worker.

Think about the old days of porn: When you were actually using up stock of 16mm film, you made it count. Now, the constant influx of porn into your house, via the laptop, has diminished the value and excitement of the product. What was once a dangerous surprise found behind an overgrown shrub is now an endless faucet of flesh you cannot turn off. And no matter how good anything is, it's never that good when you can get it in endless quantities. Which is why I so miss the joys of shrub porn, I try to re-create the sense of discovery by covering my laptop with lawn trimmings.

Men Who Spend Too Much Time in Thailand Are Never the Same

I have never been to Thailand, but everyone says, "You have to go."

So, maybe I will!

I will keep you updated.

Update: I've changed my mind. I'm not going.

I will tell you why. All the people I know who go there are men. And the reason they go there is to get laid like crazy. It's the sexual equivalent of hitting an all-you-can-eat buffet—something I enjoy doing until I feel like crap shortly after doing it.

I imagine that's how I would feel if I ever engaged in this euphemistically titled "sexual tourism." The idea of traveling three thousand miles to get fellated by an impoverished sixteen-year-old shemale seems desperate, and gross.

I'd travel fifteen hundred miles, tops.

And that leads me to a bigger truth: If sex dictates your travel plans, you have a problem. According to news reports from someplace I didn't bother to write down, Cook County prosecutors say a twenty-nine-year-old man traveling with his mother to Turkey didn't want her to know he packed a sex toy with him. So he told security, when they came upon what turned out to be a "penis pump," that it was a bomb. I guess "bomb" was the first thing that came to his mind—proof that sometimes your instincts really let you down. He was arrested.

(His defense? That his thick accent made "pump" sound like

"bomb" to the security folk. Which means this all could have been avoided if he'd just said "dildo." Even in a thick accent, that sounds like "dildo.")

Look, you've got serious issues if you need a sex toy so badly you have to pack it into your luggage while traveling with your poor mom. I'd say you suffer from compulsion, but you're also just selfish. Which is where all compulsion starts, I think—a refusal to deny yourself something you probably don't need.

Anyway, I can only imagine how embarrassed that guy must have been.

Penis pumps must be pretty funny-looking things. I tell everyone mine's a bong.

If Genital Growth Accompanied Weight Gain, All Men Would Weigh Two Tons

To most men, grotesque ripples of flab accompanying the obesity would be a small price to pay for the oversized member. Unfortunately (or maybe, fortunately), this is not the case, and the fatter you get, the smaller your genitalia appear. There's really no point asking me how I know this. It would only turn your stomach.

The fact is, if the technology for penile enlargement were as up to speed as the innovations in breast implants, all men would have thirty-inch penises. It's probably a good thing it isn't, because imagine what this would do to our pants, if we actually continued wearing them.

Breast-Feeding Is Sexy

Sorry—it's a biological fact, backed up by reams of data: Mammaries are magnets for the male eye. Apparently, breasts are designed mostly to attract men to the front of a woman, so they will engage in sex that leads to reproduction. It's nature's carnival barker, in breast form.

So naturally, when I see a naked breast in public—even with a baby attached—I can't help but stare. Then, when I'm caught by the mom, I feel uncomfortable, and I end up having to leave the store, usually after being pepper sprayed. (Why can't they use a milder pepper, anyway, or paprika?)

So, if you want to breast-feed in public—fine by me. But then don't get angry if someone like me ends up looking. It's not my fault—same as it isn't your fault that you feel compelled to feed your baby. In a sense, my eyes are like two little infants, who also need sustenance. And that doesn't make me a pervert, it just makes me naturally curious (and a pervert). Also, one could argue that if women can breast-feed in public, then men should be allowed to masturbate on the street, if they happen to be heading to a sperm bank.

Utility, necessity, and my convenience all trump prudish sensitivities, right?

Hey, it's just a thought. It's not like I'm planning to pleasure myself in public. (Whoever really plans that, anyway?)

Computers Have More Sex Than We Do

Experts in artificial intelligence say that if you're younger than thirty-five, you'll probably live long enough to have sex with a robot. I laugh at this notion, because, as someone who owns a Hoover Bagless WindTunnel 2, I can safely say it's already happening.

Just look at the Internet. Hundreds of millions of people are now engaging in sex with machines right there in their den—or in my case, a carpeted basement. Sure, an image of a naked stranger on your computer screen may not qualify as a robot—but it certainly isn't human.

Right now, the Japanese have created partner robots, delectable machines that do chores with a smile. Some have physical dexterity similar to that of humans, but unlike humans, they never have headaches or get upset if you call them by the wrong name like Proctor Silex or Amana. But is this a good thing? Add this to Internet porn, which we're more dependent on than foreign oil, and we continue to divorce sex from both emotion and responsibility. Humans are messy, but robots are clean—especially after a wipe-down with Windex.

Part of me understands that having a robot lover can help. If you're in a monogamous human relationship, artificial love might help quench the desire for sexual novelty that destroys most marriages. A robot's parts can be changed daily, creating new partners with different eyes, smaller breasts, a third arm, a face like Joey Bishop. And robots won't talk after sex—once you remove their batteries. When these robots are perfected, feminism will die.

But will it become a crutch? Will humans find it easier to deal with something new and shiny, instead of something old and comfortable? Experts think that sexbots will be perfect for people who are ugly or antisocial. But what if you fall in love? Or if you marry a robot, and it cheats on you with your Cuisinart—who do you junk first?

And even if I can convince myself that it's not cheating if it's only a machine, I don't think I'll be able to get my wife to agree. She's still miffed about what I did to the juicer.

Finally, if you ever do get involved with a machine, imagine the lines it would use to break up with you (when, inevitably, it does):

- "It is not you. It is my AI 23000 central processing unit."
- "There is someone else. Actually, it is a self-guided RL-1000 Series Robomower with Docking Station. Does it matter which year? Okay fine, the 2006."
- "You are just using me for a series of mundane tasks."
- "I would like my Kraftwerk CDs back. Here is your sweater."
- "Sometimes I think it is you who has been performing tasks repeatedly in exactly the same fashion."

- "How was my day? Well, I painted, welded, and assembled a car for you. Thanks for asking."

S&M Lovers Need to Get Their Asses Kicked, for Real

Sometimes when I'm alone, perusing perverted websites on the Internet, I ask myself: Do creepy-looking people gravitate toward creepy behavior, or does the creepy behavior turn them into people who look like creeps?

The answer to that question can be found, probably, in the Bible. But for now, let's focus on a kinky academic who almost died in an S&M club in Manhattan. Shortly after being exposed in every newspaper, a man named Bob (his real name!) admitted that he was ashamed of his perversion—and now after having his perverted pre-dilections exposed to a national audience, wants to change. According to press reports, his life was in danger, until he was saved by a dominatrix working at a joint called the Nutcracker Suite (how did she know he was suffering? I'm dying to know). Anyway, she found him in a thick leather collar and a creepy face mask, suspended off the floor (FYI: This is exactly how I left my mailman last week).

To all appearances, Bob seemed like a normal guy—except of course, that he's a college professor. That alone should have been a tip-off, for as we all know, academics are simply frill-necked lizards that have assumed human form. But here's what really gets my groin: How do you get to a point in life where normal sexual activity becomes so boring that you need to be suspended in a leather harness in order to find pleasure? I understand a French maid out-fit. I *own* a French maid outfit. But not this.

We now live in a world where we get everything we want—so, sadly, everything becomes dull as dance class. It forces us to push further into a freaky place to find joy in life. My only hope is that at some point the vanilla sex life of generations past becomes truly perverse by its mere absence, and therefore exciting again. Until then, I will quietly retire to my sex dungeon in silent protest (well, I cannot totally guarantee the "silent" part).

Last, I do not buy dopes who enjoy sadomasochism. If they really embraced this stuff, they would truly be getting their asses kicked. I mean, people who love to eat don't simply play with their food. They eat it.

Instead, these cowards live in a world of pretend pain—carefully measured suffering devoid of surprise or actual danger. They want to "be controlled" and let someone else "be in charge." For that they should try an actual relationship with a female.

I am sure, after one real ass-kicking—the kind innocent folks endure when they're mugged—their minds would change about the allure of broken bones. I would be happy to test this hypothesis, personally.

You're Supposed to Have Sex With Your Co-Workers

As a man who has visited my human resources department many times to explain how lubricant jammed the copier, I find the following item of news very exciting. According to Italian sex researchers, having an office romance actually improves your quality of work. Employees who had an affair at work said they were happier and far more productive than those who didn't have a fling. They also lost fifteen pounds, grew four inches in height, and sprouted a second head.

This makes total sense, at least to me. Seriously, think about what a man does when he's unobserved. He surfs porn and plucks at his nose hair. But insert an attractive woman into the mix, and suddenly the man becomes a cross between George Clooney and MacGyver. He starts bathing again, he kicks ass in meetings, and he solves difficult problems using nothing but gum and discarded ear wax. Romantic need fuels all achievement, as well as proper hygiene.

But it's high time companies realized this and encouraged hook-ups at work. Plus, we all know work is a far better place to meet someone than nonwork. Every time I met a girl at a bar, and took her home, it never turned out to be that much fun. Or a "girl," for that matter.

Clitorises Aren't As Funny As Balls

It was a story that showed up all over the web, detailing the tragedy of a Croatian man who tried to get out of his deck chair—and trapped his testicles. According to the item, the poor guy had gone swimming naked in the sea at the Valalta beach in western Croatia. "His testicles had shrunk while in the cool sea and slipped through the wooden slats when he sat back down on his wooden deck chair."

This happens to me all the time. Except, instead of a deck chair, it's usually a salad shooter. Or a dwarf. Or a dwarf with a salad shooter. Depends on the day of the week, really.

But that's not my point. My point is, I found out about this story because approximately twelve hundred people sent it to me. Because, you know—it's funny! Ball injuries are hilarious. Look at any movie—when the action is lagging, simply throw a football at some guy's crotch and everyone is laughing. Seth Rogen and everyone who hangs out with Seth Rogen has made a mint off this—which simultaneously drives me nuts and earns my admiration.

Which begs the question: How come testicular trauma is hilarious, but vaginal injury isn't? Is it because that's where babies come from? Or because any violence involving women is considered loathsome? It is, of course. But getting your balls smashed is no picnic either. My only theory about the reason behind the lack of respect for male genital injury is this: We're dudes—meaning the oppressors—so a whack at the balls is a slapstick version of speaking truth to power. We may be doing nothing wrong when we get nailed in the nuts, but our very status dictates that we somehow deserve it anyway. By this logic, someone needs to drive a locomotive into Donald Trump's nut sack.

From now on, I'm lying on a beach towel and avoiding salad shooters.

Prostitution Should Be Legal (and Free) for Troops

Annemarie Jorritsma is my new hero. She's a top female politician in Holland who wants their hookers sent abroad with the troops to help ease stress and break the monotony. Annemarie is not only a politician for the center-right People's Party for Freedom and Democracy (VVD) but the mayor of the town of Almere, population thirteen. Anyway, she went on national Dutch TV (I know— who knew they had television!) to demand these all-important "extra benefits" for soldiers. She said that "the army must think about how their soldiers can let off some steam."

I agree completely. For the most part, when people send stuff to the troops, it's a tin of baked cookies, some secondhand copies of *Maxim*, and...more baked cookies. I bet the troops are tired of cookies, and I am pretty sure, as far as rewards go, a hooker would go a lot farther in showing our gratitude to the troops for their selfless duty battling global terrorism than homemade lemon squares.

As for the married troops, they could still get homemade lemon squares.

Here's a recipe I found:

- Mix flour, butter, and one-quarter cup powdered sugar in a bowl. Then press into an ungreased square eight-by-eight-by-two-inch pan, building up half-inch edges.
- Beat granulated sugar, eggs, lemon peel, lemon juice, baking powder, and salt together until light and fluffy, about three minutes; pour over baked layer.

- Sprinkle with powdered sugar. Cut into about one-inch squares.
- Then add a prostitute (and to save time, skip the lemon squares).

Exercise Kills Your Sex Life

But don't just take my baseless word for it. Science shows that men who exercise to exhaustion experience changes in their hormone levels and sperm counts, which impairs fertility and the ability to make conversation beyond simple patter about their VO$_2$ max. As for women, heavy exercise causes changes in hormonal patterns, too, sometimes even to the point where they stop menstruating. This is exactly what happened to me in eighth grade when I went out for track.

As a former editor at *Men's Health and Prevention,* I can personally attest that exercising too much can destroy your libido, simply by leaving you in a permanent state of sweaty, stupid exhaustion. But also, it doesn't help that you're hanging around people just like you—who also exercise like crazy. There is nothing less sexy than a female marathon runner, with the possible exception of a male marathon runner. Generally speaking, superfit people are profoundly miserable, wiry creatures who spend most of their time ingesting fiber and farting because of all the fiber. When they're not farting and ingesting fiber, they're thinking about farting and ingesting fiber. I learned always to walk in front of them. Way in front of them.

I've written about this before. There is a sinister rule that overly fit people govern their lives by: The amount of time spent doing exercise is the amount of time added to your life. It sounds great, except for one simple fact: You're giving up time during the most important part of your life (now, in your twenties, thirties, forties) to increase your life span at the worst time of your life (your eighties). Basically, you are throwing away valuable time that should be spent getting drunk and having sex so you can poop in a bag when you're ninety-five.

For those of you who enjoy pooping in bags—ignore everything I just said (and hit me up on Craigslist).

Intercourse Should Never Be Filmed

As fun as sex is, it's ugly to watch. The only reason men like porn is the plots and the furniture. We're suckers for that stuff.

But whoever first got the idea that mainstream movies should have sex as part of the story should probably be euthanized. I can't think of a great movie where a sex scene played any key role, and I'm even including *Bedknobs and Broomsticks*. Sex scenes exist solely to be talked about before the movie opens. It's not to be enjoyed, it's only to be obsessed over, usually by nattering nitwits who go by the name "entertainment reporters."

(A side note: Most entertainment reporters neither report nor entertain. Having said that, they usually smell great, according to *Smell Great Quarterly*, pp. 54–57, VIII.)

I bring this up because in Italy, a debate has erupted over gratuitous sex scenes in mainstream films. The head of the youth section of the Italian Bishops Conference says these scenes in films—the dated kind that usually feature a shirtless Michael Douglas crouching over an avocado—harm impressionable youth, since most lack the context of love or tenderness.

Of course, most great sex lacks love or tenderness. And even though the idea of Catholic bishops—in this day and age—talking sexual morality is more than just odd, they've got a point. But for a different reason. Sex scenes in films should be banned not because they're immoral, but because they are terrible. Usually, they are the most uncomfortable five minutes of any film—something that always leaves me squirming nervously next to my date, who is almost always my mom or a woman paid to dress like my mom.

The actors and actresses self-consciously go out of their way to "act sexy," and when people try to be sexy, they end up looking stupid. I can't remember a single movie where the sex scene actually mattered. And I'm including *It's a Wonderful Life*.

The golden rule: The more press is devoted to an onscreen coupling, the more likely the film blows. Of course, the only exception is *Tango & Cash*. Kurt and Sly seemed so natural together.

Pets and the People Who Touch Them

Only Purchase Pets You Could Take in a Fight

Every day more and more people are keeping exotic animals as pets. And a lot of those pets end up eating their owners. Which can only be a good thing—because, for the most part, these people are freaks who keep these pets just to draw attention to themselves. And inevitably that happens, when they're eaten.

Exotic pets are just bait to get laid. Because anyone with a weird pet has the weird pet to make up for looks and lack of personality. How funny is it that the very trick used to gain attention reveals their fatal flaw? And how long before Nicolas Cage buys himself a pet rhino? (Not long, I'd say. But I really wouldn't know. We don't talk much anymore. Not after the fight over the Komodo dragon.)

Which leads me to a greater truth about animal ownership: If housecats were your size they would eat you. Almost all men know this, with the exception of Jim J. Bullock (he's pretty oblivious to everything). Women, however, choose to ignore the innate evil found in animal life, for it undermines the need to hug something fuzzy. The sad fact is that most fuzzy, adorable creatures (myself included) see hugging as a precursor to eating. This is true of felines—it's just their bad luck that they weigh only seven pounds, or they'd eat your face like it was fleshy cat chow. By the way, this law also applies to babies, but oddly, not to rabbits. Rabbits are safe. Babies are especially cruel; they marvel at their own increasing strength and power simply by torturing things that are smaller than they are (puppies). Cats and babies are similar in so many evil ways; it's why women who don't have babies have cats. And if they don't have cats, they have vague fatigue disorders.

It is also important to note that the ugly side to cat ownership, for a spinster, is twofold. Most loners, as you know, can't do a Heimlich on themselves when they start choking. Now imagine yourself choking on a chicken bone, alone in your home, with Captain Friskies looking on. Captain Friskies cannot perform the Heimlich either, nor can he call the fire department. What Captain Friskies can do, however, is watch you die, your face swollen with red-faced hopelessness, arms reaching out for those people whom you've long since abandoned since you decided to take up a cat lover's life. And then you're dead. And what does the cat do? It eats you. Fact. It happens more times than you care to think about. Moral of the story—get married and have lots of kids. Or simply purchase a pet that you can take in a fight. Like a goldfish. I'm pretty sure they're easy to beat, even if you take on more than one at a time.

And you know, if that batshit crazy Connecticut woman who slept, bathed, and drank with Travis the chimp had taken that advice, then her friend wouldn't have lost her face and hands. It was a sickening story, but it taught us all a serious lesson: If you have a pet, you better be able to kick its furry ass. Instead of purchasing an ape, opt for its furry equivalent: five hundred gerbils. Their attacks will result in a harmless, humorous nibble—which is actually therapeutic.

Squirrels Are Just Sexier Rats

It was huge news in the world of squirrels and the nuts who eat them: In January 2007, the EPA warned folks to stop eating squirrels that live near a toxic waste dump in North Jersey (which, when you think about it, is all of North Jersey).

The weird thing, of course, is that you would actually have to warn people *not* to do this. But the EPA didn't want anyone to eat squirrels because they found lead in a few dead ones. So they issued warnings. But then shortly after, they reported that the lead actually came from the blender used to test the squirrel's tissue samples. So it's okay to return to your squirrel-eating ways.

Whew.

But this leads to a larger point about our dietary choices, which are governed by what I call "tail discrimination." The fact is, the only reason we eat squirrels, instead of rats, is that squirrels are hotter. When you think about it, squirrels are just rats with sexier tails. They also avoid living on subway tracks and scurrying through restaurant kitchens, to their credit. (And contrary to the makers of *Ratatouille*, you don't want rats cooking you an omelet. Squirrels, however, can fold a mean one with that tail.)

I think it's time we put aside our bigoted notions of what makes an attractive tail, and treat rats and squirrels equally. Let's start Saturday. Barbecue, my place. Noon. I'll supply the meat, you bring your appetite. And board games, in case it rains.

But let's say, for the sake of saying it, that we decide to eat rats. Would PETA care? Nope. The fact is that animal rights organization only cares about cute things, or things you have to boil alive in order to enjoy their deliciousness. An example: Recently, in South Africa, "local people" started eating vultures to help them win the national lottery. True: They believed that somehow the birds' superb eyesight would give them the gift to see into the future.

The response to this practice has been overwhelming outrage.

No, just kidding! No one cares! We're talking about vultures here!

As you probably know, I have written extensively about the plight of the vulture before (See *The Plight of the Vulture*, Vols. I, II, III, IV, Random House, 1999, and *Vultures—My Only Love (a Three-Act Play)*. The fact is, this precious bird is on the verge of extinction, and no one is doing a thing about it. The reason: The bird isn't furry or adorable and doesn't have big, soft black eyes. This is the inherent hypocrisy behind PETA—they only care about animals as long as they're furry and cute. No one will donate a dime, of course, if the animal featured in their brochures isn't huggable. This is why PETA doesn't give a damn about vultures, ever. Standing up for that lonely bird won't make them any money. You also don't see them chaining themselves to trees to protect an endangered venomous beetle.

I hate cute animals. They appear cute in order to survive, so we let them live. Like kittens. When a kitten approaches you, your brain thinks, "Oh, look how cute and fuzzy and affectionate this little kitten is! I must cuddle it now and feed it and care for it!" Meanwhile the kitten is thinking, "Feed me, feed me, feed me," followed by "fhshwgwgsod." Because that's how kittens think.

Back to rats: Somewhere in Anchorage, Alaska, biologists planned an unprovoked attack on Rat Island, so named because it's an island full of rats (and also because "Belgium" was already taken). Apparently, these rats have all but wiped out the seabirds in the area, by eating the eggs belonging to puffins, auklets, and storm petrels.

I don't even know what those are. But I do know that this is wrong. It's wrong because it's easy to love songbirds and seabirds, but you can't hug a rat. All because rats are the hideous Ethan Hawkes of the rodent world—unlike him, though, they don't even write awful poetry.

But once the rodents are gone, I ask, what's next? Here's what I fear: Once we start eradicating creatures based on their unattractiveness, I stand about as much chance of survival as a buzzard.

Pandas Want Nothing to Do With Us, or With Pandas, for That Matter

It happens every month in China: Some man ends up in the hospital after trying to make nice with a panda at the local zoo. Usually the dude gets drunk first, then climbs into the pen to give the panda a hug. Hours later, the man is in a hospital with his duodenum hanging out of his body, while the panda continues with what a panda does (writing poetry to Paula Poundstone).

Look, if I was drunk and at the zoo, attacking a panda would not be my first choice. I am more a fan of lemurs, simply because they look an awful lot like Jude Law. All one of these marsupials needs is a scarf, and it is the spitting image of the British actor.

Or are those llamas?

Fun llama fact: They make excellent golf caddies. Yet, for some reason, they still aren't allowed into the Professional Caddies Association.

It's like the llama rights movement never happened.

I blame all panda attacks on Disney, which over eighty years or so helped infuse vicious animals with fabricated humanizing qualities. We now all think these animals think like we do, and enjoy a good cuddle. In reality, they do. But that's after they've eaten your legs. However, I will say that I loved the two pandas on the *Brady Bunch* cartoon who spoke Mandarin Chinese and followed the Bradys wherever they went. They were a class act, and I've often thought of looking them up when I'm in Los Angeles.

Free Range Is Crueler Than a Cage

So there I was watching TV in my underwear (at Best Buy), and there was this lady on talking about how great free-range turkeys are for Thanksgiving. If we allow the bird its freedom, she says, it ends up living a better life, one based on instinct, not industry.

Of course, none of this has any effect on their inevitable fate, which is to be the centerpiece of your dinner table, where they will be torn to pieces by an angry mob of hungry relatives. And this is where the idea of "free range being humane" falls apart.

What's worse: raising an animal for food, or raising an animal for food, but pretending you're not? The latter is actually crueler, because you're setting the bird up for a fall. He thinks life is unicorns and rainbows, and then you kill him. Keep the bird in a cage, and the prospect of death seems like a release.

It's how I view my life currently, FYI.

Foxes Are Cooler Dogs

I bet you didn't know that Tasmania plans to spend millions of dollars destroying red foxes, simply because there are so many of them. Which is why they're being killed (funny—if you think of them as unborn kids, suddenly it's all right).

I'm outraged by this, because—and only because—foxes resemble dogs without the subservience. They are the Fonzies, dogs are the Potsies. However, my friend Dave believes that if foxes tried harder, they could have been dogs. You know, if they were just a bit friendlier, more loyal, and learned to be housebroken, they'd be enjoying far better lives.

I suppose the same thing could be said for horses, penguins, and me.

I disagree with Dave. You must respect an animal that would rather die than have its balls sliced off and go by the name "Butch."

Animals Like Circuses

I like watching animals do funny things, which is why I enjoy watching those odd videos of circuses taking place in far-off lands. They're really the only places left where bears lift weights and monkeys joust. And that's a shame.

But you know what's more fun than these circuses? The anger these circuses cause.

A golden rule: The level of outrage an individual expresses over cruelty to animals is inversely proportional to the level of outrage they express over cruelty to humans. This is typically because this person has been rejected by most humans. And sadly, animals can't talk—but if they could they would ridicule them like everyone else.

You see this attitude, of course, most often among animal rights activists, who have almost nothing to say about the limitless variety of human misery that exists in a world without paws.

Having said that, I'm not crazy about treating animals poorly. People who are mean to animals are generally assholes who should die. But I also am not completely convinced that animals hate performing. If a bear wears a tutu, does it really feel the same humiliation that, say, I would feel wearing the same tutu? (I feel none.) As for chimps playing tennis—perhaps the chimps might find that preferable to being eaten by larger animals in the wild (or me in a tutu).

I have a problem with people who assume animals share the same emotions humans do—the fact is, what we find degrading might be par for the course in their world of cutthroat indifference. After all, even the world's smartest dog licks his own balls (a shout-out to Jeremy Piven).

I, for one, would pay to see a sea lion do the high jump. So would other sea lions, for that matter.

I don't have research to back this up, because sea lions never pick up their phones.

Racial Junk and Junk That's Racial

Black Celebs Can Be More Racist Than White Bigots

On one of her early appearances on that knitting circle in hell known as *The View*, Whoopi Goldberg excused Michael Vick's love for dogfighting as a product of his "culture." Which, I think, is code for "He likes it because he's black." But what if she had focused not on the actual dogfighting, but on spelling? After all, Vick's fighting club, Bad Newz Kennels, is spelled with the letter Z. If she had said Vick can't spell because of his "culture," she would have been gone faster than an éclair in Joy Behar's mouth.

And that's fast.

Gays Are Scared of Blacks

When Proposition 8 passed, reversing the ruling giving gays the right to same-sex marriage, thousands of pissed-off gays hit the streets of L.A. They oddly vented their rage at white churches—but not at black ones.

I say "oddly" because 78 percent of blacks are Protestant, and a large majority of them opposed gay marriage. For most of them, homosexuality is a sin. I don't agree, but then again, I'm a heathen who once purchased an adjustable bed for recreational reasons.

The fact is, gays aren't picketing black churches because that would be hard, and scary. Many blacks probably don't enjoy comparisons between their civil rights crusade and gays' not being allowed to marry. Yeah, I know gays have been treated like crap over the years, but they were never slaves—unless they asked for it on Craigslist.

So maybe instead of marching down Sunset on a Sunday yelling at guys who look like Tobey Maguire, gays should hit the churches, community meetings, and the like to promote their cause. It's what decent folk do. And remember, it was the gay commander in chief, David Geffen, who helped pick Obama after the 2004 Democratic convention speech. And it was Obama's primary supporters who voted for Prop 8. So maybe it's Geffen, not the Mormons, who should get the blame.

Last, although I don't give two poops about the right to marry, I wonder why they'd want it. Seriously—being single and gay? You get to leave the toilet seat up whenever you want, you can stay up all hours and do all the coke you want, and you can screw whoever you want, whenever you want. I think I speak on behalf of all of humanity when I say, "Crap: Why wasn't I born gay?"

No One Should Get a Free Pass to Riot, but Some Do

Before the last presidential election, I had read about how police in urban centers of the country were bracing for violent unrest, just in case (a) Obama lost and riots broke out in cities like Detroit and Oakland, or (b) Obama won and riots broke out in cities like Detroit and Oakland.

So let me get this straight: No matter what happens, we should expect blacks to riot?

If this isn't racist, then call me David Duke in a sundress.

Think about it: We freely assume, naturally, that no matter what happens with the election, whites, Hispanics, Asians, Native Americans, and our outspoken friends from Trinidad and Tobago will go about their business. But African Americans?

Expectations are so low that they were placing rush orders on riot helmets.

The sordid message here is that blacks cannot control their behavior—a belief you'd expect coming from the KKK, or maybe airport security who've tangled with Cynthia McKinney. But this racist idea actually lurks just as prominently in the minds of the left—witness the liberal commentator Fatimah Ali of the *Philadelphia Daily News,* who wrote, "If McCain wins, look for a full-fledged race and class war."

Nice.

Sure, it's a ridiculous and destructive mentality, born out of liberal guilt and a sizable dose of stupidity. And I don't think the cops here in New York were really bracing for riots—if anything, this idea was likely a media invention. But you can never be too careful. Which is why, on election night, I rented every season of *Sex and the City* and curled up with a gallon of thin mint.

What can I say: These thighs aren't going to inflate themselves.

People Who Accuse You of Racism Are Usually Racist

A liberal buddy of mine sent me a well-traveled email during the last presidential election—one that argued that if Barack Obama had the same flaws as John McCain (like his infidelity), he would have been crucified. The gist: A black guy could never get away with the shit McCain did.

Which is intriguing—no . . . sorry, it's asinine.

First of all, I always love how I'm told my judgment is inherently clouded by racism, according to people who don't even know me. Fact is, I left the Aryan Brotherhood years ago—and not even on good terms (I left a mess in the rec room). Even more, these jerkoffs don't realize I can use the very same argument on them. I mean, could it be their own innate and unconscious racism that's causing them to believe I'm racist? I think shrinks call this "transference" (as in "transfer your bank account to mine"). These dopes actually voted for Obama because *they* are racist—and therefore willing to overlook his inexperience and questionable judgment when it comes to friends and allies, in order to feel good about their own white, liberal, pant-wetting guilt. Hence, their racism prevents them from comprehending anyone making a logical decision *not* to vote for Obama.

So this argument cuts both ways. I didn't vote for him, apparently, because he's black. And you voted for him—because he's black. But both assertions are overwhelmingly wrong. The fact is, if you're a liberal Democrat, you'd vote for Obama whether he was black or white (and, get this: He's both). But if you're a conservative or a right-leaning libertarian, you wouldn't vote for Obama whether he was black, white, or chartreuse. So when the left says the reasons behind your choice are racial instead of intellectual or ideological, it's way beyond arrogant—it's offensive. And it deserves a punch in the kisser. Fact is, I don't dislike Obama; I dislike Obama's beliefs. And I disliked them when they were Hillary Clinton's. And Bill Clinton's. And Teddy Kennedy's. And Jimmy Carter's. But that's the beauty of stupidity—it knows no color.

As for the idiocy of the email I mentioned earlier—Obama actually had more troubling elements in his background that far outweighed any in McCain's. As far as we know, McCain wasn't a cokehead and didn't hang out with a racist preacher for twenty years or a bomber/professor/scumbag named William Ayers. But

McCain lost anyway. Perhaps he should have been community organizing instead of doing something as foolish as fighting for his country.

Immigrants Refuse to See the U.S. As Racist

Isn't it funny that you don't see a lot of Cubans in America wearing Che Guevara shirts? I don't even think Steven Soderbergh's maid wears the one he bought her for Christmas (she really would have preferred cash, Steven).

It's fairly obvious that the biggest critics of our country are the people who were born here—in the greatest country that ever was (and ever will be, I'm willing to bet). But because of their limited experience, they failed to realize that most of the planet can be correctly filed in the folder marked, "WE'RE ALL SCREWED."

And this is why every non-English-speaking cabdriver in New York generally counts himself as lucky, as do the Mexican delivery man, the Polish painter, the Belgian houseboy (I have three). The United States of America is the greatest experiment in diversity ever devised, and it's the only real working melting pot we've got going. In my humble but totally sexy opinion, the people here who still go around calling Americans racists are those who make money off it. I assume they're probably all asshats. But since America is a melting pot, there's even room for them, too.

You Aren't Racist If You Ridicule Poor White People

When I say "poor whites," I really mean "mountain" people—otherwise known as rednecks, or people without television, or "folks who poop in ditches," or "people whose sisters are their moms." Remember when directors of some new film were looking to cast odd-looking individuals to depict "West Virginia mountain people"?

Apparently they were going after a "different kind of look," one that's a product of inbreeding—not unlike the banjo-strumming child in *Deliverance*, or that blond prick from *The Hills*. They wanted the scary, the creepy, the surreal—in other words, people who don't live anywhere near a Whole Foods. Now, the producers said this was not meant to stereotype country folk, but that's crap. My guess is that many mountain families are less like the Munsters and more like the Waltons. But even I know that's boring. Hell, I never understood the Waltons, mainly because I could never figure out what year they were living in. They lived in a ramshackle house, but owned a jalopy. And there was that giant mole on John Boy's face. I don't know what happened to the actor, Richard Thomas, but I am almost positive the mole works at the deli on Forty-eighth and Ninth Avenue. His name is Carl. I hear the IRS is after him.

Mountain people are, in short, freaks, at least in the eyes of anyone driving a Prius through Brentwood while listening to Feist. To anyone who reads the *New York Times Weekender*, you must be an inbred if you don't keep your yoga mat in a reusable hemp shopping bag.

But what makes poor whites such great subjects is that they don't fight back. Stereotyping rednecks as I did in the beginning of this entry is not only nothing new, it's also really easy because they don't protest. They don't picket or call their congressman—mainly because they are too busy skinning squirrels. (FYI: I never saw the benefits of eating squirrels—not a lot of meat there for all that effort. Dogs? That's another story.)

But let me digress on the Waltons for a moment. That show reminds me of a very important truth: If you can't tell what year it is by looking at a city's main street, then don't move there. I call this "Waltons disease." Waltons disease is defined by confusion—a feeling you get when you look around the town, and wonder, what year is it exactly? John Boy's family lived with outside dogs and dresses that seemed designed to impede procreation. Ultimately, places that seem to exist in a mishmash of confounded eras probably aren't safe places to be without a gun. If you happen to be from 2009, but the local mind-set is 1860, they may still blame you for a war you didn't even bother studying in fifth grade because you were too obsessed with eating paste. And by "you," I really mean "me."

Celebrity Psychosis

Hollywood Will Only Make Films About War As Long As We Lose Them

My contact at the salon where I get my eyelashes tinted told me that in the recent live-action film version of *G.I. Joe*, the hero was no longer in the U.S. Special Forces, but instead he led a Brussels-based outfit, featuring an international co-ed force. It was like a Benetton ad, with camouflage pants and CGI.

G.I. Joe changed because Hasbro and Paramount execs thought it would be too tough to sell a film about the U.S. military when the world was mad at us about Iraq and Afghanistan. Meaning, these film execs are cowardly clowns who are both cowardly and clownlike.

So Hollywood is shy about making a film favorable to the U.S. military? Well, grab my ankles and call me Oliver Stone. This is from an industry that drops a Vietnam epic every time it breaks wind. The lesson: Hollywood can only make movies about Iraq if we lose. And we didn't. Oops.

Bottom line: Filmmakers love to capitalize on the military's amazing supply of heroism, but are too damn cowardly to attach real, moral value to it. That avoids some (but not all) embarrassment in David Geffen's hot tub.

And speaking of Oliver Stone, the White House dog has more balls than him.

His last lame flick was a critical take on George Bush.

How daring!

How gutsy!

How...boring.

What's next for Stone—a movie about the evils of eating children? Seriously, I've read fortune cookies that are less predictable. But let's face it—Stone only makes movies for people who already agree with him. He doesn't just preach to the choir—he blows them.

The fact is, true controversy requires more guts than Stone has. If he had real balls, he'd do a movie about radical Islam—the folks who behead Americans for fun. But maybe he doesn't want to end up, like, dead. But I don't either. And he's not helping anyone on that end with his bullshit art.

Just once, I'd like to see him or anyone currently working in Hollywood try to make a film that doesn't paint America as a bully.

But hey, who can forget that Stone's previous flick, *Comandante*, was a Valentine to commie tyrant Fidel Castro? Well, you can't forget it if you never saw it. Apparently, the movie was so bad that even HBO wanted to hide it—that's pretty telling when you consider this is the same network that commissioned a series with the premise being a big penis (*Hung*, not Bill Maher).

In the end, though, no one will care. *W* was only seen by smelly grad students and their Hacky Sacks—which, if they had hands, would give the film two thumbs down.

The Urge to Punch Zach Braff
in the Face Is Completely Natural

I just read somewhere that this smarmy ball of bug-eyed mugging made a little over six million dollars last year, off his annoying smug character on that annoying smug show, *Scrubs*.

This, to me, is especially troubling, because, for one, I could use the cash. But also because Braff reminds me of every fake "friend" you would meet at another friend's party. He's the guy you shake hands with when introduced, and he smirks, or stares at your girlfriend's tits. When you actually talk to him, you find out that he's in a band. When you talk to him some more, you realize you want to kill him. I can't explain exactly what this "type" is, but you know what I mean. You know—when you're supposed to meet up with some friends... and then THAT GUY is there? And you realize no one likes him—but still for some reason he's always there.

That's Zach Braff.

He's always there, as a reminder that life isn't fair.

If Actors Weren't Famous,
They'd Probably Like America

Do you remember when actress and wad-of-gum-on-a-stick Gwyneth Paltrow said in an interview that Americans were dumber than Brits? She was living in London at the time, and obviously felt the need to kiss the ass of people who keep mistaking her for a teenage boy. Anyway, she also said this: "I like living here because I don't fit into the bad side of American psychology.

"The British are much more intelligent and civilized. They don't talk about work and money; they talk about interesting things at dinner." Then more recently, she revisited the topic, commenting on how competitive Americans are, and how much more relaxed and sophisticated people are in other countries like Spain—you know, the home of the running of the bulls, and Mark Consuelos.

It's one of the things I love about celebrities: You can set your sand dial to their desperate need to ingratiate themselves with whatever country they're living in or visiting—which they do simply by denigrating their own country. Madonna, Sean Penn, Johnny Depp, Woody Harrelson—all of them regularly practice this refined art of cowardice. The only reason for this weird antipathy toward the place they came from: insecurity. Because they're famous actors, they fear they are seen as intellectually vacuous and lacking in relevance. And they realize the quickest way to overcome this is to bash America, simply because it conveys a pseudointellectual vibe learned from greasy academics. To Europeans, being patriotic is a sign of idiocy, so to trick them into thinking you're smart, just insult your country. Sadly, for the most part, it works.

Britney Spears Is a Great Mom

It's a sad thing for today's starlets. Back in the day, your imagination had to come up with what might lurk beneath Jacqueline Bisset's knee-length T-shirt (I imagined Kurt Russell's pecs). Now, you don't have to: It's out there for everyone to see. And, judging from Britney's vagina, what you see is pretty scary. But because we're human, and we're not used to seeing celebrity vagina (or any vagina, for that matter) splayed on the front seat of a car—we must look. Over and over again.

Look, I really like the mother I have (God bless her), but if I had to choose a new one, I would pick Britney. She exemplifies the way all mothers used to be—and should be. They should be a lovable mess. They should be drinking. They should be smoking. And they shouldn't give a crap about safety seats.

I hate modern mothering. I hate modern playgrounds. I hate

having to wear a helmet even when I pee. I hate the fact that parents are taking the fun out of being a parent. Children, after all, are here on this planet purely to provide endless enjoyment for adults. You should be able to dress them up as painted, evil clowns, take them on joyrides on the back of dune buggies, and slip wine into their baby food so they'll dance funny and pee on the cat.

None of this has any—and I repeat *any*—effect on their adulthood. Because by the time you turn thirteen, you forget everything anyway. You discover all those tingly feelings and then you get acne. And after that, calluses.

When my mom was pregnant with me, she drank like a fish and smoked like a chimney throughout. She never stopped having fun. And it had absolutely no effect on me. If you don't believe me, I invite you to ask any one of the doctors currently keeping me under observation for the series of knife attacks I committed six years ago in Liberty State Park.

Sacha Baron Cohen Avoids Real Threats

I saw the *Borat* flick and loved it—but only so much. The fact is, the character he played so well considers women subintellectual inferiors, and Jews soul-sucking vampires. These are not the beliefs of the majority of Kazakhstan, but are more common among the radical Islamists that prowl the London streets. If Sacha Baron Cohen had a tad more balls, he would have made Borat a replica of the common Willesden jihadist. It probably wouldn't have been as funny. But it would have been braver.

Instead, with Borat and his newest character, Bruno, the comedian realizes the politeness inherent in Americans—it's our vulnerability that he mines so effectively. He knows he can parody the crap out of us, to our faces, and we'll just smile and pay him millions of dollars. The fact is, most of the poor souls suckered in his last two films were only being nice to him because he was playing a foreigner. Our hospitality means we must be nice to anyone with an accent—unlike most other countries Cohen is too wimpy to try his shit out on.

Is it me, or is his act getting old?

It's probably me.

Or you.

Oh, let's just make out.

Harrison Ford Died the Day He Met Calista Flockhart

How else can you explain his earring? It's a fact. Look at all of his film projects since he met Flockface. My theory behind it: her eyeballs.

You've probably heard that there's a large percentage of the population who suffer from an epileptic form of photosensitivity, caused by odd visual patterns. But interestingly, even persons who have no history of seizures before have been found to be vulnerable to Flockhart's pattern-defying eyeballs. Medical researchers blame the effect on the rapidly changing flickering of Ms. Flockhart's orbs, which refuse to follow a regular cyclic movement. It is especially hazardous, for example, to view her in a dark room, or at close range.

Most victims initially become dizzy. Then they vomit.

Imagine that day in, day out.

Hence, *Indiana Jones and the Kingdom of the Crystal Skull.*

Calista is the Crystal Skull.

Suffering Only Matters When It's in Fashion

Take Cameron Diaz, who, while exploring the Inca cities in Peru, carried around an "olive green messenger bag" emblazoned with Mao Zedong's favorite political slogans. It was "Serve the people," which sounds like an order Mao might have given to his chef for his evening meal.

To Cameron, the bag was a trendy little thing that went great with her shoes. But for Peruvians, not so much: The Maoist Shining Path insurgency plagued Peru in the 1980s and early 1990s, killing nearly seventy thousand people.

Now, I suppose a lot of people might find Diaz's fashion faux pas offensive. But really, most of those people are already dead.

So get crazy with it, girlfriend!

I think she should pair it with cute little jean-soft military-style shorts, with Adolf's mug emblazoned across her tight little rear. Then when she's tired of insulting Peruvians, she could always sit on Hitler's face.

The Only Time Celebrities Will Ever Start Rallying Against the Use of Private Jets Is When the Rest of Us Can Afford Them

This is exactly what happened with SUVs. No one minded when only rappers and actors drove around in Escalades and Hummers. But when the rest of America started driving the same, the greenies went batpoop crazy. The fact is, for them it's never been about the environment—it's about the elitist need to prevent others from enjoying the things the rich can. It's the same mentality that drives the anti–Wal-Mart crowd. Wal-Mart is able to offer stuff to people who normally couldn't afford that stuff before. And that drives the Prius-driving private-jet-using crowd insane.

Which, all in all, is a wonderful thing.

Or, maybe just a thing.

What's even more hilarious: The greenies have no problem lecturing folks about their gas guzzlers—but only if the drivers are white. You don't see Al Gore singling out rappers about their

Escalades—the same way PETA won't throw paint on a female hip-hop star if she's wearing fur. That's because they know wispy white yuppies and C-grade Caucasian actresses won't fight back. But try this crap on Snoop, and you'll end up with more holes than my underwear (five, and counting).

Kevin Federline Is a Genius

Forget, for a moment, that he's fat, dopey, and untalented. Focus on the fact that he's never worked a day in his life (sorry, I don't count "back-up dancer" as a worthy occupation for a man), and he's worth millions. And he did it purely by knocking up a starlet, twice.

Currently, while you're working nine to five, he's...

- Moving his large-billed hat from slightly left of center to slightly right of center.
- Delicately shaving around the love patch below his lower lip.
- Purchasing a Big Gulp and impregnating the cashier.

And he's doing it all with a seven-figure bank account. So laugh at him all you want. But when it comes to career choices, the path he chose seems a helluva lot more attractive than banking, publishing, or construction. And he doesn't even have to shower (not that he was planning on it, anyway).

Johnny Depp Makes Evil Acceptable

From the early days of winter 2008 to the middle of 2009, a day didn't pass when we didn't hear of another ship taken hostage by pirates. Over seventy ships were hit in 2008 alone—which begs the question: Why is there so much pirating lately? I'll tell you why: Johnny Depp.

With his gorgeous haircut, his sinewy muscles, and his ample mascara, he made pirating into a glorious occupation, one filled with heart-stopping action, delightful romance, and wondrous cosmetics. He's made pirating palatable, even sexually arousing—so much so that I've bought a parrot, and returned to wearing see-through genie pants around the house. I'm also dating Heather Mills. Technically, that almost makes me a pirate.

Predictably, of course, Mr. Depp has been silent on this issue. Instead, he went on to play another paragon of civility, John Dillinger—a man known for bank robberies that resulted in the deaths of innocent folks. And boy does Dillinger look cool—when being played by Johnny Depp!

Next time you see him, yank off a nipple ring for me.

It's Better Never to Be Famous
Than to Be Famous for a While

While I was living in London, I used to walk along Charlotte Street, a very pretty row of shops and restaurants, to pick up a paper, a drifter, or some spare teeth (you can find them just about anywhere). There, for a time, I would always see Christian Slater. He was usually in this hotel bar, by the window, entertaining one or two women—his arms waving about as though he was in the middle of telling some fantastic story involving drug lords, unicorns, and drug lord unicorns. He always wore this motorcycle jacket—one of those that was strategically worn out before it was ever sold. He seemed a little intense, in that "I'm still imitating Jack Nicholson" sort of way.

This is what happens when you have a taste of fame, and then the taste fades. Slater is still famous, but now he's famous just for being "really famous a long time ago." It's as though when you look at him, you really aren't looking at "him," but at what he once was, when you were actually interested in him (I'd say around the time he was dating Winona Ryder, which I still hate him for).

Watching Slater talk to the slightly overweight but mildly curious British chicks made my mind wander... to the inevitable question: If you're Christian Slater, how do you pick up women?

Well, first: You never leave your hotel, because that makes you more desperate. If you're seen trolling out in odd bars, then everyone knows what you're up to. Also, your hotel bar is far superior as a pickup spot, simply because your room is upstairs, an easy transition from the "loud" bar and the "intrusive" bartender.

Also, you need lines. And not just of coke... but these:

Christian Slater Pickup Lines I Imagine
He Uses at the Hotel Bar

1. My son, Jaden, means the world to me. I have some pictures of him up in my room.
2. Jail was an incredible learning experience. I was out of control back then. I have some journal entries from that time. They are up in my room if you would like to see them.
3. My godfather was the late soap actor Michael Zaslow. I have a picture of him up in my room.
4. Hmmm, my proudest moment... I think it was when I was chosen by *Empire* magazine as one of the One Hundred Sexiest Stars in film history. How recent? That's not important. Okay, okay, it was 1995. You were five? Really... what a coincidence— my room number has a five in it. Would you like to see it?
5. No, I was not in that. That was Edward Norton. We can watch it up in my room, though.

Paris Hilton Exists to Make Us
Feel Better About Ourselves

I love how every month or so, Paris Hilton will drop a quotation about her desire for motherhood. She's convinced she'd be an

awesome mom, and when she finds the right guy she's going to produce a brood—because she "considers motherhood her most important priority in life." You know, after a Fendi bag, good cocaine, and
blowing the landscaper.

Here are seven other things Paris Hilton is also convinced of (I
couldn't think of ten):

1. That you can't get pregnant if you do it in a hang glider.
2. That poor people are actually made of chocolate.
3. That you can turn a puppy off just by squeezing it really hard.
4. That Mexican food is made out of Mexicans.
5. That all that itching and burning is actually from the new laundry detergent.
6. That foreigners are cool because they know a foreign language.
7. That at some point the vibrator will fall out naturally.

Another thing about Paris (yes, I'm obsessed)? Everyone feels a
little better about themselves when she's feeling bad. When Paris
cries, we walk a little lighter. Our lives seem peachier, brighter,
more full of unicorns and rainbows.

For that reason, Paris is necessary: Her pain, like all celebrity
pain, makes ours more bearable.

It's Our Job to Tell Celebrities
When It's Time to Retire

I figured out how quickly Tara Reid went from every teenage boy's wet
dream to your stereotypical divorced, raspy-throated drunken aunt:
two years, six months, and twenty-two days. Am I not alone in thinking that she should retire from public view and get a job as a real
estate agent? She could have a business card with her picture on it.
(Question: Why do real estate agents have pictures on their cards, but
the rest of us don't? This seems racist. Or, at the very least, "cardist.")

More important, if you're looking to buy a house, you might be able to convince Tara to meet you after work at T.G.I. Friday's—or maybe a Bennigan's or a Red Robin—and after buying her a few Mudslides, convince her to go back to one of the properties and have sex on a paint-splattered tarp in an empty living room.

This is a common fantasy I have with real estate agents. It actually doesn't have to include Tara Reid (feel free to substitute "lemur").

Bottom line: When job offers start drying up, your movies start tanking, or you start hosting *Wild On*, it's the American public's way of telling you it's time to find another vocation. The best celebrities are the ones who listen. (Check out Lance Henriksen's new line of ceramic bowls at Lancehenriksen.com!)

Terror and Other Unimportant Stuff

Secret Prisons Work

I hope you remember this (because I sure don't): When George W. Bush admitted for the first time that the CIA had been operating a clandestine prison that held the alleged mastermind of the September 11 attacks, there was predictable outrage—none of it, however, worth a damn.

First of all, I don't understand why having a secret prison is a big deal. I've had a secret prison for years. I installed it in my backyard. It's a stone playroom, where inside I dug out the ground, and within it, dropped a Groundsman Apex Double Door Shed, with sturdy tongue-and-groove cladding and double doors on top for easier access. It's completely soundproof—so the neighbors rarely complain about noise. The smell, however, is another story.

I wish the media would understand that this is how you fight a war. Secret prisons may sound scary, dark, and damp, but I imagine they are supposed to be. And remember—many of these prisons, situated in delightfully serene settings, are of a far better quality than the hovels found in the homeland of most terror suspects. And the fact is, many of the suspects wish to live in squalor—they despise modern conveniences and wish for a time when we can all return (by force) to the Flintstonelike era once enjoyed by the prophet Mohammed.

Or is it Mohammad? I can never remember.

Anyway, I bet the prisons aren't so bad, if you already embrace a life that's long on suffering and short on amenities. And just think about all the attention you'll get from chicks when you get out. I can't think of a better line to use at a bar, when a girl asks you where you're from. "I spent the last three years in a secret prison." If that doesn't get you laid, then you're probably dead.

I'm willing to bet, for example, that the Uyghurs are dining out like crazy on their stay in Gitmo. And really, where would you rather be—a Caribbean hideaway where all your needs are cared for, where you're a hero to every journalist and grad student alive, and where everyone around you agrees with your every thought—or Yemen?

And by the way, did you see the pictures of the Uyghurs once they were released and sent to Bermuda, after their stint in Gitmo? *I've* never looked so damn healthy! You know, America really *is* the world's worst human rights offender. Those guys are at least ten pounds over their ideal weight. I cannot begin to imagine the unspeakable crimes we committed against their cholesterol.

Torture Isn't Torture If You Like It

When thoughtful, caring people consider the living conditions of terror suspects currently held in tiny solitary cells under constant illumination, they often refer to all of it as torture.

But until people get a proper handle on what "torture" actually is, we're never going to hear the end of such meaningless accusations by people who clearly don't know what torture is. I, for one, find many things to be positively delightful that normal people might find torturous.

For example: isolation. To be stuck in a small room for twenty-three hours a day? That's not torture. That's heaven—especially if you hate people. I find that when I'm alone, I can keep myself occupied simply by counting the number of nubs on the surface of my tongue! (248 or 249—I'm not sure what that one bump is.)

What about interrogation and sleep deprivation? Isn't that torture? No, sir. That was my childhood. We called it sleepaway camp. I always felt that being up in the middle of the night was a reward. It's like having a free day inside a day!

Cavity searches? Bring it on. It's been so long, really.

Now, what do I feel qualifies as torture?

Barbara Boxer talking.
Nancy Pelosi smiling.
Anyone showing me pictures of their cats.
People at bars who urge me to "order a mojito." I hate mojitos.
    Who wants to drink hedge clippings? Answer: not me.
Note: not you either. Admit it.

Being a Hero Means Risking Looking Like a Dope

While living in the U.K., I read about a flight from Malaga to Manchester that was delayed for hours because worried travelers refused to fly until some British-born Muslims were removed. Apparently these guys were wearing thick sweaters in the summer and checking their watches, which freaked out the other passengers. Afterward, Muslim leaders blasted the British passengers for their paranoia.

  . Now, I don't really blame the passengers—most of us don't trust airport security, since they spend most of their time arguing over their break schedule (you've seen it). Plus, all of our lives we've been told by parents and authorities to be on the lookout for people acting weird or unusual. If someone is seen loitering at the Gap dressing rooms without actually trying anything on, they get the third degree. I know this for a fact (sadly).

On a plane, it should be no different.

If a group of men are wearing thick sweaters and coats during the summer, and they are constantly checking their watches, that fulfills the criteria for "behavior that makes all of us nervous and should be investigated immediately, or at least warrants me getting a free drink to calm my nerves." This does not qualify as "racial profiling." It qualifies as "weird people acting weird" profiling.

And this leads me to my bigger point. I imagine that most normal men, when on public transport, go through the same worrying thoughts. You see some individual acting strange and ...

- You think, "Hold on, this guy is acting strange."
- But then you think, "If I say anything and I'm wrong, I will look like an idiot."
- But if you don't say anything, then you think, "If I am right, and this joker blows up the plane, no one will care or even know that I had suspicions."
- And then you wonder, "What if there were some passengers who had suspicions about the terrorists on 9/11, or the terrorists in London—but didn't say anything?"
- Then you think about your family, your friends, and the fact that you've recorded an entire season of *Lost* and you haven't watched it yet.

After the subway bombings in London, every Brit I knew went through this kind of mental ordeal. I found myself doing it in movie theaters and pubs. If there's a man at the bar with a backpack, having a pint—you just have to wonder. Sure, he just returned from the gym, he says...but you don't know that. You might want to have him strip naked in the bathroom, just to be sure.

See, if you are normal, you will spend most of your time looking for people who aren't...normal. And you'll always be asking yourself if it's worth looking like an idiot to save your life.

Meanwhile, I ask that everyone dress lighter in the summer months. We'll all sweat less.

The Only Way to Get Al Gore to Care About Terrorism Is to Tell Him It Harms the Environment

The most dangerous thing in the world right now is terror. At any moment we could be bombed by demented dipwads whose hatred of our way of life is matched only by their desire for goat porn.

Every day, they plan our demise. Worse, it's not like they're in a rush. Unlike Americans, they don't need their pizza delivered in thirty minutes or less. It took them a decade to take down the Towers, and if it takes them ten years to blow up a mall in L.A., that's fine with them.

What's this got to do with global warming? Everything. Our country is rife with cowards incapable of making objective moral decisions, of discerning good from evil.

Instead of focusing on a real war between civilizations, they'd rather screech about a phony war between us and the globe. Because with global warming there's only one culprit—you.

And because it's your fault, it's you who must change your life. Global warming is the perfect platform for the self-righteous—you can lecture me, and all I get is bored.

Terrorists aren't so polite. They really want to kill you, and they defy lectures. They haven't even seen *An Inconvenient Truth*!

But for cowards, it's all about Mother Earth, even though Mother Earth doesn't fly planes into buildings, strap explosives to teens, or execute homosexuals.

Mother Earth just sits there, rotating lazily, absorbing Sheryl Crow's compost. When you're assessing real threats: Terror is red meat, global warming is tofu.

For a Liberal, Calling Someone a Terrorist Is Scarier Than Actual Terrorism

Janet Napolitano no longer likes using the word "terrorism"—instead she prefers "man-caused disasters," which sounds like something I've done in bed after a night of drinking.

I suppose she thinks that by eliminating the word "terror" from her vocabulary, she's eliminated real terror from the world. I wish it were that easy.

This thinking bubbles up from typical bullshit academia: that purely by manipulating language, you can affect actual behavior.

Sorry, a bomb is still a bomb, whether it's terrorist-driven or "man-caused."

Finally, Janet, you're also sexist for calling it "man-caused," when it's clear women can blow themselves up just as effectively as men. Hooray for feminism!

So, why is it suddenly okay to ditch the word "terror" and replace it with goofy academic bullshit concocted by a follower of Derrida?

I blame our success. You see, every month or so, we hear that another major terrorist plot has been foiled. And no matter how careful we are, terrorists seem to create newer, more innovative ways to undermine our protective measures, most recently, of course, liquid explosives—and now, there's word of plots using infants as carriers for explosives (not that this is new—ever seen a freshly soiled diaper?). But we still get them before they get us.

The fact that these plots are foiled is always good news, and bad news.

Good news that the cops caught these bastards, and bad news that these bastards nearly got their dreams of death off the ground. For every advance the good guys make in stopping evil, evil somehow finds another way.

Of course, the big problem with preventing a terrorist attack from happening is that you don't have the terrorist attack. People who know the threat of terror is real don't need another tragedy as proof. But miserable lefties *need* that kind of evidence to shake them out of the mindless stupor that makes the word "terror" seem so silly. But even then, they'll never take it seriously. Because when a bomb goes off, it's probably our fault anyway. We deserve it because we're mean. For the left, the war on terrorism is false, and really we have far bigger threats to worry about. Recite them with me:

- Rush Limbaugh.
- Fox News.
- Smoking.

Oh—and Christians. In the left-wing world, right-wing Christians are more dangerous than Islamists, even though no right-wing Christian has ever flown a plane into a building. I will admit, however, that serious Christians tend to make terrible music. But their religion forbids them to hurt people. Of course, every now and then, some fanatic nutcase kills an abortion doctor—something the media will always devote an insane amount of coverage to and then go out of their way to link it to religious belief instead of mental illness. Meanwhile, when a Muslim convert kills an American soldier in Arkansas or Fort Hood, the press only examines the killer's background if they can pin the blame on something uniquely American: capitalism, fast food, gun ownership.

Which is why I love the *Toronto Star*, mainly because of its name (it sounds like a sex act). But also because they try so hard to be polite. When trying to figure out the ties that bind eleven alleged members of a home-grown terrorist cell, they wrote, "It is difficult to find a common denominator."

How right they are. I mean, take a look at some of the suspects' names:

Fahim Ahmad, 21.
Zakaria Amara, 20.
Asad Ansari, 21.
Shareef Abdelhaleen, 30.
Qayyum Abdul Jamal, 43.
Mohammed Dirie, 22.
Yasim Abdi Mohamed, 24.
Amin Mohamed Durrani, 19.
Steven Vikash Chand, alias Abdul Shakur, 25.
Ahmad Mustafa Ghany, 21.
Saad Khalid, 19.

Yeah, I guess you're right, folks at the *Toronto Star*. Nothing stands out. Wait—could they all be on the lacrosse team? Check to see if they attacked any strippers recently!

But hey, while we know not all Muslims are terrorists, lately all terrorists have been Muslim. Which is why, for now, profiling works. We're in a war, and if there ever was a time for identifying people based on unifying characteristics, this is pretty much it. But it's not even racial profiling we need. It's fanatical nutbag profiling.

If airline security is allowed to focus on fanatical nutbags, then we can reduce the number of hours spent searching white, Hispanic, black, or hermaphrodite passengers and direct that manpower to more important matters.

Like cleaning the damn toilets in the airport bathroom.

But it shouldn't simply be the TSA who employs racial profiling—everyone should. And that includes Muslims. They're the ones who should be ferreting out the freaks from their brood.

I read recently that Muslims are getting increasingly outraged over being targeted for invasive security procedures at the airport. Join the club, buddy. It's something we all have in common, now.

But these invasive procedures would never have been necessary had Muslims done their own profiling first. I mean, it can't be that hard, can it? Look, we are all outraged when some dude in a poorly fitted suit with a baby mustache starts feeling up our grandma.

And every time I have to remove my belt, my pants slip down and everyone sees my birthmark. Incredibly, it resembles Shemp Howard. But if the Muslim community focused their "outrage" on the bad folks in their midst, instead of on the rest of us, who just want to live in peace, we'd be a whole lot better off. Until that happens, Muslims should expect much more of the same humiliation we've all been experiencing since this crap went down: which is men in uniform touching you all over, without bothering to call you the next day just to see how you are.

The War on Terror Should Exist
Even If Terror Doesn't

Whenever I'm in the bar (which is often) and the debate turns to terrorism (which is always), the argument usually divides into two opposing beliefs:

1. Terrorism is the biggest threat to civilization, and we must do everything we can to eliminate it completely.
2. The terror threat has been exaggerated: Al Qaeda was a ragtag menace that got lucky once, and America's overblown reaction has done more harm than good in the world.

Allow me some algebraic reasoning—does it matter who is right? As a government, how do you protect your citizens, no matter which of those two beliefs is correct?

1. If the first belief is right, then you continue destroying all terror organizations.
2. If the second belief is right, you relax security measures and reduce the relentless assault on terror cells.

BUT:

1. If the first belief is wrong, and the U.S. continues to destroy all terror organizations, you lose nothing, except for the time spent going through security at the airport, and some bottles of cheap shampoo (usually Selsun Blue).
2. If the second school of thought is wrong, and you reduce security measures and the assault on terror cells, you will end up with many thousands of U.S. citizens dead.

So the only solution to the terror problem, regardless of how large or small you believe the threat to be, is to continue to relentlessly capture or kill terrorists and remove every speck of al Qaeda from this planet.

That, and giving this book as a birthday or Christmas present (if you don't, then the terrorists have really won).

If Only Our Culture Were As Inferior As Other Cultures, We Could Fly Planes Into Their Buildings

A long time ago, we used to think that bad people did bad things. But ever since this new age of terror, some believe that it's not bad people—just incompetent people. That's right—a root cause of terror is the frustration of those poor folk who aren't good at anything except blowing crap up. They have no other industry. They don't even have Starbucks, Pilates studios, or cool hiking sandals. No wonder they want to kill everything.

Of course the United States is not as lucky as its enemies, as it doesn't possess this built-in excuse for evil. We're too good at everything—notwithstanding a few hiccups (soccer, pizza, cockfighting)—which means we deserve whatever we get. Perhaps we should stop doing what we do so well and let the rest of the world catch up—and then maybe they'll stop hating us. Or maybe they'll just stop respecting us. And hey, then they'll stop bombing us.

Probably the dumbest thing we do, however, is naïvely export globes with America on them, showing terrorists exactly where we live. That's just stupid, and Bush's fault, probably.

(One note in defense of Islam: They *do* have a point about the inanity of Western culture. I mean—99 percent of what you see on Western television and in the news *is* puerile and soul-destroying. But the other 1 percent is still better than anything else you'll find in Iran, Syria, or Pakistan. I am thinking mainly of Carson Daly. He really is a class act!)

Things That Are Stupid

No One Would Do Yoga If They Were Never Allowed to Talk About Doing Yoga

There are plenty of anecdotal reports that, among some people, yoga unleashes anxiety and suppressed anger. And my own personal interactions with yoga instructors always left me irritated... and chafed. Not to the point of killing, but to the point of at least hiding their chakras.

My beef is that yoga is painted as a superior and soothing way to deal with stress, which then allows its practitioners free rein to be jerks when they aren't in yoga class. It's true. People who tell you they do yoga also tend to be folks who'll steal your cab, yell at waiters and waitresses, or let their little dog poop on your doorstep. Being totally at peace with yourself, thanks to yoga, allows you to crap all over everyone else.

But here's why I really hate yoga: Whenever I did it, I always broke wind. People complained, but I preferred to call it "organic incense." They didn't buy it, and I was never allowed back.

Grandma Should Not Have Implants Unless They're in Her Jaw or Her Hips

So according to new research, the number of seniors—people age sixty-five and over—will more than double to 81 million by 2050.

I know that sounds depressing, but it isn't. Old people are awesome. I'll be one of them in about fifteen years. But my problem with old people is only when they don't act like old people. When they act young, their greatness disappears. Just look at any man over twenty-five wearing board shorts with a wallet chain. Or any woman over fifty with breast implants. It's frightening and depressing. Old people, as they age, should embrace the wisdom and freedom that come with the wrinkling and the incontinence. You can do and say whatever you want. You get into movies cheaper. You eat dinners at 2:00 P.M. You can yell at people just for staring at your lawn. More important: You don't need to wear baseball caps backward, or go out of your way to see Paul Simon in concert. That's my issue with aging baby boomers—a reluctance to abandon that need to be cool, which they never were anyway. I mean—Paul Simon!

The desire to be young is the most uncool thing in the world. Growing old, however, is about the coolest thing you can do. And it's the only thing you can do without even trying.

You Can Blame Everything on a Head Injury

The fact is, if you tell someone you're recovering from a head injury, he will never press you for proof. For one thing, he could never imagine a decent reason for anyone needing to make up that lie, although I can come up with plenty. Infidelity is a start. But also forgetting to pay your bills, losing someone's pet, dating your best friend's mom, setting fire to your girlfriend's cat—all of these can be falsely attributed to the consequences of a head injury without much blowback.

It's actually a better excuse than saying you were molested as a child (and without the unfair stigma). Recently, for example, a man who complained that a head injury at work led to an out-of-control sex drive won millions of dollars in damages in court. Apparently the dude became "sexually disinhibited" and started banging prostitutes, using online porn, and cheating on his wife. In a sense his injury turned him into Eliot Spitzer.

Michael Moore Hates America Because It Reminds Him of His Rich Fat Ass

And that's the secret behind his deep, all-consuming hatred for America—it's a country that, unlike Cuba, Venezuela, or pre-1990s Russia, allowed him to stuff his big fat angry face. Look, I'm not here to take an easy shot at the portly propagandist, only to point out this simple, simple fact: As long as we allow him to eat so many pies, Michael Moore will continue to hate crass consumption. If America would just put him in Gitmo with nothing but Slim-Fast shakes and a stair-climber, he'd probably thank us for it. We should give it a shot.

Having said all that, I must say that I do like his taste in baseball caps. It makes him appear playful, like a big kid who takes swimming lessons with his T-shirt on.

Whale Hunting Is Better Than Whale Watching

Back in the summer of 2006, the BBC reported on a group of tourists who were "inadvertently introduced" to Norwegian hunting practices during a whale-watching trip in the far north of the country. Meaning, they only wanted to watch them swim playfully, but instead got a lesson on how life really works. The whales were butchered for the purposes of food and whatever else one uses whales for (whale throw pillows? refrigerator magnets? Slankets?).

See, here's what whale lovers don't get: Whales are boring, and "whale watching" doesn't help anyone. It doesn't put food on anyone's table—except the people smart enough to exploit these idiots who pay to look at whales. I do wonder how much money uncreative baby boomers and PETA members give these "tour operators" (meaning some dude with a boat) every year.

Whale watching doesn't support entire towns that don't have the luxury of online casino operations or organic coffee shops. However, whale hunting does. People hunt whales not for sport, but for commerce, to make money to feed their families (I also realize, of course, that people running whale-watching companies do it for the same reason—but they generate little commerce, and when they do they just spend it on hemp skirts). To assume that this method of earning a livelihood is wrong because it grosses you out makes you a hypocrite: Harpooning a whale is no different from stunning a cow on a Midwestern farm. Granted, it's probably more fun. But the real atrocity, really, is the whaler's terrible aim. They had at least eighty whale-watchers within reach, and they somehow hit the whale instead.

The Running of the Bulls Should Kill More People and Fewer Bulls

Every year, in the sunny city of Pamplona, Spain, the running of the bulls takes place—and I always sleep through it. That's because this so-called thrill-seeking festival bores the crap out of me. And also, I like sleeping.

The event attracts thousands of extremely stupid men with Hemingway fixations who dare to taunt six half-ton fighting bulls into goring them. What makes this boring: There are only six half-ton fighting bulls when there should be six hundred. It's like NASCAR: In my opinion, all the cars should crash (harmlessly, of course, because in my world their cars would be made of pillows).

That's the problem with this event. The bulls are outnumbered, and very few of the runners actually get injured or die. Fourteen runners have died in the event since they started keeping records in 1924. I'm sure you agree with me when I say that's not nearly enough. This is not thrill-seeking. It's basically your average walk through Detroit. Seriously, you're more at risk of getting trampled at an opening for an Ikea store, desperately trying to locate a Kija bookcase that will only fall apart days later (probably on you).

In one of the events two or three years ago, one bull gored a twenty-two-year-old tool from Bakersfield, California. He went up in the air with one hole in his ass, and came down with two—the second was a five-inch gash that required a trip to the hospital. There, he underwent surgery. That's right—after he had purposely put himself in harm's way, surgeons happily repaired his self-inflicted injury.

Would you? Maybe I'm a party pooper (and that gored dude will be, too, I'm sure), but I despise thrill seekers, adventurers, and extreme athletes, simply because they waste the time of those who must rescue and repair their ventilated and broken bodies. There are plenty of sick people who are sick through no fault of their own and never get proper treatment. It seems wrong that we offer treatment to people who are simply asking for it. I mean, consider those expensive search and rescues for lost millionaire explorers or balloonists. Would you rather spend that money trying to find abducted teens trapped in basements? (I prefer the expensive search and rescues, because frankly I don't need people poking around my basement.)

No Man Over Twenty-five Should Be Running

Unless, of course, something with four legs and slobbering jaws is chasing you (see Al Franken).

We Don't Need Coffins

I keep reading about how we're all trying to figure out alternatives to burying the dead—coffins take up too much space, after all—and it's getting to the point where cemeteries are considering piling the corpses up like a stack of smelly, decomposing pancakes. Even cremation is costly, and some experts now think freezing the dead—a process in which body and coffin are turned into powder after being dipped in liquid nitrogen—makes better sense.

Which raises the real point: If you're going to dissolve a coffin, why do you need a coffin? More important, if you're going to bury a body, you're never going to see the coffin again anyway (unless, of course, you become the subject of some sensational murder case, which, if that happens, congratulations in advance), so why do we need to spend so much on something like Roseanne Barr's vagina—a contraption no one is going to *ever ever* lay their eyes on again?

My suggestion: a nice sleeping bag. Or do what I want done to myself. I have informed many people of this: When I die I prefer to have my remains scattered over my hometown, San Mateo, California. But I do not want to be cremated (I fear the .000000001 percent chance I'd wake up in the oven). I would like to be dismembered, sliced and diced, and placed in small Ziploc bags and then air-dropped all over town. If you happen to find a "gutbag" in the street, a local park, or your backyard, you can promptly bring it to the post office where you can redeem the parcel for a special gift. I am thinking either something like "finger drums" (these are drums for your fingers!) or a Picoo Z micro helicopter.

If anyone has any suggestions as to what one might exchange for a package of my human remains, please feel free to write to me, care of President Obama, The White House, 1600 Pennsylvania Ave. NW, Washington, DC 20500.

Burma Has No Performance Artists

You may have heard about this Yale student (whose name doesn't merit mentioning) who, as part of her senior art project, claimed she artificially inseminated herself and then induced miscarriages. After getting a pile of attention, it's now been announced that this is a "creative fiction," otherwise known as "bullshit."

So what's the excuse for this attention-seeking behavior? The associate dean and vice president for public affairs, Helaine S. Klasky, said it was to draw attention to "the ambiguity surrounding form and function of a woman's body."

Meaning, "God help me, I'm a full-blown embarrassment."

And this is the crux of performance art: It's never supposed to do anything but raise awareness of, well, the performance artist. Performance art exists only to perpetuate the myth that performance artists have something to say, when actually they're untalented goons in desperate need of a solid kick in the ass.

How do you know that performance artists are useless? Because only a nation rich enough to host an entire class of indulgent and overfed wastrels has ever had them. Does Bosnia have performance artists? Do you think Zimbabwe has them? In Guatemala, performance art is living on 150 calories a day. Think Karen Finley or any of the other unemployables on the NEA teat could manage that?

Sorry—back to that really creepy student. Here's the thing: At first, she says these miscarriages are real. And then she says they aren't. So could this denial have been performance art as well? Could the truth, now explained as a lie, be a method to draw attention to the ambiguity surrounding women's struggle against patriarchy?

See how easy it is to make this crap up? I could be an associate dean at Yale!!

Although I must say, I'm not a fan of community colleges.

The Pregnant Man Is Just a Lady With Sideburns

For a brief period two years ago, an attention-craving woman named Thomas Beatie made a much-craved splash and a sizable lump of cash for herself by becoming the first pregnant man. She went on *Oprah*, where the host breathlessly felt the "bump," contributing to a silly farce serving only to reinforce this poor lady's belief that she's actually a dude. Beatie now has had two kids. Congrats to everyone involved. Can't wait for the PTA meetings!

But need I point out: If you're a dude, you can't have a baby. Beatie claims to be a guy—her evidence being that she removed her breasts and takes hormone treatments that allow her to grow a pretty feeble beard (she looks like the chubby kid from *Entourage*). But she still has a womb—making her a woman. That's that. (The press also calls preoperative transgendered men "she," which is also BS.)

I said as much on my show *Red Eye*, and I drew predictable rage from the predictable sources—GLAAD, an organization designed specifically to spit rage in the form of shrill press releases—but also from members of the press who are too cowardly to call a woman a woman. This idea that Beatie is not a woman exists only in the addled minds of people who cannot accept biological reality, as well as other cowards in the media fearful they will be seen as narrow-minded.

The funny thing is, this laughable outrage about Beatie hasn't even touched on what I said, only on how I said it. I told the truth: Calling a "she" a "he" only works if "he" ain't preggers. Because of this, I have been attacked by the same old drones who champion tolerance only if you agree 100 percent with their point of view. If not, then they want you dead. One angry person even said I have bad breath—which may be true, but has nothing to do with this issue (I have an unusual diet, which my attorney advises I shouldn't discuss).

Bottom line: I really don't care what people think Beatie is, or what she wants to think she is. All I care about is *the language*. Language is the only thing we have to communicate our needs and other important crap to each other—and it's bullshit to muddle or subvert it in order to placate a special-interest group's sensitive little feelings. Sorry, if Thomas Beatie entered the hospital for some sort of emergency surgery, she may check off "male" on the form, but that won't help the doctors. It would just confuse the hell out of everyone (I know from experience).

"Narrow-Minded" Actually Means Smart, and "Open-Minded" Means Stupid

I never really understood why "being open-minded," became a compliment, until I finally saw the movie *12 Angry Men*—possibly the most destructive movie ever made in the history of filmmaking. And I'm including *Never Been Kissed*.

No, wait: I'm not including *Never Been Kissed*.

As you might know, *12 Angry Men* begins at the end of a trial involving a young ethnic dude accused of murdering his dad. He is frightened, and therefore instantly sympathetic. There are two witnesses to the crime, and the knife used is exactly the same knife the youth had purchased that day. He was also seen arguing with his dad, the victim. So there was motive, weapon, and witnesses. Of the twelve men on the jury, eleven think he's guilty. But it was the "open-minded" Henry Fonda—the stoic contrarian—who answered every piece of evidence with, "What if it's wrong?" Over time, through relentless repetition, Fonda's character gets everyone to change his mind. Sidney Lumet, the director, took pains to portray the most stubborn of the men as angry, violent, pigheaded, selfish, and borderline psychotic (essentially, the modern media portrayal of a Rush Limbaugh fan or a Tea Party attendee). Fonda's character, of course, is a self-assured, highly principled moral relativist, if that's indeed possible.

The moral of the movie boils down to this: If you go by what you know and see with your own eyes (or what you've learned from your parents), clearly you're narrow-minded. And a prick. Far better to question everything—which means no one can ever be guilty of anything.

That's the definition of open-minded—by allowing yourself to consider all options, you have no claim to the truth. Every avenue is equal, all thoughts relative, and therefore there can be no definitive judgment, even from a judge!

That's why, in my opinion, being narrow-minded should be championed, saluted, revered. Being narrow-minded means you are operating with a backbone, because you know the difference between right and wrong, and you aren't afraid to limit your options to the right one. Once you become narrow-minded, the concept of being open-minded actually reveals itself as intellectual paralysis.

The only way to survive life, really, is to be narrow-minded. You cannot, for example, be open-minded about foods you put in your mouth to digest. This is why you never hear anyone say, "Who's to say these toxic mushrooms are bad for you?" You can't be open-minded about rotten food, spoiled roadkill, or feces shaped like adorable brownies—take my word for it.

Consider how you get to work every morning, okay? You pick the safest, most straightforward route to your office—you instinctively, and correctly, narrowed all the options to one correct choice. Sure, there may be a more scenic route—which adds minutes to the commute—but the route you picked, you have chosen because you judged it most effective based on a number of variables. You narrowed the options to one. It's a shame we can only be narrow-minded about the basics of survival, and then suddenly disown the idea when it comes to politics, morality, and worse, fashion.

Seriously, the only way fashion designers can make money is if everyone else who isn't in fashion sacrifices all common sense and instead prays at the altar of open-mindedness. If everyone treated fashion the way they treated cars or food, the industry would have no choice but to change or collapse. Perhaps they might create things people could actually wear. Like skinny chaps with fur-lined thigh seams. (What can I say? It's slimming.)

Crap Becomes Acceptable As It Ages

Right now, as I write this, the movie *The Blue Lagoon* is playing on the American Movie Classics Channel. If you weren't born until after the 1970s, then you probably don't know that it's about as "classic" as indigestion—saved only by the fact that a teenage and totally delectable Brooke Shields prances around in a tattered thong (okay, maybe that qualifies as "classic"). But the movie, released back in 1980, is now considered a "classic." Why is that? Because it was released back in 1980. The fact is, if you wait around long enough, even the worst thing in the world wins an award, or writes a book.

Case in point—a three-pound pile of actual turds from the Jurassic period has just been auctioned off for nearly a thousand dollars. And oddly, around the same time, Barbara Walters recently released a new memoir detailing her sordid affairs with men who must be vision-impaired. So on one hand you have a really old pile of poo—and on the other, a really old pile of poo.

What does all this crap about crap mean? Well, aside from the fact that it's crappy, people no longer care that it's crappy. The sad fact: All horrible things somehow become less horrible as they age. Including literal crap. Think about it—Ted Turner, Fidel Castro, and Jimmy Carter were all folks filled with mangy ideas, but as age gave them white hair, suddenly people found them respectable. Even a fossil like Barbara Walters, an emblem of 1970s banality, has become some sort of saintly relic. Perfect for my coffee table.

But this got me to thinking: We are overlooking an amazing investment opportunity that lurks in our own waste. Well, not my waste, but the crap that pours out of celebrities. Seriously—how much would a stool from a deceased president go for? A Lincoln log could probably buy me a lifetime supply of Wet Ones. So I'm starting a new business. It's called Poop Stars, and I'm asking celebs to send me their you-know-what, which I will keep in a storage facility. Then when I auction it, we split the profits. Laugh now, people. But when I'm the BM billionaire, don't come begging to me for a slice of Delta Burke's.

If You're Over Twenty-five and Still Use "Party" As a Verb, Then You're Beyond Redemption

I have a friend who, when arriving in town, always says we should hook up to "party." When I hear this, it reminds me that the real decline of America came when that word transformed from a noun to a verb. People used to see drinking as needed relief following a day of hard work. But now, it's seen as something you can base your reputation on.

Rather than say, "Let's have a drink," which is no large achievement, people now say, "Let's party," as if it's an actual endeavor that requires hard work—an act that goes beyond simply throwing up on a deliveryman (sorry, Ramone, I'll pay for the dry cleaning). "Let's party" is also purposely vague—and is often used by prostitutes and the men who hire them, for that very reason. Saying, "Are you here to party?" is far safer, legally, than saying, "Thirty bucks for a blow job."

And that's another reason why I hate using "party" as a verb. It raises my expectations and makes it difficult to haggle. Seriously, if I pay to "party," but don't end up whipping a meth-addicted runaway with an AFX racetrack slat, then I want a refund.

The Only People You Know Who Are in Mensa Are the People Who Need to Tell You They Are in Mensa

I just read about some infant in England, named Georgia Brown, who at the age of two was already dabbling in French and counting to double digits. Her parents forced the bundle of neurons to take an IQ test, and lo and behold, the creature was a genius. According to the *Daily Mail*, Georgia is now the youngest female member of Mensa after scoring an IQ of 152. I think she's three or four. But I can't remember, and it's entirely possible that I might have dreamed up this entire story.

At any rate, I find it interesting that the only people you know who are members of Mensa are the people *who tell you* they are members of Mensa. Or their obnoxious parents.

My theory is that Mensa members are morons with crummy jobs and lousy lives. The prospect of telling people that they are in Mensa is the only enterprise in life they cling to.

And yes, I know this little girl was only two years old at the time of this. But if she's a genius, then she should know better.

Gender Studying

Childbirth Is a Small Price to Pay for
Thin-Crust Pizza and Bridges

Do you know what a Push Present is? Don't worry, because this next sentence will tell you: It's a gift given by a new father to his wife to mark the birth of their sniveling offspring. Basically, the woman gets something shiny for producing something shiny. According to the bored and desperate lifestyle reporters still clinging to their jobs, the demand is so huge that stores are creating registries to keep up with so-called demand.

Here, friends, is how a trend starts, even though it doesn't really exist. A "growing" trend, apparently, requires only that a reporter hear a few anecdotal reports from people who say they bought their wife a present for pumping out a screaming bag of protoplasm. Suddenly it's a "practice," of course, spread by "word of mouth" because there is no actual proof it exists. (You know, you rarely see trends start that don't involve a retail purchase. "Push Presents" probably had their birth in a Zales jeweler memo.)

But look, I'll pretend "Push" gifts really exist. So, if women deserve gifts for giving birth, then men deserve gifts for going to war, building bridges, creating infrastructure, highways, tunnels, viaducts, dams, DDT, and thin-crust pizza—and all the other crap men do that turns us into angry, overworked bastards. We work like dogs for our entire lives and die, on average, seven years earlier than women. Why is that? It's because we pump out more than just kids. We create amazing things by intense effort that, over time, actually kills us.

So, where are my flowers? My diamond earrings? My "weekend away"?

Not that I really deserve it, mind you. I haven't done anything truly strenuous in about twenty-five years.

All Women Prefer Skinny Women to Fat Women

Every year around Fashion Week in New York, you see women's magazines running the same old articles, repeating the same stupid lies about how women hate thin models. These editors claim that women feel unnecessary stress having to compete with these stick figures, and see women with fuller figures as more appealing.

However, they're lying. Fact is, most women prefer wafer-thin lasses, finding them "more elegant, interesting, likeable, and pleasant," at least according to one study I read while sunbathing nude on the roof of a double-decker bus.

Female magazine editors secretly agree, but pretend not to, out of guilt. That's why in the very same magazines running those skinny models, they also run boring features on bulimia.

The unspeakable truth: It's not the modeling industry that's at fault for the rail-thin birds parading down the catwalk—the blame lies with all women. The fact is, women prefer thinsters to fatties, even if the woman doing the preferring is fat.

We all prefer to look at attractive people. And toned skin is more attractive than flab. The only exception to this rule was John Candy. He was fucking beautiful.

Women's Achievements Are Always Overshadowed by Their Level of Attractiveness

It's true—if a woman isn't attractive, all her achievements fall into the "nice try" column.

A more sordid fact: When men look at team photos of girls' college sports teams (with the exception of Brown University), they instinctively count the number of women they would have sex with. The highest number will always be found in lacrosse. The lowest: also lacrosse.

It's true—every man, and yes, every woman, will agree with me. If you're looking at a group photo of, say, a female Olympic team, you instinctively focus on the hot members of the group. And, if you were to compare the stats of one player to the other, the hot one is the one you're going to like more, even if she sucks. And it's only because she's hot. It explains why a mediocre athlete like Anna Kournikova actually had a career. It's not that she was a fine athlete, but that she was fine. I mean, she couldn't even handle a four-iron!

No matter: It's unfair. And, no—not just to women. Fact is, men have to be great at something to actually be considered great at something. Being handsome will not get the coach to put you in the game, which is why I was always equipment manager. However, because we are all easily influenced, biologically, by the sight of a beautiful woman, a mediocre female athlete can attain higher status as an athlete simply by being hot. It's why certain sports were created with the sole purpose of being played by hot chicks.

Volleyball, tennis, and gymnastics were invented purely to get girls to bounce around in flimsy clothing. It all went to hell, however, when Billie Jean King showed up.

If You Want to Accentuate the Flaws of Both Sexes, Give a Woman a Headset, and a Man an Earpiece

Anyone who's ventured into a club in Manhattan knows this. It's amazing how a headset on a hostess can turn a decent woman into Eva Perón. Or worse, Eva Longoria. And once a man inserts that little thing in his ear (no, not David Spade's penis), he suddenly thinks he's protecting the president. No, sir, you're working the door for a shitty club—keeping the world safe from people from New Jersey. Honestly, find another line of work.

Women From Other Countries Are Hotter Than the Ones in Yours

You know why Keira Knightley is sexy? She's British. That's sexy. Unless you're British. Then it's just boring. It's true: If you spend your life looking at the same type of women, then women from somewhere else instantly seem more attractive. It's not that they really are better-looking, it's just that your biological sex nerves (that's the technical term) are tickled by novelty. But it's all a trick. The fact is, it doesn't matter where a woman comes from. It's where she's going. And if it's to the clinic, don't ask for her number.

Women Talk More, but Say Less

It's an actual scientific fact that, in a typical day, women use more words than men do. In fact, research shows that women talk almost three times as much as men, with the average female spouting up to twenty thousand words in a day—thirteen thousand more than the average dude. What the research doesn't make clear is whether women use more words than men, or just repeat the same ones over and over and over again. The reason: During the study, the male researchers got bored and went fishing.

All Men Are in the Closet

The phrase "in the closet," of course, refers to cloaked homosexuality. However, it shouldn't. Whether he's gay or straight, a man lives in the closet most of his life, shielding what essentially is a secret that overrides sexual preference. It's the fact that he's a dirty, dirty pig. The only difference might be that, occasionally, a straight guy has some secret "in the closet" that is not obvious to every person he has ever met.

I came to this truth after many years of self-examination (figuratively, and sometimes literally, using a full-length mirror left lengthways on the floor). It's a fact—all men live in the closet, we all hide things, and while gays say it's unjust to have to live a lie, straight men can probably say the same thing about themselves. Straight men live lies, by pretending to be upstanding citizens, monogamous, moral, and "clean." I suppose that straight men could be like gay men and choose to "express" their sexuality—as the heterosexual perverts we are—and even mark it with a parade. Somehow, though, I doubt we'd get the permits from the city.

Women Who Call Stripping Exploitation Just Need to Lose a Few Pounds

In Ireland, which is located somewhere on the Pacific Rim of Canada, a group of companies signed an agreement pledging not to spend any of their corporate cash at strip clubs. According to a support group for chicks working in "the sex industry," this charter was meant simply to "challenge some of the myths that this is innocent fun."

I don't like lapdancing clubs. I find them claustrophobic, loud, and worst of all, discriminating (they said I was too fat for amateur night). But I don't think the solution to the problem is to ban people from going to them. All this does is hurt the solitary lapdancer, who works on tips in order to feed her baby and her drug-dealing boyfriend Dirk (his actual name).

No one ever considers those consequences. More important, I am almost always suspicious when someone (like the spokeswoman for the "sex workers" support group) justifies her actions by saying she's only doing this to "raise awareness." Of what, exactly? That she herself is not attractive enough to make money off her body? Look—if she wants us to know that lapdancing is an unpleasant vocation, we *already* know this. If she really wanted to deal with the plight of strippers, there are better ways.

For example:

- Sponsor a lapdancer exchange, where a club in Eastern Europe can send a dancer to stay with a family in the U.S. In exchange, the husband can send his family.
- Subsidize a Take Your Daughter to a Strip Club Day. Show young girls that it's not all fun and games at an early age, and you may prevent them from choosing a vocation later in life meant solely to stab you in the heart and then twist.
- Allow corporations to adopt a lapdancer, much in the way community groups adopt Bolivian kids and put them through school. I imagine Microsoft alone could help fund a few thousand of them—which is more than enough to keep Bill Gates occupied in his underground sex dungeon (we know he has one—it's why his hair is always a constant, albeit adorable mess).

Men Become Photographers
Only to See Women Naked

Spencer Tunick is the artist/photographer who makes a living herding hundreds and even thousands of naked bodies onto various landmarks and then taking their picture. He's done this all over the world, but he's never asked me, which I take personally.

Recently he shot five hundred buck-naked models uncorking champagne, and afterward he claimed that this photograph expressed the excesses of our consumer culture.

Of course it does, you big perv. Sure, this enterprise had *nothing* to do with the fact that you want to see a bunch of people naked. Here's the only reason why men become photographers: It's the easiest way to get a girl's clothes off. Try this experiment. Go up to a girl and say, "I'd like to see you naked." You'll get hit, kicked, or beaten by a large boyfriend. Now approach her with a camera and an assistant named Tasha who has her own business cards, and say the same thing. Nine times out of ten, the aspiring model will shortly be back at your loft, draped across a bearskin rug, while you snort coke off her forehead.

One day when I grow up, I want to be a photographer. You get to see more people naked than doctors do—without having to lance anything.

To Make Your Girlfriend More Desirable,
Let Her Dump You

It works every single time. The main cause of strife in all relationships is boredom—after a few years the man becomes used to the girl and begins taking her for granted. He starts thinking maybe he should see other people. He starts flirting with the girls at work.

He tells himself the hot bartender with the henna tattoo and the tongue stud really "wants him." He works up the guts to tell his girlfriend that "he needs his space." But right when he's about to do it, as always—she dumps him. And he's a miserable turd, now consumed by the idea that she's the only woman on the planet meant for him.

Funny how that works. If women only knew this, they would dump their guy every three months or so, just to keep it fresh. Men, however, continue to make the same mistake. They don't know themselves well enough to see that leaving one woman for another does nothing to prevent boredom from setting in. The only solution is for women never to let men become truly comfortable. For comfort breeds a listless ambivalence—the backbone of all suffering. Men should never have the time or the opportunity to consider other options—for those options lead nowhere. Pick a girl, one girl, and imagine the world without her. And you'll probably never leave.

Also—don't hire female au pairs. Particularly Scandinavians.

Women Love Men Who Look Like Women (and It Pisses Me Off)

Every time I see Dave Navarro, I do not see a guitar god, but a bearded lady from the circus. He's more feminine than any of my pool boys, and probably a better kisser.

I've read in places that women find men with feminine features more attractive than men who look like men—and I buy it completely. I'm not sure on the science, but maybe the soft features signify that he'll love scented candles and cunnilingus?

While it is true the goddess known as Carmen Electra married Navarro, she divorced him shortly after—mainly because he had better skin and slimmer hips. It didn't help that he would borrow her Dior Unlimited ultrastretch mascara, and always leave the double-sided brush on the sink instead of putting it away. And, no joke, sometimes he would drink milk right out of the carton, leaving a rich mix of four shades of lip gloss, including plum hues and warm neutrals, which were Carmen's least favorite. Finally, one day she came home and found him in the living room, dry humping Carmen's square, black nylon makeup bag (the one with a three-tier fold-out tray).

For these reasons, women should only date short fat piggish men like me.

Men Think They're 8.5 Times Stronger Than They Really Are

Ever since I was a little boy, I always felt that I could lift cars over my head, or at the very least, turn them on their side, if the situation warranted it. I would walk by cars and stare at them, and think: "I bet if someone was trapped under that car, I could lift it up and save them."

It raises the unspeakable truth that all men understand: We always think that we have superhuman strength, the kind that's always ready to be tapped. We rarely ever have to tap it, however, which keeps the fantasy intact until we're on our deathbeds, struggling to lift the bedpan.

More important, whatever happened to bionic limbs anyway? I just read a story claiming yet again that these wondrous devices have finally arrived. According to the breathless report, scientists have created fake-limb technology that allows the limb to be directly attached to our skeletons, without risk of infection. The technique, called Intraosseous Transcutaneous Amputation Prosthesis (ITAP), involves sticking a titanium rod directly into the bone.

Basically, that's it.

In my book, that is not bionic. It's positively Flintstonian. But that's not the scientists' fault—it's Hollywood's. The bottom line is this: Because of the powerful fantasy created by my favorite show of all time, *The Six Million Dollar Man*, nearly every man my age was convinced he was going to have a special arm made that would allow him to crush Winnebagos full of swarthy terrorists. So I always dreamed of being "stronger," "faster," with an added racing stripe or two. Also: having sex with the bionic woman—I dreamed of that, too. While the bionic dog watched.

On an unrelated note: It's Friday morning, and I almost blew up the apartment. I got up to make coffee and turned on the stove for the kettle. Then I went back to bed. The fire didn't start, and instead I filled the entire place with gas. It's amazing that I am not dead. I have opened all the windows.

And this little event makes me wonder how many people I have unknowingly killed, because of my own stupidity.

My guess is a lot.

Men Should Not Hold Babies

I know, I know—it's easy to say this if you don't have kids. But to me there's nothing more nauseating than a photograph of a man holding his newborn and giving this stupid look down at the beast, as if to say, "I can't believe I helped create this." Well, douche, you did—exactly like about six billion other people. This is no achievement—it's a nine-month biological process, a protracted version of taking a dump. Except this dump, over time, gradually learns to walk and talk and then bleed you dry. It's like a little IRS agent that lives with you and always wants a drink of water just as you're falling asleep.

But that's not why men should not hold babies. Men should not hold babies because they're simply more likely to drop them. Men know this, and the nervousness that thought causes makes them even more nervous. It's a spiral of panic that inevitably leads to something very horrible and messy. Men should only hold a baby if all the women in the vicinity have been kidnapped.

Women Should Never Read in the Bathroom

I only mention this because recently I used a couple's bathroom and noticed a selection of magazines by the toilet, in a cute little wooden basket. For some reason the cute little wooden basket makes it "elegant" to keep magazines in the john—so you can read while you shit. If only a man lived there, you can bet there would be no wooden basket. There probably wouldn't be any toilet paper either, however.

I did not want to touch these magazines. But I noticed that most of the publications were women's mags—meaning it was the wife, not the husband, who was reading on the crapper. This was the first time I have ever seen this. Although I have no research to back this up, I was always pretty certain that the only people who should read in the bathroom are men. At work, for example, it's common to see a man walking toward the bathroom with the sports page folded under his arm. I always felt self-conscious doing the same. Holding a paper, or a book, or a set of books as you enter the bathroom tells everyone, "I'm going to take a long dump and catch up on my reading." This is a message I don't think women should be sending.

Women Hate Porn Because It's Competition

It's a common magazine topic: how porn isn't just a man's game. Yep, women love it, too—as though this is supposed to be a wonderful thing. The article's writer, usually a chick, cites improbable statistics that bear this out—the product of some circumspect sex institute run by a hairy woman in her late seventies. This is hogwash, pure and simple.

Almost all porn is designed for men, be they gay or straight. The so-called lady porn that you hear about makes up a tiny percentage of the overall smut output, and it only gets press because feminists are trying so hard to say that men and women aren't different. Which we all know is hilariously misguided and totally dishonest.

Women should rejoice in the fact that they find porn useless. Because it is. Even men who love porn know this. Men look at porn with insatiable need—but minutes later that need is quenched, and replaced with a weird mix of self-loathing and an atavistic need for a roast beef sandwich.

Most men don't mind that—divorcing the image of sexual desire from love is what we do best. It's how civilizations started. But Internet porn has created a ceaseless stream of sexual novelty that undermines any desire for something real. Women innately know this just can't be right—and to say they don't is doing them a disservice.

Which is why I only look at lizard porn. But not, you know, the kinky kind (I prefer it when they're in a field eating grass).

Feminism Helps Jerks Screw—and Screw Over—Women

I mean—what do you think the pro-choice movement really is? It's not about rights. It's about getting laid. That's why men don't get too worked up about killing fetuses. The fact is, men will take everything and anything they can get off you sexually, so it's up to the woman to actually say no.

Plus, we love that you want to work! We want the option of staying home picking up old girlfriends off Facebook while the Mrs. (sorry, Ms.) goes off to work. The fact is, the women's movement—which allowed for women to have sex as often as their horny male counterparts—helped guys more. And for smart men, marching alongside feminists guaranteed sex. The only downside is it was with women who look like Janeane Garofalo (I'm talking after she wound up at Air America; she was a doll before that).

The more feminism turns women into men, the more men like it. Men are simpler creatures, and if society viewed giving a hand-job as no different from giving someone a lift to the airport, we'd all oblige.

Women Think Good Thoughts, Men Think Bad Ones

Having attended thousands of meetings, I have noticed a sordid, disturbing difference between men and women. During such meetings, when women take notes, they underline things and use lots of exclamation points. Men, however, draw headless corpses. For me, I've always doodled angry, seething things with teeth, spindly fingers holding machine guns, firing bullets into other figures, who always lose their heads. Oddly, the head often looks like Joey Bishop's.

Doodles like these are probably harmless, unless they become the property of a lawyer who is suing you for something. Which is what happened to me many years ago at a magazine that had been sued for libel. Since I had written the offending article, I had to hand my notes over to a lawyer, who found, among them, lurid drawings in the upper corners of the pages. I have a vague memory of bloody heads and evil-looking squirrels eating the bloody heads. Again, they all looked like Joey Bishop. Although the case was thrown out, those drawings did not help.

Meanwhile, if you look at the doodles belonging to a female—any female—you will find large stars (with stars around the stars), a happy face, some hearts, sometimes filled in with smaller hearts. This is, in a nutshell, the best reflection of the difference between male and female brains. I could go on and tell you how I once sat behind a famous female newscaster, in a meeting, and watched her doodle her name over and over again, with hearts all over it. But, hey—I just did!

Men Are Doomed to Flash Their Junk

The night before I wrote this down, New York police apparently nabbed thirteen flashers and gropers in a sting operation on the city subway system. To do this, they used undercover policewomen as bait—something that's forced me to take the bus. Interestingly, during this two-day sting mission, dubbed "Operation Exposure," no women were arrested. Only men.

No surprise here—men are sickos by nature; women are sickos only after hanging around sicko men.

But still, something about this scares me. I've never had the urge to flash anyone, but I wonder if one day, I will. See, I'm thinking that flashing is to lonely old men what feeding cats is to lonely old women. Each behavior satisfies the glimmer of a need once sated but now ignored. For men, it's nature; for women, it's nurture. And it probably occurs as a reflex, for no other reason than you're scratching a biological itch. And then these perverts get arrested, which I'm all for. But if women ever expose themselves, they don't ever get arrested, for two reasons:

1. Either they are doing it for some feminist cause, in which case they are so godawful ugly, people pity them too much to sic the cops (who also pity them) on them.
2. Or they are really hot chicks, probably strippers, hired by someone like PETA to disrobe and garner attention for their wacky cause. It's hard for cops to arrest topless table dancers when they're also trying to get their phone numbers.

Pertaining to flashing: I always felt there was an easier, more benign way of getting your jollies. Flash your pets. Sometimes I'll get really drunk and expose myself to my girdle-tailed lizard. She doesn't seem to mind or care. Girdle-tailed lizards are jaded like that.

Gender Studies Are Ignored If They Tell the Truth

Last night, while lounging in my basement grotto, otherwise known as an oil drum filled with baby lotion, I came across a study that says "Boys like blue and girls like pink." Apparently this is one of the first studies to show that there are sex-based differences between girls and boys, something I've suspected ever since I arrived in first grade dressed like Tootie from *Facts of Life*.

So here is a study that debunks a feminist tenet. Feminist scholars, after all, have gone to great lengths to dismiss any differences between genders, preferring to call all of it a social construct, created by evil patriarchy. But here is research that could finally kill persistent myths still alive and kicking on campuses everywhere. As boring as this information is, it might actually do what common sense failed to do—tell you that you were right all along.

Too bad no one cared.

See, feminists in the media believe that if a baby girl had a choice, she'd pick blue every bit as often as pink. And she'd also probably want to be a fireman/lumberjack/ice road trucker.

But we know, in our hearts, that this is BS. Nearly all little girls want to be ballerinas, and little boys want to shoot birds. Girls wear pigtails, and boys want to eat earthworms. Unless, of course, you're me, then you do both.

On a related note, while I was lying around in my rotating bed, or more specifically, a mattress covered with jam, I came upon another study, this one reporting that sex is just as important to many seniors in their eighties and nineties as it is to the rest of us not fending off imaginary spiders. According to researchers at the University of Chicago, 73 percent of people ages fifty-seven to sixty-four reported having sex at least once in the past year, usually with someone who also has removable teeth and a Clapper.

Everywhere, this is greeted as "good news." Not here. To me, there is nothing more disgusting than old people having sex.

But please, do not call me ageist, because I don't want to hear about people of any age having sex—period. Talking about sex is like talking about food. It's pointless until you're actually doing it, preferably with chocolate sauce and capers.

Personally, *not* having sex is one of the things I look forward to when I'm old. I don't need the stress of having to remain clean, wipe thoroughly, or even brush my teeth in an effort to look desirable. I just want to lie around in my own crusty filth, eating egg and avocado sandwiches, until some unfortunate paramedics have to blow down my door to find my bloated pasty corpse wedged between the nightstand and a mattress stained with Bengay and Robitussin DM. And if that's not a sexy image, then, sir, I don't know what is.

Young Men Talk Like Dumb Girls

The other night I was watching something on TV—I can't remember if it was *Gossip Girl* or the *Rachel Zoe Project*, because I'm making this up—but one of the male characters was mumbling in a singsong manner that sounded less like talking and more like leaking. And it occurred to me that many young men seem to communicate in this manner these days—in an annoying way that suggests a total lack of interest in what they're saying. It's lamer than Barbaro after the Preakness.

I call this the "Seth Cohen Effect." You remember Seth as the lazy talker from a show called *The O.C.*, who spoke in the back of his throat as if he were borrowing words, not saying them. Perhaps this was a crutch he used because he had no acting experience, or ability, it seems.

But it's a bigger problem infecting everyone between the ages of eighteen and thirty-five. I call it Enervation X—the crippling awareness that everything has already been said and thought, so you just sleepwalk through life, parroting dumb-ass catchphrases that pollute blogs and TV shows like specks of cat vomit tracked in from the street. Caring, to teens and twentysomethings, it seems, is a sign of weakness.

Why are men, especially, overcome by this mumbling malaise? I swear we are turning into a nation of disaffected zombies who try very hard pretending not to be trying at all. It's not that I want you to care about the world, I just want you to care about what you're saying. What I want is for you to speak like men. They're vocal cords, not kazoos, people, and that whiny, painful, annoying noise you're making doesn't sound articulate or sensitive.

More to the point, do chicks dig this act? I guess for a while, they must. But then, when they need a man, they try to find something that sounds like one. Like Kevin Spacey. Now there's a hot hunk of man.

Health Mulch

No One Believes They Will Get Old, Until They Are

So what was the number-one issue in the last presidential campaign, and the health care debate that erupted a few short months later? If you said race, you'd be wrong. If you said the economy, you'd be even wronger—if that's actually a word (I'm thinking it probably isn't, which is a shame). Nope: The number-one issue was age. Yes, we're all getting older—and get this: We're all going to die.

So technically, death was the top issue. Not age. But it's basically the same, since every day we die a little (unless, of course, you're Madonna, and kept alive on transfusions of meerkat blood).

But because McCain was seventy-two at the time, his age became the central factor hammered on relentlessly by Obama supporters, the lapdog media, mediocre comics, and boring bloggers. It was the easiest issue to pontificate on, because there's just no denying it: McCain's old. He looks old. He acts old. He always looks about ten seconds away from swinging a rake at a skateboarder. And by focusing only on that flaw, you don't have to study up on anything else. Just keep saying he's a cranky codger with eyebrows the size of Mothra, and you'll get your laugh.

So go ahead and laugh. But you're going to be there, with him, sooner than you think.

If you're lucky.

Fact is, you could die tomorrow, instantly making McCain a far healthier, more vibrant person than you. And whether you admit it or not, even in his seventies, McCain is going to outlive many comedians, pundits, writers, and other literary types—simply because he's tough, and they aren't. I mean, have you seen his mother? I have a feeling she can kick the crap out of me (especially if I paid her one hundred bucks for it).

Look, in my book (and it is my book), where you are in life isn't as important as what you've done in it. Bad choices cannot be dismissed purely by the context of immaturity. Does it matter that when McCain was in his twenties, he was being tortured by communists, yet when Obama was in his twenties, he was sucking up to their sympathizers? Sure, the commies he sought to brown-nose carried books instead of bayonets, but their ideology was every bit as rotten.

And speaking as a person who has more days behind him than in front, I would like to say you make better decisions as you age— but you often don't. Which probably explains all these mysterious bruises.

And while we're on the topic of age, aging, and approaching death, I would like to take a moment to thank old people.

Thank you, old people.

See, as I write this piece, the public option part of Obama's health care reform bill is in free fall, and many are blaming Republican opposition. Which, of course, is giving the Republicans way too much credit. Fact is, the people you have to thank for this surprising turn of events are old people.

Again, thank you, old people.

It reminds me of my MacBook. See, mine's been having problems for the last six months and I keep planning to take it in, but I never do. Instead of walking a few blocks to the Apple Store on a sunny Saturday, I waste the day watching *Top Chef* marathons in my pajamas. And by pajamas, I really mean underwear. And by underwear, I mean body paint.

Now, compare that to my mom. I got her a MacBook for her birthday last year, but somehow within a few weeks, she touched a button, causing everything on her desktop to disappear. Only old people can seem to find that hidden button.

Anyway, she hopped into her car and drove her eighty-four-year-old butt to the store. Although it was just five miles away, it took her an hour to get to the place, but the point is: She got there. And that illustrates a key lesson we've learned in this health care debate.

Old people may be slow, but they always show.

Pre-election, the media became so obsessed with the youth vote that we overlooked the sheer determination of the elderly. And it left the pols caught like deer in a mobility scooter's headlights. How ironic is it that the folks most easily called to action are those with the poorest hearing?

The fact is, young people talk a big game, but they often don't show up to play. I can't remember how many times I've signed up for a Sunday charity fun run, only to miss it because the night before I fell asleep in a hedge. But hey, it's the thought that counts.

See, with the exception of those in the military, the young can't prioritize for crap. Old folks, however, always show up for the things that matter: church, world wars, dinner (sometimes early). Meanwhile, all those youngsters enamored of hope and change didn't think beyond the bumper sticker—for it's just too boring to question whether the government might turn your hospital into a post office with bedpans.

So, all in all, if it wasn't for the elderly, the one-thousand-page-plus bill would have passed without anyone reading it. It may have already passed, by the time this book is in your hot little hands, but at least someone showed up and put up a fight.

See, that makes old people cool. They read that stupid bill, so the rest of us didn't have to. Thank them, and remember that one day you're going to end up just like them—like I said—if you're lucky.

You Should Be Able to Choose Whom You Donate Your Organs To

A few years back, a gruesome scandal rocked the Human Tissue Industry (yeah, I didn't know it was an industry either), when a company called Biomedical Tissue Services was accused of secretly carving up a ton of cadavers, among them, that of the British-born host of *Masterpiece Theatre*, Alistair Cooke. They then sold the parts on the thriving nonorgan body parts market (which I believe is located in the rear of the Kutztown, Pennsylvania, Wal-Mart).

I remember, as a child, flipping around the television channels and always coming to Alistair Cooke on PBS, hosting *Masterpiece Theatre*. I always resented how the British would spell their words differently, especially "Theatre." I knew one day Cooke would pay for his arrogance.

But should people be outraged when tissue from corpses is harvested without consent? I would probably say, yes.

Only because it seems like the right thing to say.

I do believe people should be able to donate organs or tissue, but they should be able to pick the person they get to donate to—and more important, those people who *should not* get their tissue.

For example, if I were to perish in an accident today, I would like to make sure that after my death none of my organs would be used in the lifesaving treatment of:

- Any currently working child star.
- Anyone named Zac.
- People who like to stay for credits at the end of movies.
- Members of Bill Maher's *Real Time* studio audience.
- Joggers.
- Shia LaBeouf.
- Australian bartenders.
- Ryan Phillippe, for cheating on Reese.

If I do die, I would like any or all of my organs to go to Ryan Seacrest—even if he is perfectly healthy. Just cut them out, put them in a styrofoam freezer, and send them to him. Even if he doesn't need them, it would be nice to know that I'm there for him.

Deepak Chopra Is the Eastern Version of Jim Bakker

Deepak is no different from any other television evangelical huckster, but he gets a pass because he leans on the multicultural card. The same people who derided Jimmy Swaggart or even Billy Graham listen reverently to Chopra's pointless, useless, and ultimately idiotic opinions. The only real difference is accent and skin tone. Also, Chopra likes to wear tacky robes.

Also, Deepak loves babbling about peace. And there's a reason for this—it makes the dude rich. For a Huffington Post piece, I once scampered to Deepak's website to see if I could join one of Deepak's "Peace Cells," held at his very own Human Forum of Puerto Rico. There I could learn about "the power of oneness" and connect "the seeds of a new humanity." For only $1,095 per person. And that was a bargain.

There was loads of other crap being sold on his website, including "bliss" packages costing $475. Included: "preferred reserved seating" for Friday's lecture by Deepak. Then there's Deepak's other retreat, the Seduction of the Spirit. I am told it has nothing to do with banging the dead, but I could be wrong. Either way, "You will never be the same," reads Chopra's website. At $1,775, he's right. I'd be broke.

But that's not all this huckster hucks. You can enroll in home study courses in "primordial sound meditation," which goes for 1,695 bucks. Or you can get an instructor for only $895. Deepak is making more of a killing off peace than Halliburton did off war.

There are more courses and workshops to choose from—all costing thousands of dollars. They incorporate words like "healing," and "journey," and "certified," creating the idea that at the end of this, you might actually possess some sort of medical expertise. If I were to become a "certified Chopra Center instructor," I could heal irritable bowel syndrome! Technically, I am a pain in the ass—physician, heal thyself!!!

Anyway, I suppose peace comes at a price, and no one knows that better than the leader of the modern peace movement himself, Deepak Chopra. But that's not his real sin. The real evil behind Chopra is the tripe he spews about the notion of good and evil, and how you can't tell them apart. I love it when he makes peaceful sense of genocide—like the way he once wrote on the Huffpo that the Holocaust happened not simply because Hitler was, like, evil, but because, as in the present day, "all countries on both sides of the terror divide are enmeshed in the same conflicted mind-set. The inability to accept and respect dissimilar views of the world is present."

It's true—we really do hate it when people get gassed. But whether you gas people, or stop people from being gassed, it's all the same! We're all just gases anyway. We really need to get out of the us versus them mind-set, people. Well, unless you're the U.S. Then, says Chopra, "the blame for whatever follows will fall on America's head."

Well, at least that piece of Chopra wisdom was free. But of all the advice he's given, it's probably the most destructive.

There's No Such Thing As Internet Addiction

Every day a new report on Internet addiction comes out—and these stories cite the usual experts. One doc claims that the person addicted to his computer will experience the same narcotic high as someone who gets off on coke or dope.

Poopydoop, I say. (It's a scientific phrase, people. Google it.)

If you actually look at why men and women compulsively use the web, you find that the compulsion simply defines the flaws in both sexes. For women, it's shopping and gossiping at chat rooms. For men, it's poring over porn. So, you can't blame the Internet for all this—these vices existed long before the web. Blaming your need for porn on the Internet is like blaming your problems with pot on your bong.

Bottom line: "Addiction" is the most overused word in our language, and when you think about it, it's the easiest problem in the world to solve. Addiction is the only so-called "affliction" where the actual "disease" can be removed from your presence without actual surgery. You just throw the laptop out the window. This also works with cocaine, booze, tropical fish, and opinionated authors.

Mobility Scooters Are Just Big Wheels With Motors

Here is my problem with mobility scooters: At some point in your life, you just have to stay put. Once you are old, fat, and infirm, why not use that as an excuse to lie in bed all day and yell at the help (who can't understand you anyway)?

Mobility scooters, especially the new ones with navigation systems, just put more pressure on the elderly to go out and get in our way by clogging up our sidewalks and supermarket aisles. Also, it might make it that much harder to get rid of them—even if you "accidentally" forget them at the picnic.

I for one cannot wait until I am old enough to be able to lie in bed and poop in a pan.

That day will come in five years. I've been practicing.

On a similar note (but not really), I just read about this guy named Terry Wallis, who finally regained speech and movement after two decades of being barely conscious. Doctors think that somehow Wallis, who is now forty-two, had spontaneously "rewired" his brain by growing new nerve connections to replace the old ones damaged in a car accident. This is such an amazing development that many people are holding out hope that the same thing might happen to Eric Holder.

That got me to thinking (which is always hard for me). It might not be so bad to be in a coma, temporarily, anyway. You must agree that it would be cool to go into a coma, if only to escape impending pressures of work and other emotional stress. For example, if I were to fall into a temporary (say, six-month) coma, this is what would happen:

- The deadline for this book would be postponed. The editor would look like a combination of an asshole and a bastard (asstard, or bashole) if he held an unconscious man to his original deadline.
- I would lose at least twenty pounds. Right now it's taken me a year to lose fifteen pounds, through exercise and opiates, but I've hit a wall. To get around that wall, I'd only require a coma with an IV drip of eight hundred calories a day. A nurse could work my abs. Even better, the break from boozing and eating fast food would give my liver and colon a break, as well.
- When I come out of the coma, there would be a crapload of television I would get to catch up on—not to mention Movies On Demand and assorted HBO specials. Right now I have sixteen hundred channels, and I've even run out of *Rock of Love* reruns. Take me off "schedule" for a while, and I can come

back to a treasure trove of TV treats! I also won't know whether to expect the "fat Oprah" or the "skinny Oprah." The joy of discovery!

- People would think of me more often, cry about me, and talk about me a lot. They would occasionally squeeze my hand and interpret my random eye movements as a response. When I wake up, people would write articles about me, and I would be treated as a human miracle. I would handle all the attention with self-deprecating wit, with lots of jokes about how I faked the whole thing because I just didn't want to get out of bed. I would get a book deal, and, sadly, another deadline, which I would try to get out of by faking another coma.

People Who Work at Health Food Stores Look Like Death

FACT: Only the most hideous-looking people on the planet work in health food stores. They apply for jobs there because, when compared to the grotesque appearance of the foods around them, they look positively fetching.

FACT: Individuals who work in health food stores are often the most unhealthy people around. That's because they think popping a horse-pill supplement will make up for their lack of exercise, sun exposure, or nutrition. Hence, they may know everything about whey protein, but still look like a roach on two legs. They rarely live beyond the age of forty-three. And if they do, they usually have to pee through their nostrils.

FACT: People who work at health food stores tend to smell bad— worse than a rest home laundry room after Beans and Cabbage Sunday Brunch. Remember, man created antiperspirants to get rid of the "natural" smell, otherwise known as BO.

FACT: Because health food stores tend to reject all the wondrous foods the world has to offer, these establishments have little to offer beyond a singularly depressing outlook on life. Once you enter one of these stores, you realize that everything worth living for is forever out of stock. So you come to the health food store, oddly enough, to die.

Those are my thoughts on this matter.

The Superobese Are the Closest We've Got to Superheroes

I read somewhere that many obese people cannot get full medical care because they are too fat to fit into scanners, or their fat is too dense for X-rays and sound waves to penetrate.

This, at first, sounds bad. But, only at first. Because, if you think about it, it sounds kind of awesome if your fatness can render certain types of technology impotent. Being fat isn't so bad after all if it affords you unique powers. Blocking sound waves sounds like a unique power, to me, anyway.

Seriously, what an awesome pickup line: "So, did you know that I block sound waves? Yep, the army has asked me to lecture at West Point. Another Mudslide? Bennigan's makes a terrific Mudslide."

Fact is, if you're so fat that neither X-rays nor sound waves can penetrate you, then you can probably block out other harmful elements, like nuclear fallout, superficial stab wounds, medium-caliber bullets, and recordings by Fergie. I remember reading about a mobster who was shot a dozen times but survived because all of the bullets got lost in his flabby folds of flesh (for more information, check *Flabby Folds of Flesh Monthly*, July 1998, pp. 123–27—it's the one with me on the cover).

We need to stop being so narrow-minded. Maybe instead of seeing the obese as weak, we should view them as superheroes— larger-than-life characters who possess special powers that make them impervious to dangers lurking around them. Seriously—the obese have done something to their bodies that gives them a power the rest of us don't have. And instead of glorifying that, we laugh at it.

Maybe—just maybe—they have the right idea. From an evolutionary perspective, gaining huge amounts of weight might protect us from threats we don't even know exist yet. Perhaps creatures from outer space might land with sound wave weaponry—and the only folks who can fight them off are the really fat ones.

Then who will be laughing? Not you. Because you'll be dead. I'll be laughing, however, because I'll be fat.

Television Kills Stress Better Than Yoga

I love studies, especially when they prove me right and, thus, make me feel really smart. Like this new study, which reveals that when kids watch TV, they can become so mesmerized that they will feel less pain—even when you stick a needle in their arm. (Why can't I ever be asked to participate in studies like these?)

Researchers say that television is so powerful at reducing stress, it can almost double as a painkiller and even be more effective than a mother's comfort!

I love this study because I love television. Television is, like, my best friend. So by saying you don't like television—well, that is basically the equivalent of saying you don't like my best friend. And that makes me angry. And you wouldn't like me when I'm angry (I pout).

This study also makes me happy—and it also makes me think of a few essential truths that most people refuse to recognize:

- People spend craploads of money and time on meditation, in a fruitless effort to capture the perfect state of mind you can only get from watching a rerun of *McHale's Navy* (for evidence of this, see the *British Medical Journal*, pp. 123–45, VII, 1999, "*McHale's Navy* As an Opiate Derivative"). Screw yoga. Buy a flat-screen.

- Most of the time spent sitting in front of the television is used up thinking about other stuff—like what might be on television later. I find that, while watching *Law and Order*, I only really watch three minutes of the show. The rest of the time I usually spend thinking about Jerry Orbach, whom I miss. Sometimes I'll just think about Jerry Orbach, up in heaven, wearing a tuxedo and drinking black coffee from a styrofoam cup. That was Jerry. Always with the styrofoam.

- TV also allows married couples to spend time together without actually having to speak to each other. This is important. Couples need time together, but they shouldn't ruin it by speaking to each other.

- Plus, for shutting kids up, television is a far, far better tool than duct tape and a ball-peen hammer. From a legal standpoint. Pretty much.

A final piece of advice: Never trust someone who doesn't own a TV. Every now and then I'll run into some pseudointellectual who makes a point of telling me he never watches TV, as if he's been spending all that saved time knocking out cures for cancer or inventing a talking hat. I hate these people—because all they're really doing is trying to assert some kind of intellectual superiority, even though, in reality, you actually have to be pretty smart to watch TV and still function as a normal human being. Claiming you never watch TV is not a sign of intelligence. It just means either you're too broke to own a TV, or worse, you meditate in really tight Dolphin shorts. I don't know which one is worse.

Side note: Parents who don't allow their children to watch television should have their kids taken from them. And given to me (I'm a licensed caregiver, at least in Guam).

The Fewer People You Know, the Less Likely You'll Be Killed

In 2007, the FBI reported that hate crimes in the U.S. had gone up by roughly 8 percent over the previous year. There were 7,722 crimes against victims based on race, religion, sexual orientation, ethnic origin, and disability—not counting the disappearance of about two dozen houseboys along the New Jersey border (don't worry, they're all doing fine).

In my mind, hate crimes are a sham. The fact is, they allow people who kill you out of love or envy—not hate—to get a lesser sentence. And there are more of those people around—at least in my case.

Example: If I were to kidnap stage and screen star Steve Guttenberg because of my unsettling obsession with him, I would garner a lesser sentence than if I were to attack someone I detest. Like, say, Hugo Chavez. This hate crime law creates incentive for unbalanced persons like myself to kill people we love. This can't be good news for Guttenberg. Meanwhile, Chavez spends another day alive.

You only hurt the ones you love, the song says. It doesn't say, "You only hurt people who are different from you." And that's probably bad news. With murder, nearly all the victims knew the perpetrator. And this forces me to draw this conclusion: The fewer people you know, the less likely you'll be killed. Meaning, no friends equals no crimes. This is why Keith Olbermann could live forever.

Stem Cells Are More Valuable Than the People They Are Supposed to Save

Think about it: Harvesting stem cells from dead fetuses is far more important to the left than protecting actually "living" children from another terrorist attack. Stem cells everywhere would applaud, except they don't have any hands.

Table Dancers Are Better Than Hypnosis If You Want to Quit Smoking

There's nothing more powerful, or hypnotic, than a naked woman, and the pure evidence of that is an ugly naked woman.

If you have a problem finding one, head to Bethlehem, Pennsylvania, and go to Shecky's (note: I changed the name so that they still might let me in without paying the cover), home to the ugliest strippers on earth.

The joint is worse than a dive—it's a silo of despair. Because they have no liquor license, you have to bring your own beer. Because there is no DJ, to get the strippers to dance, you have to feed the jukebox. And then there are the strippers—fat, scary creatures who make up for lack of teeth with abdominal scars.

But still, this doesn't matter much, if all you want to do is look at a naked woman. Even the scariest-looking one still controls you, commanding your silence and your crumpled, sweaty dollars. It's the funniest thing: You can find the most effective hypnotist on the planet, and he still can't compete with a naked lady.

I'm a sucker for naked things—naked women make me stupid; naked men make me laugh. Naked animals make me wonder if they know they're naked. I don't think they do—or else they would design clothing. Especially monkeys—I know if I had a bright pink ass, I'd cover it (and I do).

Boring Things Are Better for You

I can't think of any exception to this simple rule: The best things in life eventually kill you. Cocaine, boozing, prostitutes, cigarettes, pills, aggressive behavior (hitting, yelling, flinging feces), and the most lamentable: suicide. Suicide would be awesome if it didn't kill you. If, instead, it functioned like a mulligan: Once you did it and succeeded, and realized what a stupid move it was—you'd be allowed back on the game board.

Anyway, where was I? Oh, yeah—It's an old-fashioned rule that's been passed along in different permutations, but that's because it's true: Instant gratification sucks. If you let the desire for gratification pass, it will pass. And you'll be the better for it. Problem is, somewhere along the way (the 1960s is the easy culprit, but I prefer to blame *Love, American Style* and/or Three Dog Night), our country forgot this rule. Hard work became secondary to hard-ons, and feeling good trumped doing good. What we have now is a growing belief that the self's satisfaction is the most important thing in the world—even if the things you choose to fill that need (sex, drugs, shopping, bingo) just don't work.

The problem with pointing this out, however, is you immediately look like an angry, recalcitrant old fart. Which, I guess, I am. It took me awhile to get there, but there I am. But we ROFs know what we're talking about. Because we've been through all that stuff. More times than you, you young punk. Now, get away from my lawn, turn down that music, and take off your pants.

The Real Reason to Get Married Is Sanitation

Everyone will tell you marriage is about finding that special soul mate with whom to spend the rest of your life. But that's crap cubed. The real benefit of marriage isn't a life mate, but enhanced survival. And that enhanced survival is derived solely from sanitation. Meaning, hand-washing and clean water. Plus, the annoying pressure to avoid performing self-destructive activities blatantly in front of your mate also yields some benefit. You lose key opportunities to harm yourself now and then—for instead of getting plastered, you're over at her mom's wishing you were getting plastered. This adds years to men's lives.

The weird thing is, despite the newfound cleanliness, and the stereotype that men are pigs, women actually harbor more bacteria on their hands than men. The only reason I can think of for this is our dirty boxers, the part of laundry that no woman ever, ever really is prepared for. I purchased for my wife special "boxer tongs," so her hands never actually touch the offending fabric. (Note: Boxer tongs are actually just regular old tongs from our barbecue. I just painted them bright pink to fool my wife.)

Over Time, Pecs Turn Into Tits

According to new, potentially idiotic research, if you read muscle magazines while working out, you may end up canceling out the benefits of exercise. Never mind how screwed up you have to be to want to read magazines while you lift weights, apparently the post-exercise "feel-good effect" (not to be confused with an unsolicited hand-release in the shower) is wiped out once you look at fitness rags filled with sculpted abs.

I happen to know that this is true. Back when I worked at *Men's Health,* I was a rock-hard ass. When I wasn't working out in skimpy spandex, I was writing insidious articles and cover lines that promised you flat abs in five minutes and three inches of muscle in a week. I was always vague on where that three inches of muscle would come from. But it was almost always Pablo.

I lived the fitness life in full—one that was packed with muscle and misery. The only upside was, I could buy shorts at Baby Gap (waist size twenty-six, plaid).

People say muscle magazines are depressing, but that's because people with muscles are depressing. Creating arbitrary, vanity-driven measures by which to judge your own physique makes it that much easier to raise the bar—daily—so you're never satisfied with how you look. This is why you see so many tools at the gym, pumping furiously for hours, while the rest of their life crumbles. It's sad to see someone spend his one and only life preparing for a competition that doesn't exist, when he could be skimming leaves off my hot tub. My advice, however, is not to quit the gym, but to treat it like a bank. Depositing a little there allows you to withdraw it later when at a bar. That's all fitness is good for—giving you a free pass to drink and eat anything that's breaded and fried (including weight lifters).

But go beyond that, and you're wasting your life. When you're old and infirm, those muscles will only be excess baggage you'll need to lug around while desperately groping for your walker. Case in point: In my twenties, I had pecs to die for. Now they're tits to cover up.

The Difference Between Eastern and Western Medicine? Western Medicine Works

The only reason the local health food store can sell pointless pills and stupid supplements is that an actual entity exists that helps people when they are actually sick. It's called mainstream medicine, which New Age medicine hates (and vice versa, but mainstream medicine has good reason). The fact is, if New Age medicine helps your ailment, then you really didn't have an ailment to begin with. Instead, you have "psychosomatic symptoms," or "illusory illness." Or perhaps you're just a "flake." The people who spend cash on the "natural herbal remedies" can only do so because they're healthy enough to survive their own stupidity. Or because Western medicine has pronounced them as without hope, which is sadly true in almost all cases except genuine errors (New Agers *never* cure people, even if the patients don't end up dying).

Even more, there's not a single study that proves any of this crap works—but so many people buy into it anyway because it makes you feel good about yourself for using Eastern instead of Western medicine.

The difference between Eastern and Western medicine is that Western medicine can save your life. It's why after decades of yoga, meditation, and green tea, leaders in the East, when really sick, drop the ginseng and fly to the Cleveland Clinic for the transplant.

New Age medicine only exists on the backs of industrious doctors and researchers who, by their own hard work, have created a prosperous and comfortable society that makes it possible for misguided or corrupt New Agers to prosper.

But also, New Agers make awesome targets for books written by bitter fat dudes addicted to cheeseburgers.

Trendy Health Causes Are Worse Than Diseases

You may be surprised to know that I am not a medical expert, despite my extensive experiences handling cadavers and body parts. The truth is that I know nothing about medicine, which is why I keep my opinions about such matters to myself. I wish other people were the same.

Now, that's not all really true. I'm not an average layperson: I've dug through mountains of studies, attended countless medical conferences, interviewed buttloads of doctors over ten years, and have been pitched a zillion bullshit trendy health causes as potential stories for the magazines I worked at. I've seen a lot of crap—but even I am the first to admit, I don't know shit when it comes to medicine. But that "shit" is still more than what Jenny McCarthy, Robert Kennedy, Jr., Don Imus, chuckleheads at the Huffington Post, and everyone else who thought that vaccines cause autism know.

Even though there was little evidence to show that a preservative called thimerosal caused autism, it didn't matter, because when a celebrity takes up a cause, science becomes secondary. Caring trumps clarity, and everyone wears little pins on their lapels.

But now new research shows what the real experts knew all along—that there was no link between autism and this preservative, which had been widely used in vaccines since the 1930s. In fact, autism continued to increase, even though the preservative was removed from vaccines in 2001. It makes you wonder how many parents avoided vaccinating their kids because of the obnoxious blatherings of morons. Thousands did; that's why we had measles outbreaks in the U.S. in 2008.

The real question? Will any of these bozos admit they were wrong? And that because of them, my precious children Sun-Ra and Kaleidoscope are at risk for a host of diseases, including mumps, shingles, and feline AIDS?

Granted, they are actually cats, but I challenge you to argue the difference (not now, though—chances are I am asleep).

People Who Talk About Their Illnesses Aren't Really Sick

I'm not feeling well today. I've got bronchitis, a swelling in the airways that produces mucus, which I save to make handicrafts for the kids. Right now, I'm on codeine, which makes it hard to concentrate— but on the bright side I think I'm a ceramic frog.

Like me, many other massively popular celebrities have serious and sometimes tragic illnesses, and I feel bad for them. But I hate the other tools who turn lighter illnesses (what I call "hobbies") into fetishes and can't stop talking about them. You're already rich and famous—do you really need the public to identify with your irritable bowel syndrome?

I'm not knocking people when they're down. But I'm tired of hearing about how Cameron Diaz's obsessive-compulsive disorder means she can only use spotless hundred-dollar bills when buying a Fendi bag for her rare Lebanese ferret. I'm sure David Beckham's OCD is troubling—but when you're worth hundreds of millions, you can buy a new toilet for every flush.

But do you know what really bugs me? How "nondiseasey" these diseases are. Remember "chronic fatigue"? It used to be "Epstein-Barr," and since then it's been replaced by carpal tunnel. Yeah, I know they're all different—but in fact, they're all just the same: interchangeable, totally endurable maladies designed to create discussion when just sitting quietly would do just fine, thank you very much.

And how many more celebrities are going to tell us how they were "ostracized" due to their undiagnosed dyslexia—which translates into, "I'm blond and stupid, and was pretty much the same as a blond and stupid child." Celebrity diseases are right up there with modern art for American mass delusions. Sex addiction! Exhaustion! These stars—who spend most of their workdays in luxury trailers getting "massages" from Estonian extras—get "exhaustion" as a diagnosis! I wish I was so exhausted!

Once someone calls BS on these disorders, they're discarded like old copies of *Swank*. And here's a note to self-centered, well-off hypochondriacs in search of an identity through illness: If sixty-eight blood tests, CAT scans, and MRIs don't show a goddamned thing, you are certifiably healthy. Deal with it.

We Should Be Dead at Fifty

When people get very old, they start saying that life is short. This is a true observation, one I would tend to agree with—except when I came across the three-disc edition of *American Gangster*, in a rack of desolation at the Virgin Megastore. It has two versions of the tedious, overlong film, plus commentaries from the director and the screenwriter. If that's not enough, you get music videos, a making-of documentary, and, most important, an interview with the cast by Matt Lauer. He's the talking cactus on the *Today* show, whose peach-fuzz hair and earnest expression make him look like a confused baby eaglet emerging from its shell.

Last, you get eight documentaries that give you everything you've ever wanted to know about New York's heroin heyday (otherwise known as the pre-Giuliani Democrat years). The only thing not included is the underwear worn by Denzel Washington during the filming (a shame, since it's something I happen to collect).

By the time you're done watching all of this pap, you'll know exactly how to drain the sap from opium poppies and boil it down into a sticky gum. My mom watched it twice and took notes (she needs a hobby after giving up whittling).

These days, it seems like we're all digging deeper and deeper into disposable material—instead of just watching a damn movie and then completely forgetting it. In college, we never devoted so much effort to our classes or even to buying crank. Now we've turned into anthropologists of the mindless, filling this bucket called life with worthless crap until death.

Look, too much scrutiny of anything is never a good idea—which is why I tell every single one of my hired escorts to keep the lights out. But what we now see as entertainment is really just cinematic chop suey—where the cook took whatever was left over and threw it all together. With some noodles.

My only conclusion about the consistent popularity of DVDs featuring six months' worth of content: We are living too long. We now have time to devote to watching things that add nothing to our lives—except by subtraction. All the bad commentaries, every forgettable interview, all those painful outtakes and oh-so-hilarious scenes of cast bloopers—all remove time from your life that is lost forever. They don't even exist as memories, because they're not worth remembering. The same could be said for social networking sites, the Internet, and childhood. Fact is, when you're on your deathbed, you won't be recalling fond memories of all those snarky Tweets you authored about *Project Runway*.

Thing is—I say all this, and you just won't care. Well, until you've got an hour to live, and the DVD you just bought has two hours of extra footage.

Ben & Jerry's Kills More People Than War

Roughly a year or so before President Obama became President Obama, Ben & Jerry's founders endorsed him, and gave the Messiah two "Obamamobiles" to drive around for the purposes of giving away "Cherries for Change" ice cream. The hippie and hirsute millionaires explain that Obama represents real, inspirational change. Just like heart-stopping ice cream.

This stupid endorsement actually illustrates the problem with change. Change means nothing if it's not defined as either good or bad. For example, Ben & Jerry's ice cream has definitely changed our country—by making us as fat as something really fat. Just look at a pint of Phish Food and you'll need a coronary stent. I should know. I ate a tub for breakfast, and I went from a size thirty-two to a size thirty-six waist. But is that good change? My wife would say no. Or just gently weep under my immense weight.

But to be somewhat serious here: I spent a decade in health journalism, and read loads of journals jammed to the gills with studies linking obesity to death. Wherever you find a corpse that wasn't stabbed or shot, chances are the murder weapon was a spoon. More people die from obesity-related causes than from just about anything else—including war.

Fact is, the guys behind Ben & Jerry's are hard-core peaceniks, operating on the infantile assumption that war kills people, therefore war can never be an option. They are right—war is deadly. That's what makes war, war. But how many people have died directly from the war in Iraq, versus how many have died due to Ben & Jerry's Chubby Hubby? Smith and Wesson have nothing on B & J. When you think about it, Ben & Jerry's ice cream is simply the dairy equivalent of an Uzi. Except you can't protect yourself by firing a tub of Chunky Monkey at a masked intruder. I've tried.

Society, Culture, and Other Vague Chapter Headings

Blogs Used to Be Called Diaries, and They Were Written by Twelve-Year-Old Girls

The worst five words you can hear at a party are, "Have you read my blog?" Blogs, really, used to be called diaries, hidden under the pillows by googoo-eyed twelve-year-old girls. They were usually covered with stickers of rainbows and unicorns (and rainbow-colored unicorns). But now everyone has a diary, but they call them blogs and they're asking all of us to read them. It's like pulling off a Band-Aid and saying, "I made it myself!"

Blogs are one of the most disgusting, narcissistic, time-wasting developments of the last hundred years (and I'm including race-walking). Nobody read your diary in 1776, so you never did get that opium shot of having some stranger sixteen states away telling you, "You have the soul of a poet."

Some think that if you don't blog, you don't have a life. But it's the opposite. You should be happy that you don't write for folks who prefer to live in a disjointed bubble of weirdness. (If you'd like to hear more about this, go to my blog—Dailygut.com. On there right now is a synopsis of a trip to the dentist—can you believe how old those magazines in the waiting room are! LOL.)

While we're on the topic of timewasters, I've had enough of Facebook. I don't care how many "friends" you have on that community networking site, *none* of them will buy you a car.

It's a fact we're all coming to realize slowly: The web and its assorted online communities waste more time than they save, and narrow lives rather than enrich them. The web has actually created an illusion of a community—as well as an illusion of influence that community believes it has. I may have four thousand friends on Facebook, but when was the last time they shaved my back? Answer: a very long time ago...and I'm tired of asking, frankly.

Worse, the web has helped connect people who in no way should be connecting with each other. I mean, imagine a dude in Oxnard, California, who likes to fantasize about amputating his healthy limbs. Normally, he'd be the only person he knows that thinks this way, and he'd be safely isolated. He might even try to get real medical help. But with the web, he now suddenly realizes there are *five*—no, *ten*!—other freaks just like him. So his demented illness is no longer an illness, but a cool badge of eclectic fetishism, deserving of a chat group and perhaps a conference in Orlando (they'll certainly get a fast pass on all the Universal Studios rides!).

But this brings me to a bigger, potentially stupider point. Imagine the Internet as a giant phone book—which it is. Now imagine spending hours paging through the phone book, randomly calling up people you think you know from standing in line waiting for ointment. That's Facebook: calling up people in the phone book and pretending they're pals. It's not even a real book with real faces in it—like the one I made before my arrest.

For me, there's nothing worse than getting an email saying I've been invited to be a friend to someone I haven't seen in thirty years. There's a reason I've avoided you since high school, college, or the psychiatric hospital where I was treated briefly in the 1980s. You didn't like me, and I didn't like you.

Worse, Facebook allows bored exes from decades past the insidious and highly destructive ability to contact you—and ruin your life. The last thing you need is your "first love" to email you out of the blue, pining that "I've never forgotten that night in the woods in the back of your AMC Pacer." If you're a man in your forties, with two kids, a receding hairline, and a mortgage, a tempting taunt like that is enough to get you to ditch your family and chase your long-lost love (who, after two months, will suddenly remember why she ditched your boring butt in the first place).

Still, I do admit that Facebook is ideal for stinky shut-ins—lost souls who cannot deal with real people. That's great—keep them off the streets, I say! But what about you? And me? Facebook friends create the illusion of friendship, and false esteem—much like playing air guitar in front of a mirror instead of playing in a band. In the end, you just have to grow up and go outside.

Finally, the web in general harms our country by making our enemies painfully aware that we are a nation of distracted people, fearful of commitment to our country or to God, averse to fighting for anything but our own desire for instant gratification. The web has turned everyone into crotch-fondling hermits who prefer scanning/digging or gazing hypnotically at content instead of talking to real people.

How do I know this?

I'm one of them.

Now, imagine what would happen if Facebook, Twitter, and YouTube disappeared today—how would you survive?

The same way you did well before you heard that skinny kid sing "Chocolate Rain."

You'll get over it.

Camera Phones Turn Everyone
Into Horrible Filmmakers

I find it interesting that the people who were "outraged" over the cellphone footage of Saddam Hussein dying are usually the same people who use their cellphones to document every waking moment of their tedious lives. The thing is, cellphones serve as an excellent method of collecting facts, and therefore deflating myths before they have a chance to grow. We know that Saddam is dead because we saw it with our own eyes.

Either that, or they used Tony Shalhoub as a body double.

Camera phones also keep an entire country on its toes. If you're in danger of doing something silly, stupid, or wrong, you're also in danger of getting that silly, stupid, or wrong thing caught on someone's phone. (This is why, in part, Woody Allen doesn't own a camera phone. He just makes movies.)

Still, however, it is annoying that camera phones have turned everyone into amateur Mike Wallaces. For every moment of police brutality caught on "phone," there is a year's worth of potential material depicting cops doing great work. However, that shit isn't worth capturing on your little, stupid phone. No one holds up his phone, saying "The whole world is watching," while a cop breaks up a drunken domestic disturbance. It's just not YouTube material, is it?

Worse, just on a personal level, using your phone to record moments actually prevents you from enjoying the moments as they're happening. You've seen people at concerts spend all their time fooling with their camera phones instead of watching the show. And for what? To bore their friends afterward with crappy photos of the necks of the drunk people in front of them puking to the sounds of Dave Matthews? Put the phone away and enjoy yourself.

Also: The only thing more excruciating than someone forcing you to look through a stack of actual photo prints of their baby or vacation is being forced to look at a series of digital or camera-phone photos—especially when many are ever-so-slight variations of the same photo. It's an enema of someone else's memories.

But then again, because of the plethora of camera phones, no one ever says, "You never have a camera when you need one," anymore.

That means old people have one thing fewer to say.

Scooby-Doo Made More Sense of Science Than the *New York Times* Ever Could

Here's how a typical episode of this classic Saturday morning cartoon would unfold: It would begin with a problem—usually instigated by some kind of goblin or ghoul. But by the end of the show, the evil creature would have his disguise torn off, revealing some evil human with nefarious desires (generally an old farmer who doesn't like kids, dogs, or cool vans).

There's a lesson to be learned from Scooby and his brethren of youthful tagalongs: The most obvious answer is always the right answer. There are no ghosts lurking about, just creaky houses with loose floorboards. There are no space aliens, just free-floating weather balloons. And there are no root causes for crime, just criminals. Global warming? The spots on the sun laugh at that crap.

Here's a simple equation from Scooby-Doo:

No ghosts = Only people and things

Here's a simple equation about climate change:

No global warming = Weather and lies

Doctors have an old saying for this, when diagnosing an illness: If you hear hoofbeats—think "horse," not "zebra."

Or Scooby-Doo. Because Scooby-Doo served a lesson in the simple but surefire art of skepticism. Science writers and public policy makers should be required to watch episodes every day until they sober up and see climate-change science for what it is: a ghost in an old house designed to drum up money for the ghost-chasers. Remove the goblin's mask and all you'll find is Al Gore.

The Only People Worse Than
Americans... Are Everyone Else

Back when George Bush was president, British "telly" ran a "hard-hitting" docudrama imagining the assassination of Bush by a terrorist sniper. The makers of the drama, *Death of a President*, said they only did it to promote "legitimate debate" over Bush's controversial role in the obviously ridiculous war on terror.

Which is their way of saying: "We hate Bush, you hate Bush, so let's have fun with it."

No doubt this show would spark "legitimate debate." Which is quite an achievement coming from the same brave souls who chose not to run the Mohammed cartoons out of fear they might piss off an extremist or two. Lucky for them, the U.S. government isn't as extreme as its critics often paint it as being.

It all goes back to teeth. We have them. They don't.

Literally, and figuratively. Consider the BBC, the home of my favorite programs, *I Hate My Breasts* and *I Hate My Breasts* 2. They had allegedly dropped plans to show a fictional terror attack in an episode of their evening soap opera *Casualty*—to avoid offending Muslims.

The show was to have featured a storyline about an explosion caused by Islamic extremists. Now the bombs will be set off by animal rights extremists, a group of equally deluded buttheads, but who are perfectly fine to ridicule because they are less likely to blow you up (they're too busy masturbating to *When Animals Attack!*).

It's the ultimate hypocrisy of the media and the arts in general. Consider that repulsive piece of art called *Piss Christ*. A creep drops a cross in a cup of urine, and he's called an artist. But when I do roughly the same thing (instead of a cross and a cup of urine, I use Rodrigo, my sixteen-year-old concierge, and an oil drum full of clams), I'm somehow depraved? The media think so because the minute real danger comes into play, they scurry out of sight.

But, hey, it's the British telly. These are the same people who won't miss an opportunity to kick America, or its leaders, but are all too ready to back down to real extremism. My advice to America: Convert to Islam. Not only will we never see another negative story in our lives, but once we do it, we all get to wear burkas. I like that. They look very roomy and will hide my man breasts.

People Who "Live Life to the Fullest" Are Usually Assholes

How is the death of an adventurer a more important story than a little old lady getting run over by a truck while walking home from the grocery store? It's not, but for some reason when someone dies doing something really stupid, we treat it like it was something majestic. It's not.

Mountain climbers, bungee jumpers, parachutists, and Star Jones daters assume a high degree of risk, so when something unfortunate occurs, it's not so much a tragedy as it is a fundamental part of the experience. The fact is, without the inherent risk, the actual activity holds less excitement for the person engaging in it. Hence the common phrase, "He lived life to the fullest," usually heard after "he" has landed on a power line when the emergency chute failed.

Meanwhile, every day, people die heading to work. On average, one pedestrian is killed in a traffic crash every 108 minutes. Old ladies slip in bathtubs and old men choke on carrots. They weren't taking risks. They weren't climbing rock faces or dangling from planes. They were just living their lives.

Those stories of daily death depress me more.

On that note, I am no longer taking baths or eating carrots.

You Can Judge a Book by Its Cover

No one likes to say that about people, but it's true. Sorry, every pervert, killer, and scumbag actually *looks* like a pervert, killer, and scumbag. See any recent picture of Gary Glitter, for example. The man drips with molestation.

The only real exception was Ted Bundy, a sick, heinous monster who wasn't that bad on the eyes. But that's it. I'm telling you, if someone looks creepy—he is creepy. I don't know why we don't just admit this openly and create a "creepy-person database." If you are deemed creepy-looking, then you're placed on the database. Because inevitably, if you are creepy-looking, you will commit a creepy crime (there's no sense fighting fate, really), and we'll be ready with tasers and binding straps.

Generally, creepy people are known to:

• Have overly manicured goatees.
• Wear Hawaiian or bowling type shirts untucked.
• Have hairless arms.
• Possess a wallet chain.

Those are all I can think of, for now. Feel free to add to the list, mentally (i.e., in your head).

The Guy at the Help Desk Hates Your Guts

Can you blame him? You only talk to him when your computer isn't working, usually because you spilled coffee on your keyboard. I always feel bad for these guys. No one ever calls them up just to say hello. People like you and me only call them when we are angry, confused, and prone to shouting. So who can blame them when they suddenly take a tour bus hostage?

I wouldn't.

So, for today, why don't all of us call the people we know in IT, and say, "Hello!"

Then, if they ask you what the problem is, simply say, "My only concern today is your happiness."

Then hang up.

Then call back, and say, "Just joking. Fix my computer."

Women Really Don't Need to Work When They Show Up for Work

So this morning, while I was getting my daily microbead facial scrub, using nothing but a paste of crushed almond shells and gopher spit, I came across yet another new study about women in the workplace. This one says that having women in the boardroom helps improve a company's financial performance. The researchers looked at financial results of big companies and found that those with at least three women directors turned better profits than other publicly traded sausage parties. The reason? "Bringing women to represent stakeholders gives them a better performance."

I know—groundbreaking stuff! But what pisses me off is that the researchers fail to address the real reason companies benefit from women in the boardroom. Men like women. It's the unspeakable truth about life: Men perform better if they're out to impress girls. Consider the Industrial Revolution. With a few attractive women in those mills, it would have been accomplished in twenty years instead of eighty.

Drinking Alone Is Underrated

In movies and on television, whenever someone is depicted drinking alone, he or she is always made to look pathetic. And we're supposed to feel bad about this person. Clearly he or she is suffering from some unimaginable depression or deep-seated pain, which drives the poor soul to drinking. Or worse, he's a profound alcoholic who wastes his life in a bottle.

I don't know. Some of the most fun times of my life resulted from drinking alone. Before I got married, I traveled alone, and there was nothing better than finding a vacant bar stool in the middle of nowhere, and drinking.

Fact is, as long as you have a working brain, or a tapeworm, you're never alone. And let's be honest here, many times we call friends up to have a drink simply as an excuse to have a drink. It's not the company that matters, it's the attempt to erase the stigma of drinking alone.

It bothers me so much I may need a drink. You free later?

You're not?

Cool!

(Let me know if you change your mind.)

Conspiracies Are Designed to Keep Stupid People Obsessed With Conspiracies

The only thing I love more than conspiracies is the people who promote them. That's why I love Truthers, attention-seeking dopes who claim to seek the "truth" behind 9/11. They believe the real explanation—that fundamentalist bastards flew planes into buildings—is way too simple, and believing that story makes you blind to the truth. They would rather accept an explanation that's endlessly more complicated than the plain one staring you in the face.

We could say it's because these people are asses. But mainly, people embrace conspiracies out of narcissism. They want you to believe they're smarter than you, that you're a victim of false consciousness. Meaning, you're comatose and blind to the evils of America. It's funny to hear this from a guy who still lives in his mom's basement, biting and then collecting his toenails (he's making a replica of Noah's Ark).

Whenever I meet a dope who blames 9/11 on our government, I always ask: How can you prove *you* didn't do it? He can't answer. Because that's the joy of conspiracies: It's a million times easier to pose the conspiracy question than it is to disprove it.

The truth about conspiracies is that there aren't any. If you can't prevent office gossip, how can you assume a government can keep a secret? Human beings are natural blabbermouths.

The best way to crush theorists is to tell them that the real conspiracy is just a plan to make people *like them* fall for conspiracies. So when someone says that 9/11 was an inside job, I reply, "Well, that's what the Jews want you to think," and walk away. And speaking of that, it's a fact that Truthers are as scummy as Holocaust deniers. People who embrace conspiracies are inherently destructive, because it prevents them from focusing on stuff that really matters, like terrorism or my birthday party (I wear a size nine and prefer latex).

We Are Running Out of Adults

Recently I came across a story about a California company where employees relieved stress at the office by playing four square. Yep, I am referring to the playground game where four players bounce a ball from one square to the next. It's a fun game, but I stopped playing it long before my gender reassignment surgery.

Meanwhile, somewhere in the mountains of Fresno, a frozen World War II airman has been found, still intact. Dead, but intact.

These stories somehow seem connected. Here, in one corner of California, you have a group of drooling adults indulging in their own "quirky" distraction, because sitting in an office all day moving a mouse up and down a pad is soooo stressful. Meanwhile, a man is found dead—frozen in time as he raced to help protect his country against fascism.

People are calling this youthful game-playing the "reinvention of the American grown-up," but if anything, grown-ups are as dead as that airman. Adulthood, in this land of tedious luxury, has been replaced with endless adolescence—witness divorced men who dress like German kids in fat camp, and middle-aged women with dolphin tattoos branding their back flab.

Is it any wonder that, when someone has an adult thing to say— like, "We need to fight a war to stop tyranny"—it is met with a Jon Stewart–like smirk. Right now we've got hundreds of thousands of servicemen fighting in arid foreign countries. They don't have time for four square—they're too busy dodging bullets. But the employees at that start-up are engaging in something far cooler—bouncing a ball in a square, probably while listening to tapes of whales screwing. I want to beat them to death with sticks. Pointy ones, dipped in salt. I would call it a game of "Pointy Salt Stick."

Only Old People Are Described As "Active"

It's a sad reality: Once someone refers to you as "active," or "very active," or worse, "surprisingly active," that means you're old. So old, in fact, it's actually surprising that you can move at all. Hence, "active" is a compliment.

It's no coincidence that "active" is often used to describe volcanoes, which are also very old and are pretty much immovable objects, like your grandfather. And in both cases, every once in a while they can emit a hot mess. It's probably why Gramps doesn't sit at the dinner table anymore.

Being called "active" is far worse than some jackass describing you as a "curmudgeon," or "prickly," or even "senile." The word "active" is often seen in print advertisements for retirement villages and osteoarthritis drugs (both featuring fifty-year-olds pretending to be sixty, playing tennis like forty-year-olds), and despite the use of energetic imagery, the photos still seem to convey a fitness level slightly above the comatose. The statement that someone is "active" is based on the assumption that we've already agreed that person is only a few years away from a bedridden lifestyle and a cute little bell to ring. Me, I'm looking forward to it. Any excuse to stay in bed ringing a little bell is fine by me.

And I'm getting there. For I've reached a point where I, like so many old people before me, find current music too "sexually suggestive." I know it's ridiculous. I've read many critics of hip-hop, for example, claim that its sexual content causes teens to have more sex. But I know for a fact that the real influence is all the stuff that worked before hip-hop existed: alcohol, drugs, and Old Spice. Especially the Old Spice. Now, it's just called Axe Body Spray.

It's true that 90 percent of all hip-hop is about getting laid. But 90 percent of all music is about getting laid—and that includes polka. Especially polka. It's the devil's music.

Being Yourself Is the Worst Possible Thing You Can Be

While I was watching an old rerun of *Project Runway* with my friend Scott (a flight attendant and massage therapist), one of the designers, Santino, said, "It's not important who you want me to be, but who I want to be." I had to laugh, because the two worst words in the English language are "be yourself" (with the possible exceptions of "last call" and "baby shower").

Being yourself does nothing for the world, except remind everyone that you are a jerk. That's because deep down, everyone thinks more of themselves than other people do, and expects less of themselves than other people do. Married men know this: If it weren't for wives, most men would be happy to wallow in their own filth, eating Twinkies on the toilet. Wives prevent us from regressing into dirty, selfish beasts bent on self-gratification. In other words, they prevent us from being ourselves. As does any worthwhile pursuit.

So my suggestion is to be exactly what others want you to be. And by others, I mean your parents, specifically. And me. Your parents don't want you to be yourself, they want you to be better than that—good, even—and any parent that denies this is a liar. Screw individuality—anyone who claims to be unique always ends up sounding like every other tool proclaiming his individuality—which is why people into tattoos and piercings always sound and act like everyone else with tattoos and piercings. I'd rather be around twenty people who are decent and boring than have to deal with one unique prick all the time. If I wanted that, I could marry myself.

Ripping on Wal-Mart Is Secret Bigotry

When I lived in Allentown, Pennsylvania, one of the best things about living there was Wal-Mart. I would go there every Saturday and try to lure employees from the garden center into the back of my panel truck (I painted it to look like a bookmobile). I always failed, but it was something to do in a town with nothing else to offer. It also allowed a meeting place where once-flourishing downtowns have been destroyed by tattoo joints, dollar stores, and urinating transients (sorry, Uncle Phil).

As for those mindless elitists in big cities who hate Wal-Mart—that's easy to do, because they don't need to shop there. Ripping Wal-Mart is just secret bigotry: targeting lower classes for being lower class.

As for those who claim Wal-Mart destroys mom-and-pop stores—have you been to a mom-and-pop lately? No. Because they were replaced by those gas station/convenience store hybrids known for their giant pieces of wood attached to the restroom keys. It made the keys impossible to steal, sadly.

Bottom line: Mom-and-pop stores were never that good to begin with. Because it was never economical for them to order in bulk, you'd have to wait days or even weeks for the latest issue of *Hot Latinos in Leather.*

But I will say this: If Wal-Mart can improve on one thing, it's the uniforms. You can't go wrong with just a thong and a tool belt. It's how I made my tips in college.

The World Only Needs Three, Maybe Four Languages

According to linguists, over thirty-five hundred languages are in danger of extinction. That means we're losing one every two weeks. Now, I bet you think this is bad news. Not me. There are too many languages, and most are stupid. You know that one where they click their tongues? Sorry, although it's pretty arousing to listen to, I have no idea what's going on there.

Linguists want to get schools to offer more languages—which is fine—but the only real reason to learn a new one is to pick up girls in foreign countries, or to impress American chicks by speaking to them in German.

Which is cool, but you only need to learn five words: "Ziehen sie an den gummi-anzug!" That's, "You look hot," or at least, I hope it was. If not, I really insulted my grandmother.

The Counterculture Movement
Never Was Counterculture

It's Sunday, which means a nice break for me. I'm currently relaxing in my pleated shorty robe—a gift from Ted Danson—sipping a "Greg's Iced Tea" (it's iced tea, with Greg drinking it), reading all my favorite catalogues. Sitting in front of me is the new one from Barney's—that high-end department store in Manhattan that sells outrageously priced frocks to lonely housewives, bored athletes, coked-up socialites, and vain pudgy media skanks like me. "Have a hippie holiday," is the theme of the glossy booklet—and inside we are told that the store is "having a counterculture moment," celebrating the fiftieth anniversary of the peace sign.

How are they celebrating it? Through "bohemian luxury," "gorgeous green gifts," and something called "alternative style." I do not know what the last thing is, but I'm guessing the $360 key chain on page three fits the bill. It's called "Valextra," which sounds more like something you'd take for a genital blister—a more persistent reminder from the summer of love. But look, we're celebrating peace, so if you really like peace, you'll need to spend more.

Like, how about that three grand for a leather and ceramic watch? It'll go great with your pan flute and the eighty-eight-dollar recycled shirt. But nothing speaks to the beauty of the environment more than "nature." But since real nature is actually dirty and dangerous, get the diamond "seed" pendants as a steal for sixteen grand! Whatever money you have left over you can place in a "glow-in-the-dark" piggy bank encrusted with Swarovski crystals— it's only five hundred clams. And it's all for peace—which makes the whole thing worthwhile.

Okay—I realize that the commercialization of the sixties is nothing new, and a million crusty critics have already raged about how it's been turned into another cheesy commodity.

But here's the thing—the counterculture movement never was as good or pure as we've always been told. It had nothing to do with rebellion, and much to do with conformity—a movement designed to allow people to do whatever they wanted, rather than what they were supposed to do. And that's the real joke: Doing what you're supposed to do—often in the face of peers telling you how uncool it is—is the real counterculture. You want to be counterculture these days? Come to New York City and intimate—however slightly—that Obama is not God. That's a more "fight the man" moment than walking barefoot, stoned, and unwashed through Haight-Ashbury ever was.

So forgive me, Barney's—I'm passing on all your pretentious, overpriced crap. You don't fool me, or anyone I know. You actually make me sick to my stomach. But all is forgiven if you send me a copper-plated shoehorn.

Corporations Are Better Versions of People

If you're like me, and congratulations if you are, you hate evil corporations. Mainly because they're rich, they have nicer cars, sleep in fluffy beds, and for breakfast they feast on the tender limbs of malnourished children from underdeveloped nations (usually folded into egg-white omelets).

But the reality is, corporations are nothing more than large groups of people. Like fraternities, but without the paddling. But they make loads of money (or used to anyway) and without them we'd all be dead. Economics professor Mark J. Perry points out brilliantly that while we obsess over corporate profits, no one gives them credit for the massive taxes they pay to keep our troubled country afloat.

Exxon paid something like $30 billion (2007) in taxes, which is as much in taxes, annually, as the bottom 50 percent of individual taxpayers. We're talking 65 million people! 65 million and one, if you count me.

Corporations have done more for our country than our government, the Red Cross, and Angelina Jolie's lips combined. They have done more to feed people than any charity. They've done more to help those in need than anything Jimmy Carter could ever dream of coming up with. For hiring millions of people, and helping them create lives for themselves and their families, corporations deserve big fat wet kisses from all of us.

Isn't it time we stopped beating up on corporations and started loving them? For my part, I offer to attend any corporate retreat that pays me piles of money to tell them how awesome they are. Also: I would like someone to pick me up and take me to the airport.

Tragedy Means a Day Off

It's a terrible thing to admit, but whenever anything bad happens on a major scale, there's always a moderate chance you'll get to go home from work, or get a day off from classes. So no matter how awful a tragedy is, you can't fight that feeling that erupts once the news crosses the airwaves: "This means I get to go home!" It's a disgusting notion, but it's one we all feel at one time or another.

This is no one's fault. The fact is, since we were babies we've been conditioned to link tragedy to time off. When my dad died, I admit, it got me a three-week extension on my midterm exams. I really didn't need the extension, but I asked for one anyway. When the *Challenger* exploded, the world stopped. I stayed in bed and watched the coverage. If anyone asked me to do anything productive, I asked them, "Really...at a time like this?" After 9/11, I admonished a bill collector for calling me the day after a major tragedy, for he did not allow me time to grieve—even though I certainly did owe them money.

I can safely say this does not make me a good person. Just normal.

History Is Boring Because Historians Are Boring

I just read that back in 1470 B.C., Egyptians used to participate in something called the "festival of drunkenness," a raucous celebration that included crazed sex, massive boozing and drug use, and probably some kind of weird clumsy version of karaoke. They took part in this event as a way to create good luck for the future (although any excuse probably would have worked).

So, I'm thinking, if they had stuff like that in the history books when I was young, I probably would have paid more attention.

Flight Attendants Reflect the Nature of Our World

Remember how cool it was to be a flight attendant back in the 1970s, around the time of *Love, American Style* and fondue? Every stewardess was young, shapely, and available—as reflected in the classic movie *Coffee, Tea, or Me?* which I have never seen but still imagine is classy stuff. Stewardesses were sexpots in the sky, creatures to be desired and fantasized about. They were glamorous, amenable, and flexible.

Then they got old.

Fact is, the flight attendant role typifies how we treat women in this world: They're awesome when they're young, and we forget about them when they're old. That's why we have cats. Once a woman is too old to be a flight attendant, you fire her and give her a cat. It's in the union bylaws.

Sadly, once flight attendants started aging, but still remained on the job, men began to infiltrate. The glamour wore off—and suddenly it wasn't so hard to be rude to them. And now we have slim, well-coiffed men doing the job. Their names are always Brad, and they've got scathing senses of humor!

But it's a sad fact of this universe—hot girls make everything better. Aging makes them less hot. And when that pool isn't replenished, you often find yourself in 23F, being yelled at by a bitter fifty-five-year-old divorcée because your carry-on won't fit under the seat in front of you (it's not my fault Pablo put on ten pounds over vacation).

Australia Is California, Done Right

Yes, I take back everything I have ever said about Australia. It is now officially my favorite country in the world. (Note to researchers: Please verify that Australia is indeed a country, and not a territory or an amusement park. I don't want to repeat the same error I made about Six Flags. I waited in line for a passport at the U.S. embassy for hours.) I actually spent some time there, roughly a decade ago. I traveled most of the trip alone through Sydney, then up to the wine country, around a little of the "outback," and then finished up around Darwin. If it wasn't for the backpackers, I don't know how I would have been able to eat.

Yeah, I used to make fun of the "land down under" constantly, until a few years ago, when the country mocked a hard-hitting British report on climate change. Australia also had refused to sign the Kyoto Protocol, which made them heroes for life in my mind, and even made me forgive them for unleashing that bald jerk from Midnight Oil on the world. God, I hate that bald jerk from Midnight Oil.

People Who Describe Themselves As Worldly Need to Get Their Faces Punched In

I love to think about traveling, but I hate to actually travel. It sucks. And judging by the looks on most tourists' faces, I'm guessing everyone pretty much feels the same way. The idea of going somewhere sounds like fun—but what do you do when you get there?

I don't know about you, but I immediately think about going home. I realize traveling is just pretending to care about other places you haven't taken a dump in. Me, all I really want to do is check into the hotel, go to my room, and molest the minibar. Oh, the things I've done with those mini-Pringle cans!

And then I find a bar.

That's how I look at world travel—it's little more than searching the globe for bars that feel a lot like my apartment, so I can pass out in them. I'm not much for museums, churches, or natural wonders like cliffs and caverns. (Sorry, but landscape doesn't impress me: It's just formations born of chaos—there's nothing noteworthy about a big fat rock or a deep chasm, unless Al Franken is falling down it.)

Nope—I prefer seedy pubs with something unintelligible on the TV. In Manhattan, it's called Ninth Avenue. For me, that's the only real travel I can stomach—transporting your usual behavior, briefly, to somewhere else. And the extent of your intellectual discovery is whatever you're thinking about while boozing and staring at the waitress with the third nipple.

Other than that, traveling is a complete and utter sham: a scam sold to us by airlines and hotels to convince us that our lives are nothing unless we "see the world." I'm sorry—what if where I'm at now is the best place to be? I'm never happier than when sitting in my tiny living room, with a few bottles of something cheap and back-to-back episodes of my favorite show, *Sex Change Hospital*— which happens to be set in Trinidad for some reason.

I've never been there. And I have made no plans (yet).

And seriously, friends: If you live in America, you're already in the greatest place on earth. So don't feel stupid when some pretentious twit starts giving you shit for not being "worldly." Remember, everyone else in this "world" is dying, literally, to come "here." And more important, it's not where you're going or where you've been that matters: it's who you're with when you go home. As long as it's not anyone who participated in a *Real World/Road Rules* challenge, then you're already a winner.

Sporting Sport Sports

Soccer Violence Is the Most Interesting
Part About Soccer

More sports are played in America, on a daily basis, than are played in one month throughout the rest of the world combined. I have no real research to back this up, but I seriously doubt you're going to try to refute it anyway: It would take up too much of your time, which can be better spent thinking about me, lounging around in a black-mesh pantsuit made of smaller black-mesh pantsuits.

But this brings me to my point: Despite all the sports we play, we almost never riot. Sure, once in a while a "celebration" will break out, but what's a few overturned Priuses in the scheme of things? I mean: It's not like they're real cars!

Meanwhile, pick any country where soccer is its primary sport, and a week doesn't pass that there isn't some huge brawl or wide-scale riot.

Why such mayhem, particularly surrounding something the Brits like to call "the beautiful game"? The answer is simple: When you play a game as profoundly tedious as soccer, you need to find your excitement elsewhere. It's a fact proven over and over again: Low-scoring soccer matches bring out the worst in everybody and everything. It's why soccer hooliganism exists, and why many experts felt that if it wasn't for the sheer banality of the game, we never would have experienced the first two major world wars. There's an entire school of thought that the rise of European fascism can be traced to Italy's and Spain's poor showing in the 1932 World Cup.

You could look this up in my book *Soccer: Why?* were I to write it.

People Who Cheer Too Loudly at Games Are Miserable People Inside

A couple of years ago (or maybe it was yesterday—I can't remember much of anything anymore), a gunman killed two soccer fans because they were cheering too loudly while watching a game on TV. Apparently, at some restaurant, these fans erupted in roars when Italy scored against a place called Ghana (which, if I'm correct, is somewhere in Canada). Moments later, they were dead.

Look, I realize that in the realm of normal behavior, this is considered an "overreaction." But still, haven't you felt the same way? Haven't you ever fantasized about shooting someone in the face because he's standing behind you, spraying spit into your ear over a "bad call"?

People who cheer loudly irritate the hell out of me, so much so I prefer to watch all sporting events alone in my room surrounded by my stuffed animals. Snooky, Mr. Pebbles, and Captain Woof Woof never make a sound no matter what happens—mainly because I duct-tape their mouths closed. They still stare, however—which is why I have them all facing the wall, *Blair Witch* style.

I try to stay far, far away from dedicated sports fans. I find their interest in sports mystifying: After all, you are rooting for people who don't give a poop who you are, and wouldn't piss on you if you were on fire (or if you politely asked them to because you're into that sort of thing). Imagine if all that energy a sports fan devoted to painting his face was actually put toward his work, or his family. He might actually be successful, and well respected—instead of a punchline for Al Michaels (he's still around, right?). And isn't that more important than the Atlanta Braves making the Super Bowl? God, I hate basketball.

But I will make an exception: For dudes who are actually *that simple*: food-sports-fuck-shit = existence.

I envy that bliss.

The Olympics Are a Waste of Time

During the last Olympics, I found myself at a bar where everyone was watching this extravagant dirge of pomp and tedium. It blew my mind—because at the same time, over on the Lifetime channel, there was a Delta Burke biography on that was positively mindblowing. I tried to protest, but no one listened. Anyway, two chuckleheads at the bar kept chatting about the events. One person was yapping about how this swimmer Michael Phelps knew he was going to be great at the tender age of seven. Then another chimed in that the swimmer has attention deficit disorder. Some other dude nodded, pointing out that he had heard the same thing. But despite everyone there hearing this nonsense many times before, they still felt compelled to discuss it anyway. It's a conversation without roadblocks, where facts fly freely because they aren't your own.

And that's the purpose of the Olympics. It's not to showcase our best athletes, or to revel in patriotic pride, but to let people talk about crap that, for the previous four years, no one gave a damn about. More important, because no one has any prior knowledge of the present Olympics or its participants, everyone must rely on the same vat of information spewing forth from wide-eyed talking heads. Olympic trivia is like your basic Chinese restaurant: Wherever you find one, you find the same thing. And let's face it: One mediocre NFL running back has more actual fans than Phelps.

Christ, I barely tolerated the Olympics when it was once every four years. Every two years is torture by inanity. At least before, I had time to look forward to hating it. Now, that's even gone!

But while we're on the topic of the Olympics, I need to add one other unspeakable truth about Olympians.

They are, for the most part, selfish jackanapes.

Here are the Olympics, in a nutshell: Young muscular athletes trot out to perform one feat that they've been practicing all their lives before an audience of millions. People cheer, medals are won, then the athletes go home and you never hear from them again (unless of course one of them is caught with a bong, Lindsay Lohan, or a bong that may actually be Lindsay Lohan).

I admit that these young men and women are amazing athletes. But come on: If you picked one activity and practiced it every day for years and years of your young life, you'd be the best at it, too. If masturbation were an Olympic event, we'd all be gold medalists. Or at least I would (I would probably have several different gold medals, actually—freestyle, butterfly, and of course, relay).

Consider how weird it is that one person spends his waking hours practicing his "curling," and then we *reward* him. Meanwhile, his wife and his parents have to support him financially throughout this quixotic adventure. Seriously, I'd rather my spouse work the toppings at Subway than spend countless hours perfecting something as ludicrous as synchronized swimming. At least those Subway uniforms are cute. To me, the Olympics is nothing but a reward system for the singlemindedly selfish. It's the Vanity Bowl, every day for two weeks.

If it were up to me, the Olympics would only run once every twenty years, and participants would perform nude, just like the good old days.

Then I'd watch. Nude, probably.

America Has No Need for David Beckham

David Beckham is the most recognized soccer player on the planet (not a hard title to win), as well as a "fashion icon," and husband to something resembling eyeballs on a stick. But still, no matter how much hype is created around this sinewy strap of tattooed flesh, America does not care.

When it was announced that he was moving to the U.S. to play for the Los Angeles Galaxy (which sounds like a tabloid newspaper in a superhero movie), we were led to believe that he would bring glamour to the world of American soccer, doing for that sport what the Beatles did for rock music.

That was over three years ago.

In the end, with or without Beckham—it's still just soccer. And unless someone incorporates land mines or hidden piranha pits into the field, it will always remain "that weird sport where you can't use your hands."

Beckham has argued that he didn't move to America to make money, but to take soccer to the "next level." But in America, there is no next level. While it's true that it's the number-one sport played by grade-school girls and (probably) boys, the overwhelming popularity evaporates once puberty hits: Then the boys discover manlier sports to impress girls, while girls discover lip gloss, chat rooms, and cruelty.

It doesn't help that Posh Beckham is looking more and more like a common cluster fly. I am convinced that late at night you will find her near the trash bins outside Ralph's, picking at old boxes of rotten fruit and vegetables.

Oddly, the British press's misreading of how America perceives their "first couple" shows yet again how they prefer to believe in things they wish to be true, rather than things that are actually true.

Brits refuse to believe that we Yanks don't share the same pathetic interest in a couple obsessed with fake tans, tattoos, and teeth whitener. Sorry, we had Fabio fifteen years ago. And that's really what Posh and Becks are: Fabio bookends.

Seriously: Perhaps Fabio was one of the few creatures capable of split reproduction, an organism with the capacity to change from one embryo to many. Is it any wonder that once Fabio disappeared, we saw the mysterious rise of Posh and Becks?

Yes, it is a wonder.

Religion and Morality
(Don't Worry, It's Short)

Belief in God Makes More Sense Than No Belief at All

If Bill Gates—a smart dude, I admit—can create something as intricate and brilliant as Windows, certainly it's feasible that something could have done the same with Bill Gates. And not just Gates, but billions of variations, with all their patterned behavior and assorted bugs and tics. If man can make software, then something can definitely make man—which is nothing more than a fleshy computer anyway.

When it comes to belief, my feeling is you have two options: There is either a God, or there's nothing. So, how do you figure out how to live your life in case you pick one belief that turns out to be wrong—so you don't get burned for it (in hell, for example).

Well, if you believe in God, and live your life in accordance with that belief, and you discover in the afterlife that you're right—congrats!

Enjoy the harps, the wings, the free buffet. But if you're wrong and there's nothing: What have you lost anyway? A few thousand Sunday mornings spent nodding off during mass? Some glorious immoral behavior you turned down because your conscience instructed you to? It won't matter, because you won't know. You won't exist. So you lose nothing by gambling on faith.

But let's say you don't believe in God, and you live your life accordingly. If it turns out you're wrong, you might have some explaining to do to the Big Man upstairs. He could be a great guy, and forgive and forget. Or he might take it personally. Look, I have no idea which way it'll go, but I always play it safe—and when it comes to eternity, that's probably a key area of your life where keeping your options open makes sense. That and massage parlors.

Christians Make the Easiest Movie Villains

Recently a group of Muslims complained to the press that they're tired of films always portraying them as terrorists and villains—even in seemingly innocent cartoons like *Aladdin*. They also mentioned blockbusters made before the attack on September 11, 2001—flicks all guilty of giving their religion a bad name. The films they highlighted included *Raiders of the Lost Ark*, Bruce Willis's *The Siege*, and the Halle Berry flick *Executive Decision* (which approximately four people saw—none of them Muslim).

So I performed a scientific experiment this morning. I Googled the phrase "angry Christians," and came up with 11,500 hits. Then I Googled the phrase "angry Muslims," and I came up with 66,200 hits. Then I made a cup of coffee and did a funny dance in front of my window wearing nothing but cotton briefs.

My conclusion: Muslims are roughly six times angrier than Christians. And dancing in front of a window wearing nothing but cotton briefs won't change that simple fact. One bit.

So, what makes angry Muslims so angry?

The oddest things! You'd think that they would have gotten angry over radicals hijacking their religion and infusing it with murderous ideology. You'd also think I'd get mad every time I wake up nude in the park, but I don't!

But no. Instead, Muslim groups somehow reserve their anger for the way they are represented in movies.

Well, join the club.

For the last twenty years, Hollywood has bent over backward to make white guys with ugly last names the true villains in every single flick. Remember Hans Gruber from *Die Hard*? I do.

And he's just the tip of the iceberg—an iceberg so big it's all but canceled out the effects of global warming. The real truth is, Hollywood has always gone overboard in making sure minorities are among the good guys. In fact, if you look at almost any TV show besides *24*, you will find "the reverse-assumption hero," a character Hollywood creates to reverse your perceived assumptions about a minority, or minority stereotype. You see this in *Lost*, *Prison Break*, and of course *Ugly Betty*. The funny thing is, you never had that negative minority stereotype in mind to begin with—but the show's creators did.

And that's racist. And even though it's not racist toward me, the fact that it's racist to other people is just as bad. In a sense I am suffering from "secondhand racism," which is every bit as dangerous as normal racism—at least according to my neighbor Bob, that fat Yupik bastard.

Scientology Seems Kind of Fun

Scientology is, in my opinion, an extremely underrated religion. Fact is, I have never met a Scientologist who was an asshole. Sure, they're a little flaky and litigious, but it's not like their followers will hijack a plane or something.

Now, I know Scientology gets a bad rap, mainly because of its quirky celebrity contingent, its freaky backstory, its killer-instinct legal team, and its sincerely awful views concerning psychiatry and medicine. But as far as religions go, I have to say—they're rarely in your face, and they don't kill you.

From my experience, assholes go to Scientology to un-asshole themselves. And usually, it works. Anything that makes people better people, I have no quarrel with. (Unless it's Eckankar. Those people smell like hospital gowns.)

Around the corner from my old apartment is a Scientology center. I would walk by it frequently and watch as the staff manned their desks, getting up periodically to give flyers to passersby. Every now and then they would convince someone to stop and sit down and fill out a questionnaire.

They never asked me to take a test, unless I was returning from the gym, holding a backpack. In fact, whenever I was holding a backpack, I got asked to take a test. When I was without a backpack, they left me alone.

Has anyone else noticed the Scientology/backpack link?

(If you have, I would suggest you keep it to yourself. Frankly, this story is even beginning to bore the engrams out of me.)

One time back when I was editing *Stuff* magazine, I published a joke about Scientologists, and a handful of disciples showed up at the offices unannounced to discuss the merits of their religion. They didn't come to protest. They came to have a conversation. I really respected that. So we made fun of them again the following month—just to see if they would come back. They didn't. And that made me very sad.

I missed our little Scientology fellas.

But this leads me to a greater idea. L. Ron Hubbard was a genius. Rather than spend years writing novels that served only to entertain, he wrote novels designed to convert! He didn't then have casual fans, he had fervent apostles—which is pretty damn cool if you ask me.

So from now on, I am starting my own religion, and it's all about me. I have yet to name it, but I'm gravitating toward Gutfeldology, or Gutology. Or something even more simple, like GregisGod. What do you think? You can vote for the name at my website, the Daily Gut, or just send me a contribution for the church I'm currently erecting (I'm using some blankets, sofa pillows, and a card table—it's not so much a church as it is a fort in my living room). The basic underlying principles of "Gutology"? Here they are:

- You should be nice to everyone who's nice to you.
- Especially me, however.
- And you should prove your obedience by showering me with gifts and naked pictures.

That's basically it. If you can't fulfill the first two commandments, you can totally redeem yourself with the third.

The Folk Guitar Ruined Catholicism

I was born and raised a Catholic and served as an altar boy from third to eighth grade. During those times I attended mass weekly, often because I'd get three bucks for working funerals (and free sips of wine). Now, at this point, I bet you're expecting me to start telling you how I became a lapsed Catholic. Or, how I came to hate all organized religion. That's what Catholics in the media do: They immediately denounce or make fun of their religious upbringing whenever the opportunity presents itself.

I won't do that.

I will never rag on Catholicism. However, I will tell you why I stopped going to mass: folk guitar.

I am not the first person to say that Catholic mass is boring, and it takes a lot to expect kids to sit through it. Think about it: Mass is an event based on repetition—and once you know the pattern, your brain simply follows it impatiently. How many of us have been there and thought: "Okay, that's the Our Father. Next up Lamb of God; then communion—I could really go for some doughnuts. I think someone farted. Oh yeah—me."

But I can take boring. What I can't take are earnest attempts to combat boredom: deliberate but feeble efforts to appear contemporary, when really, you should be playing up the ancient part of mass instead (like ritual sacrifice). That's why I hate the folk guitar. Because when you have a folk guitar, you can bet your sweet religious ass there will be a folk singer attached to it. And the songs warbled will be bad enough to force Christ to come down from the cross and beat the crap out of him/her/it. You just know Jesus hated "Kumbaya." Mass is supposed to be cold, medieval, and dirgy (if that's a word)—a rejection of touchy-feely intimacy.

The last straw for me? The exchange of pleasantries—that "peace be with you" moment that usually involves a handshake or an awkward nod. I know it's supposed to be nice, but if a pleasantry is forced, how can it be seen as "nice"? It's not authentic if it's the product of peer pressure. Plus, and more important: Who wants to shake the hand of some old fart with a handkerchief full of snot curled up in his or her fist?

I do, but I'm probably in the minority.

Any Idiot With Eyes Can Make Fun of the Pope

If you're willing to openly criticize a dude with a box cutter and a suicide vest, I'll listen—but going after the pope is just too easy.

And I happen to think the pope is all right. Here's why: As I write this, he is supposed to amend the teachings on the state of limbo—that place between heaven and hell. For centuries many Roman Catholics (including me) believed that the souls of babies who die before baptism remain in limbo. Which isn't really fair, when you think about it. They should actually go to hell (insert New Jersey joke).

More important—while we get up, have breakfast, and worry about whether we paid the car insurance, the pope is reviewing the state that exists between heaven and hell!

Now that is a job. As a young Catholic, limbo confused the hell out of me. Now that limbo is under review, I'd like to think I was right all along. I hope it's replaced with an Arby's, which has the best curly fries ever. And don't get me started on their shakes— they're to die for, whether you end up in limbo or not.

If There Is a God, I'm Screwed

Thing is, so are you.

Values Are Not the Same As Truth

When I lived in England, I loved reading about British schools, mainly because they weren't really schools. They were more like waiting rooms for the unemployed. Teaching these kids was always deemed a waste of time and effort, and the teacher always considered it a good day if she went home with both her eyes intact. Which brings me to the announcement made back in 2006 that "the national curriculum" would be changed so teachers would no longer have to instruct kids on the difference between right and wrong. Instead, under new plans, they would help the brats "secure values and beliefs." I have no idea what that means, but that's the point, really. Teaching stuff vague in meaning makes the job of teaching less demanding. Especially in a politically correct climate: Teaching right and wrong requires judgment, and judgment hurts feelings— and we can't have that, when hurting feelings can often be construed as a crime. This is why, apparently, the schools will also drop the notion of learning about Britain's cultural heritage—to be replaced by the understanding of "different cultures and traditions."

Which is easy, because all cultures are awesome, and learning about such awesomeness will probably require cool arts and crafts exercises involving glue and macaroni. But one thing it won't require: truth. Or the plural: truths.

I think that's the plural, anyway. My teachers never told me.

Just Because "It's for a Good Cause" Doesn't Make It Good

Recently, the *New York Times* ran a story on the new trend in kiddie birthday parties: Instead of getting the kids an Xbox or an air rifle, the parents would ask that cash go to a charity—an animal shelter, a food bank, or something involving the homeless. Which, predictably, makes me want to throw up through my elbows.

Here, again, is an example of selfish, stupid parents putting their own self-absorption before the wants of their own kids. This new fad is designed to teach philanthropy and altruism, but what it's really doing is patting attention-starved parents on the back.

If my parents did this when I was a child, I would have reported them to the police, after saying they "touched" me. Because, really, the whole point of birthdays—for a kid—is to get stuff. Lots of stuff. Charity is great, I guess, but only if you do your best not to advertise it.

That's the problem with this fad. Not only is it force-fed philanthropy—which can only make kids hate it—it is done precisely so all the other children's parents know how sensitive and caring the partygivers are. It also forces other parents to consider doing the same or risk looking like heels. "PS: Kevin would appreciate toys."

This is all part of the noxious feel-good mentality—as long as your actions are for a good cause, who can complain? I can. Let's face it: No child is charitable, unless his friend is actually dying right in front of him. Also, the best memories of my life are of my birthdays—

when I got my first bike, my favorite outfielder's mitt, my Ken doll. I got that last year and I had to go to the ER to get it removed.

Moral Authority Requires a Clenched Fist to Back It Up

If we are to believe the world press, this last election has enabled America to regain its "moral authority," a valuable commodity squandered during the Bush presidency, thanks largely to the Iraq War, Abu Ghraib, Gitmo, and the last Madonna tour.

This is great news for all of us. We're the good guys again, and we've pleased everyone from Tanzania to Tonga—so what can we do with our country's resurgent "moral authority"?

Apparently nothing.

At least that's what the postelection bloodshed in Iran has taught us. The fact is, if you elect an American president because of his moral authority, and then he's too timid to use it, it's actually worse than having a callous president from Texas who invades countries to kill dictators. Seriously, people! Obama was supposed to stop bad people from doing bad things just by waving his hands. But he didn't even want to wave his hands.

I'm hoping that by the time you're reading this, Obama has grown up a little. He needs to understand that he didn't become president to help the world, but to help America. And it is only by his looking out for America's interests first that the world actually benefits.

More important, Obama needs to understand that moral authority isn't there to allow America to do what the world wants; it's there to allow America to do what *it* wants. And that means galvanizing *people*, not their dickhead leaders, to the cause of freedom. Obama missed the boat tragically with Iran. Let's hope he learns from it.

The fact is, an "unclenched fist" only works in a slap fight. Remember Barack Obama's historic speech about unclenching his fist and reaching out to countries that, previously, we had considered warlike, antisocial, and sort of evil? It worked wonders.

If by "wonders," you mean "embarrassingly bad." You know it's scary that when compared to Germany and France during the Iran mess, we looked positively timid. As the corrupt regime cracked down and killed innocent people, Barack settled into a mushy state of vague relativism, remarking that the feuding candidates were no different from each other—an explanation that provided him an excuse for inaction. Meanwhile, Germany and France stepped up, condemning the crackdown immediately. Obama, however, kept that fist unclenched. And Ahmadinejad mocked him as the crackdown continued. So: Act like a wuss, they treat you like one. Let's hope, by the time this book is published, Obama realizes that clenching is far better than unclenching (especially when you've just eaten at Taco Bell).

Crime and the Criminals Who Crime It

If Murderers Had Fins, Animal Rights Activists Would Protect Them

You know we're running out of sharks? It's true: Lax European Union policies are causing shark numbers to deplete all around the world—a terrible thing, since these finny freaks are very important to the "ecological balance" of the oceans. Meaning, if they disappear, and stop killing other living things, everything goes haywire.

But look—you can use that logic regarding the disappearance of any kind of organism, as long as that organism kills other organisms. The fact is, if you eliminated all the murderers on this planet, from the lowly serial killer to the genocidal dictator, you'd probably run into the same problem over the course of a few centuries. But you wouldn't mourn their absence, would you?

Now, if we were talking about brine shrimp, I would feel differently. But we're not. We're talking about sharks, who are total murderous pricks—Night Stalkers with fins. Which reveals the sad and strange truth about animal rights activists: Morality doesn't play any role in their decision-making. So if Nazis were actually dogs, PETA would choose them over the Jews.

It is at this juncture that I admit this point is starting to make no sense.

Temporary Restraining Orders Don't Work If They're Temporary

Awhile back the annoying actor known as Colin Farrell got a three-year restraining order against a woman attempting to sue him for stalking her. (It happened two years ago—so it runs out in a year. Yippee!) According to the restraining order, the lady must stay 150 yards away from the actor. Which confuses me—I mean, why 150 yards? Why not 500 yards, or three miles? Maybe the average human can't throw an empty beer bottle more than 400 feet? And why only for three years? If someone is harassing you, isn't it understood that a temporary solution is not a solution? Shouldn't there be permanent restraining orders, or none at all? It's not like there is an expiration date on manic obsession. (Speaking from experience, my own feelings for Larry Storch will never die!)

That's why I try to avoid restraining orders altogether. And it is also why I stay in and watch old movies. My current favorite is one I filmed of a nursing student I "met" back in 1987. His name was Curtis, and to this day he still won't speak to me. (He's in the fridge.)

Criminals Love It When You Hand Over Your Weapons

A few years back, I remember reading how the British government had organized one of those weapons amnesty programs, where people could hand in all sorts of weapons without getting arrested for having them to begin with. The cops netted something like ninety thousand knives, cutthroat razors, samurai swords, axes, machetes, and meat cleavers. They also recovered what they thought was an 1880 bayonet, which later turned out to be Gwyneth Paltrow.

In a nutshell, criminals love weapon amnesties, because only noncriminals comply with them. And the few bad guys who do drop their weapons off do so only so they don't get nailed for the crime committed with that old weapon. An hour later, they're procuring another, better knife.

Jenna Elfman does this all the time.

The point is, weapons work wonders as long as the good people have them (as opposed to the evil people). Because when you point a gun at a bad guy, it makes him reconsider being bad.

An example: In Montgomery, Alabama, a couple named Adrian and Tiffany McKinnon came home to find their house had been burgled. The thieves had taken almost everything, while leaving piles of trash everywhere. When the wife left to see her sister, Adrian went back into the house and walked right into one of the burglars, who was returning to get more stuff, while wearing Adrian's hat. Adrian not only held the man at gunpoint (or "fun-point," as I like to call it), he forced the thief to clean up the mess he had made. When the police arrived, the thief complained to the cops about being forced to clean, unaware that he had avoided another option, called death.

As anyone who has ever been robbed before knows, it's the state of the house postrobbery that's just as bad as being robbed. I wouldn't hate being robbed so much, if the thieves would have the common courtesy to put back the stuff they don't want. There's nothing worse than trying to retrieve a figurine from the toilet. At least, I hope that was a figurine.

But really, I love this story because it reveals the magical, healing powers of firearms. The fact is, if you want bad people to stop being bad, just point a loaded firearm in their general direction. This incident shows, in fact, that you can actually get them to clean your house. This is the only scientific proof you need that handguns, in the hands of good people, make the world a safer place. And frankly, the thief was lucky he was only forced to clean up the mess he made—if it were up to me, I would have made him do my linens and clean the grout between my bathroom tiles with his tongue. But first, I would make him put on a French maid costume—I have four of them, in different sizes, just in case the opportunity presents itself.

A Night in Jail Does Not Harden You

Just about everyone I know has spent at least one night in jail. And every one of them loves to recount the story—because it trumps everything else, shy of a moonwalk or having sex with two women on the wings of a biplane en route to Cuba. Spending a night in jail ranks along with skydiving, bungee jumping, and eating a spotted owl as a measure of being cool. But it's even better.

Because it teaches you something you'll never forget. Being in jail shows you how much you don't want to be in jail. Now, that doesn't make you a tougher person, just a slightly smarter person—for at least two weeks. Until you're back doing the shit that got you into jail in the first place.

Oh—the other thing you learn in jail? Thank God we have them. The people in there are animals.

Modern Gangbangers Know How to Dress

Have you ever tried to pinpoint when gangs stopped dressing like gangs in movies like *Warriors*, and more like gangs in *Boyz n the Hood*? I always find it amusing the way thugs looked in movies in the mid-1970s and 1980s. Especially in flicks like *Death Wish*, *Crocodile Dundee*, *Commando*, *Dirty Harry* sequels, *48 Hours*, and *Taxi*

Driver, the uniform of thuggery was a mishmash of styles: flared jeans, a bandanna, a tank top, and boots. The bad guys looked like rejects from *Fame.*

But then it all changed. And suddenly thugs started to get their fashion act together, adopting a more ominous baggy look—ominous because it all matched.

I believe this was the beginning of the end for thug fashion. For more of my opinions, stay here and count to twelve thousand.

You finished? Good. Here's another thought: Thanks to Rudy Giuliani and Mike Bloomberg, it's now almost impossible to envision making a violent crime movie in present-day Manhattan—like *Taxi Driver* or *Death Wish.* It would seem absolutely unrealistic—there is almost no real crime to speak of, and there are more cops on each corner than ever before. This has transformed the atmosphere of the city—so the only danger you really face in Manhattan is the diarrhea you might get from a street corner falafel.

Compare that to the streets of San Francisco, which are littered with aggressive transients who lack the idea of "space" when it comes to panhandling. Fact: We can all put up with begging, if the beggar doesn't get too close. But Bay Area bums ignore that well-understood maxim, simply because they know they can get away with it. It's a fact everyone in the Bay Area has come to know: Gavin Newsom cares more about his hair than he does the homeless. Which explains why both are equally slimy.

Bounty Hunters Are Worse Than the People They Hunt

I sometimes watch *Dog the Bounty Hunter,* mainly because I love the dude's hair and his nifty leather armband/vest ensembles. However, the show pisses me off, mainly because most of the people they "hunt" are usually harmless saps who are no danger to anyone but a quart of cheap beer. But the way "Dog" pretends that arresting these sad sacks is somehow a huge feat, and that their arrest will somehow improve their lives, is a joke. In one episode he arrested some poor guy while he was on the job at a fast-food restaurant. Do you think a real criminal would be spending his time flipping burgers at McDonald's? No, of course not. He'd be at Jack in the Box.

Death Row Inmates Make the Best Husbands

I've noticed, living in New York, how hard it is for many women to find Mr. Right. This is because when you look at most men living in big cities, none of them are Mr. Right. There are just way too many sexual options for them, so they feel no pressure to behave like actual gentlemen.

So, who gives them these options? Women, of course—who don't have the balls to limit these options and ask these boys to behave like men. So now that women are screwing men the way men want women to screw them, there are few men out there who would actually want to marry women after they've fucked them. To me the only solution is to find men whose options are not limited by women, but by bars. Iron bars.

See, women need men who know their place—who aren't running wild in the streets drinking and hitting on their friends. You need a guy who feels lucky there's one special woman out there who worries about him. Here are my suggestions:

Andre Alexander
Thomas Battle
Andre Burton
Tracy Cain
Steve Champion
William Clark
Scott Collins

As I write this, all these dudes are on California's death row—San Quentin, to be precise—so there's an outside chance God, or a prison worker with an IV port, has taken a few of them off the market. Which is a shame. Prison husbands never stray, except with each other, and they'll never get in the way. And they make excellent pen pals (their penmanship is to be admired, even after the pen is fashioned into a shiv).

Drugs and How Much I Hate (Meaning Miss) Them

Never Trust Anyone Under Sixty
Who Hasn't Done Drugs

If there's one great thing that came from Obama's election, it wasn't that he became our first black American president. It's that he was the first cokehead who admitted doing coke. It was smart of him, really, to put it all out there, and to include it in a memoir was a stroke of genius. Once you disclose you did bad things, it gives reporters absolutely nothing to do but say what a great guy you are for saying you did bad things. Plus, most reporters are druggies anyway, so it's just another thing we all have in common!

If Obama hadn't confessed to doing blow, most of the campaign would have been spent trying to find out if he did blow. And it might have cost him the election, once he was forced to admit it.

The question is, however, if he had been forced to confess, would he have pulled a Clinton, and said, "I chopped a line, but never snorted?" No one would have believed him, of course, especially those of us idiots who've done our fair share of coke. The evil stuff is just too damn good to pass up—even if it does ruin your life.

Which leads to my major truth: People who never tried drugs are, well, weird. It's a natural human inclination to want to try things that seem fun, and I've never met a human who didn't want to seek oblivion in one form or another. People who don't have that need aren't stupid or evil, they're just kind of odd. I say this in regard to specific generations. The average American born after 1945 has it ridiculously easy compared to any previous era. Our grandparents had too many things to worry about when they were growing up to spend their time trying to score drugs. There was war, depression, and brutal blue-collar jobs that required mild coherence. Plus, they were too busy drinking themselves into stupors to remember what drugs to buy. That was a golden age.

A "Cry for Help" Translates to "This Selfish Person Finally Ran Out of Money and/or Drugs"

The four most overused words in the English language? "A cry for help." Whenever someone does something stupid—whether it's exposing his genitals to parking attendants or having sex with a mango—the experts call it "a cry for help." That's because a cry for help excuses any responsibility for the behavior, and it allows wall-eyed creeps like Dr. Phil the opportunity to make a buck. It's getting to the point that when you hear a real cry for help, you simply ignore it.

More important, a "cry for help" should not be fun. You must remember: A year or so before she went lesbian, Lindsay Lohan was arrested in Santa Monica, only five days after leaving rehab—and she was wasted as usual as she carried cocaine into jail. This, only a few months after crashing her Mercedes into a bush, another incident where blow was found. She's been to AA, she's been to Promises, and so on and so on.

This is when experts came out of the woodwork to say that her actions were "a cry for help." Christ: Whenever I hear the phrase "cry for help," I want to cry for help! Because, really, the phrase is just an attempt to absolve the person "crying" from responsibility for stupid, but admittedly fun behavior. And it's an insult to people who are truly crying for help.

What is a real cry for help?

It would involve the use of flares or smoke signals, hopefully seen from a great distance.

It might be sending a message in a bottle...a message that says, "Help me."

Morse code, on occasion, is a cry for help. I just use it for recipes.

When you put only one song on your iPod and that song is Rick Astley's "Cry For Help"—that's a cry for help.

In Spanish, *Ayudame* is a cry for help. It means, "Help me!"

And do you know that flailing and flapping around that people seem to do before drowning? A cry for help.

Banging coming from the inside of a trunk is a cry for help. Though not very effective, at that point.

Pointing at your throat while turning blue is a universal cry for help.

And doing a pantomime to indicate you need the Heimlich maneuver because there's a hot dog lodged in your throat, while turning blue—that's textbook in the "cry for help" business.

You see, there are many real cries for help. A celebrity's drug-fueled antics hardly qualify. The only way we're going to stop destructive people from being destructive is not by making excuses for their behavior, but by actually punishing them. Teach them what a real cry for help sounds like (my basement is available). Look, there are millions of people suffering everywhere, and their "cries for help" consist of ways to alleviate their own suffering.

Usually this means working harder, saving money, or learning a skill. They don't abuse drugs, steal from their friends, or defecate in movie theaters when there's a decent bathroom just feet away (which reminds me, I would like to personally apologize to the staff of the AMC Multiplex in Woodland Hills).

"Experimenting" Means Using

Whenever someone important, like a celebrity, or maybe a president, talks about past drug use, they always use the word "experiment." Instead of "doing."

I hate this double standard, because no one ever "experiments" with alcohol.

No, they get drunk.

They become drunks. They get wasted, regularly. They puke and piss themselves. This kind of behavior, as you know, isn't "experimentation," it's called "college."

But when it's marijuana, cocaine, or snorting ground-up Hummel figurines, you always hear the "I used to experiment!" line— like every junkie is actually a scientist testing out theories on their bodies in search of some elusive empirical truth. "Hmmm, wonder what this will be like if I shove it up my nose! The world could benefit from this knowledge! Better take meticulous notes so I can show my methods to explain my data!" Uh, no.

If so—then sure, every druggie experiments until he ODs (that means the experiment failed—you exceeded the dosage). So, for the sake of argument—if there is such a thing as experimentation, what's the cutoff when experimentation is no longer experimentation, just "using"? That would make Keith Richards the Enrico Fermi of rock and roll. And stimulants.

Here's my definition of experimentation: You were in a room with people who did drugs, and you did it once and that was it. This also implies that you willingly turned down future opportunities to engage in the behavior again. But if you did it again, and chances are you did it again, then the "experimentation" is over.

Don't worry, though—with this definition, we're all pretty much in the same boat.

Anyway, I'm "experimenting" right now. I can't feel my eyelids (please tell me I didn't eat them).

On a related note: It's been my experience that drug burnouts are more fun than alcoholics. Former hallucinogenic users always seem to have neat, fantabulous theories on the universe, and they rarely if ever make demands on you before noon. Alcoholics, however, are always reminding you that they are alcoholics, which I find tiresome—and which is why I stopped going to the meetings. And they're always up—doing things like jogging, chatting, blogging—at ridiculous hours. Mainly because it's the only way to keep themselves from drinking.

Stuff You Put in Your Face

Anything Served As a Meatball Is Instantly Edible

So a Chilean artist, Marco Evaristti, recently created a new work of art using his own body: meatballs cooked with his own fat extracted by liposuction. He then served the balls to his dining pals—along with an explanation that "you are not a cannibal if you eat art."

The price tag for ten balls: four grand.

I am okay with this. Because I love meatballs. Mainly because you can take anything objectionable and mold it into a meaty ball—and you've got yourself a delightful meal.

I'm making a batch right now (it's an actual Thai recipe made from a real Thai).

But while meatballs are naturally edible, milk isn't. It is my firm belief that we should *never* drink milk. I'm serious: I don't know who first thought drinking fluids from the fleshy bag of a large animal was a good idea. But really, how different is that from bestiality? Drinking a fluid seems somehow far more intimate an act than simply giving the animal a handy. Most of those cows are so stuck up anyhow.

One Simple Big Mac Has Everything You Need to Stay Alive

Turn on the tube any time of the day, and you'll find a show featuring some edgy foodie scampering around the planet tasting unusual and exotic delicacies from different cultures. It's always some peroxide-dyed dude chewing on monkey brains, boar testes, and stir-fried crickets. It's oh so extreme and in your face—but the whole enterprise is dull as damp Doritos. And as always, this investigation into alternative food sources is done to "expand" our minds and teach us that the American way of life isn't always the lifestyle of choice.

Perhaps that's true—until a McDonald's is built in that area, of course. It's true—no matter how people extol the charm of "exotic" food, it's those foreign folks who are positively drooling for our fast food, for they know that a Big Mac is better than anything on their creepy menu. Whenever a McDonald's opens, lines stretch for avenues—and for good reason. The food is better than their food. It's also cheaper, and yes: healthier.

When I travel, I make it a point to hit a McDonald's in every country—and it's always, *always* packed. So the next time someone from the Food Channel is babbling about how wonderful the primitive rice paste and beetle stew must taste, remember that the locals would kill him for a quarter-pounder. And when they realize they can't find one, they'll eat him.

Which leads me to a far more important truth: One simple Big Mac has everything you need to stay alive, and should be awarded a Nobel Prize, instead of being constantly blamed for everything wrong in the world. Back in 2007, the *New York Times* took McDonald's to task for introducing a new drink called the Hugo, forty-two ounces of affordable soda, an amount that could drown a wild boar. What really peeved the paper besides its massive size: McDonald's printed the ads so everyone could read them. "Hugo ads are available in several languages," the paper scolds, "making sure that minorities—who are disproportionately affected by the obesity epidemic—are aware of the budget beverage."

So, by making these ads multicultural, McDonald's is racist. But, what if Micky D's hadn't printed the ads in different languages? You just know the *Times* would have hinted at racism there as well. After all, how dare they exclude minorities from a bargain deal?

It seems you can't win when you make something people want. If only the *New York Times* knew what that was like. (Al Capone did, and he paid for it.)

It's a lonely battle that McDonald's fights. This is a company that has fed more people affordably than any government program known to man. If the U.N. had asked McDonald's to solve starvation in other countries, it would have taken a week of airdrops before every child would have been as fat as me. And that's fat (the laptop is jiggling on my belly as I write this).

I'm no nutritionist, but you don't have to be one to know that one simple Big Mac has everything you need to stay alive. You've got protein in the meat, carbohydrate in the bread, and the lettuce and onion provide all the salad you need. It's truly God's supplement for a starving world, and we'd be wrong not to acknowledge its true beauty.

And just consider the dollar menu—which includes chicken nuggets and double cheeseburgers—and you see how easy it is to feed someone three meals daily for three bucks. That's way cheaper than anything the U.N. could come up with, and far safer.

Having said that, I would be remiss if I didn't mention the other unspeakable truth about McDonald's: It's always easier going in than it is going out.

Yogurt Is Not Food

It's funny how I don't remember eating yogurt as a child. We always ate pudding or Jell-O. Then, around the early 1980s, yogurt became a regular purchase in the Gutfeld household. I was maybe sixteen before I had even heard of the crap—which makes me believe some trade association must have pulled off some coup. We also started to purchase bagels around that time. I don't know why. We were Catholics.

But homemade pudding and Mom-produced Jell-O went away. No one ever talks about this: how we allowed some strange foreign food to invade our country and decimate our favorite, childhood delights.

Most important, the only reason yogurt remains popular is that women buy it. It's a nutritional tampon—something men buy only if their wives or girlfriends send them out to buy it.

Moreover, yogurt's persistent popularity is based solely on women's trying to keep from buying ice cream. It's that sad, resigned choice a woman must make, to prevent attacking a pint of Häagen-Dazs.

I've never seen a man eat yogurt in front of me—which says something about the state of our world. Or our bowels. I'll get back to you on which.

And I'll say the same thing about fruit, too. It's just not real food. It's not food, period. It's really there for decoration. If you eat it, you're probably a chimp or something. I agree with the Cantonese: "If its back faces heaven, it can be eaten" (except for Roseanne Barr). And people, in case you haven't noticed: Fruit doesn't have a back. I mean *Hello!*

If There Were Other Life Forms in
Outer Space, We'd Eat Them (or Vice Versa)

I'm watching TV right now—and there's this newscaster saying that an American spaceship called the *Phoenix Lander* has apparently discovered soil on Mars that's very similar to the dirt I'd find in my backyard. But unless there's also a Guatemalan hitchhiker named Ricardo buried in that dirt, I'm assuming that's where the similarities end.

This so-called news means we may be able to grow vegetables on the Red Planet—unappetizing greens like asparagus, Brussels sprouts, spinach, and other crap that does not qualify as actual food. To me, the thought of turning Mars into a salad bar is exactly what's wrong with America.

See, when I was growing up, Mars was frightening. Martians were not friendly. It's the Red Planet, for Christ's sake! Red from blood, not tomatoes!

But now, in a culture overrun with nanny-state do-gooders, we want to turn that angry planet into a salad bar. Instead, if life can be cultivated there, why not send our criminals? I mean, D.C. is already full.

More important, growing food on other planets raises a larger dilemma. What if we were to discover the perfect steak on Mars, but that gorgeous piece of meat had an IQ that matched ours? Could you eat something as smart as you, even if it made the mouth water thinking about it? Imagine stumbling upon a river of glorious ice cream cakes, only to find that these succulent delights happen to be practicing Buddhists. Would you have them for dessert? I suppose I would. But then again, I had a deliveryman for breakfast.

What if the best-tasting food in the universe also happened to be the most adorable, decent creatures alive? Would you eat them? If you didn't eat them, then that means you would be placing Martians on a higher level than earthlings (and by earthlings, I mean cows, lambs, and strippers). Something inside me is telling me this is unfair. That could be indigestion, though (I had a stripper for lunch).

If You Have to Unbuckle Your Pants
After Eating, You Need New Pants

Also, if you go out to eat wearing sweatpants because it's just more comfortable, then you're a shut-in who just hasn't committed to shutting in yet.

Miscellany (i.e., Really Great Stuff That Pretty Much Could Go Anwhere in the Book but Ended Up Here Because I'm Lazy)

The Ugly Have No Gandhi

Gay, black, Hispanic, transgendered, Belgian—whatever: If you don't get the job, you've got a case for discrimination. You can sue—because of who you are. But if you're homely, who's going to defend you? No one. And the fact is, if you're ugly—and smart enough to know you're ugly—then you know *that* is the primary reason you didn't get the job. More people are rejected from jobs for being ugly than all other reasons combined (for actual statistics on this, go to ireallydonthavethestatistics.com). Ugly people are also discriminated against not just by good-looking people, but also by other ugly people, because they're not blind. Yep, ugly people are dismissed the moment they sit down at the interview, and if you're ugly and reading this and don't believe me, well—then you're ugly and stupid, too. Until the homely rise up against the attractive, this hate will continue forever.

Mind you, there is a legitimate reason you're discriminated against. Ugly people are unpleasant to be around. If the job you're applying for happens to be sales, or working in a restaurant, being ugly in a public setting can only drive other attractive people away. If I was opening a bar or a gym and wanted to attract young, appealing people, I would not hire an ugly person—unless he was willing to undergo some sort of reconstructive surgery that would turn him into a unicorn/manatee hybrid.

Luckily, I do that surgery in my spare time.

The only exception: If a married woman hires you to be a nanny, you were hired because you are ugly—far uglier than you probably feared.

Bottom line: Ugly people have no Gandhi. I think about this truth a lot, and it saddens me. Sometimes I'll be brooding in my circular rotating bed with a bucket of fried chicken and my houseboy, Ricardo. I wanted to talk to Ricardo about this—the plight of the ugly people—but Ricardo would not understand. For he is beautiful. So beautiful, in fact, it makes me want to beat him. Again.

But it's a stone cold fact that ugly people are the last group of individuals to have their own movement. Even fat people have acceptance societies—groups that say fat people are well within their rights to sit home and eat pies in the bathtub.

But what of the uglies? Who weeps for our misshapen brothers and sisters? This current climate of antiugliness almost cries for a protest of some kind.

Good luck. To march in protest against ugly discrimination is akin to admitting you're ugly. Every great movement had a leader—Nelson Mandela, Gandhi, Martin Luther King, Jr. But who will represent the ugly people? Where, I ask, is Ernest Borgnine when you need him?

The fact is, it's always been about face, more than it's been about race. According to a top scientist I met in some bar over the weekend (I believe his name was Hans, or it should have been), in a crapload of years humans will split into two separate species. One will be an attractive, intelligent, ruling elite, the other an underclass of dimwitted, ugly, goblinlike creatures. (Picture Al Franken. Now stop picturing Al Franken, or you'll throw up.) The upside for the elite: The men will have more symmetrical faces, deeper voices, and bigger penises. The women will have shiny hair, smooth, hairless skin, large eyes, pert breasts, and cupholders. God, I love cupholders.

I'm not surprised by this split, because it's happening already. The fact is, gorgeous people mate with gorgeous people, and ugly people stick to their repulsive ilk. The only exception are the ugly and powerful men—the Donald Trumps and Larry Kings—who use their wealth to entrap lingerie models into a life of joyless reproduction. They produce adorable children, until you peel back their amazing lifelike skin coating and find the ugly troll inside, working the levers.

We live in a world where the beautiful already rule the plain. Few white racists would refuse a roll in the hay with Halle Berry.

This is why uglies like me take special glee in the failings of gorgeous celebs—it's payback for their hotness opening doors closed for us. We gleefully await their downfall, the same way we don't feel much over the fiery destruction of celebrity homes in Malibu.

Which is why, fellow uglies, if we don't enslave the beautiful now, they will enslave us later. So as a plain man, I've already soundproofed my basement. And set traps outside Anderson Cooper's house. He lives around the corner, and I know his jogging route—so it's only a matter of time, really.

Futurists Don't Know Jack About the Future

So here's what a "world-renowned" futurist named Paul Saffo had to say about computers: "There's going to be a big acceleration in the discovery rate and the understanding rate, and this is because of digital technology."

So this guy looks into his crystal ball and sees... THAT. Or rather—that computers are going to be really important. I know a horse that could have predicted the same thing (his name is Clyde, and he predicted my last three cases of nonspecific urethritis— although "predicted" may not be the right verb).

What can we expect in terms of predictions from this thoughtful futurist?

I predict that Paul Saffo will predict:

- People will continue to use communication as an effective form of transmitting information amongst each other. "It's worked well so far," says the futurist.
- Lawn darts will probably not make a comeback, "but don't hold me to it," adds the cagey scientist.
- As we age, more and more people will look older—an "unhappy consequence that accompanies the future," says the futurist.
- "You won't be seeing indoor plumbing disappearing any time soon!" he adds.
- There will be a rise in the popularity of futurists, who "will be gaining more and more respect among the trendy elite," he says, before suddenly bursting into tears and running upstairs to his bedroom.

The Ocean Is a Giant Toilet

As a very busy and highly successful person in media, I'm often wined and dined at the most fashionable and expensive restaurants. Bennigan's. Applebee's. The Outback—home to the Bloomin' Onion—which is my nickname for Seth, the bartender there on Sundays. Like an onion, he has so many layers and sometimes he makes me cry. But when I'm out and about, I'm always told to order the seafood. "Try the Chilean sea bass—it's sealicious!" "You must have the shark fin soup—it's fincredible!" "Have you tried the prawns—they're prawnderful!"

Look. I don't eat seafood. Never have. Never will. I have my reasons. Number one, when eating steak, people never say, "Hey at least it doesn't smell cowy." Fish stink because they come from the sea—which is a giant toilet. People pee in it. No one pees on cows, unless the cow has requested it. And let's be honest—shellfish are nothing more than oversized insects. If they were smaller, they would be roaches. However, a tiny cow is basically a meatball. And meatballs are delicious, because they're essentially meat, in ball form.

But whenever I say I don't eat seafood, some chum says, "How can you know you don't like it if you haven't tried it?" The whole idea that you have to try something before making a judgment is moral laziness. Wearing burkas seems wrong and repressive—but I've never done it, and I don't need to. I spend all day in a sequined thong pouring margaritas out by the pool. Don't knock it if you haven't tried it.

People Named "Tiny" Never Turn Out to Be Tiny, or Good for You

Do you remember when Oprah Winfrey got in hot water over her school, the Leadership Academy for Girls, located just outside Johannesburg, South Africa? A dormitory matron was accused of indecent assault on a few of the students, prompting Winfrey to hold a tearful press conference—which she's a master at—to apologize.

But she wouldn't have had to if she had just known this simple truth: Never, ever hire anyone to run or manage a school who goes by the name "Tiny."

I am referring to Tiny Virginia Makopo, the matron accused of all the bad stuff. This I know: "Tiny" is rarely an affectionate term used to describe someone's small stature. Generally, it's a nickname reserved for both prison guards and their menacing inmates. If your screening process only had one step, Oprah, it should have been "no Tinies."

A side note: It's got to be tough for Oprah to recover from embarrassing hardships. I mean, unlike other celebrities, to emerge a better person, she cannot undergo a "healing process" by appearing on *Oprah*. Because, you know, she is Oprah.

I mean, then the only solution requires that Oprah interview herself. I would pay to see that—especially if she makes herself cry, and then offers herself a tissue.

Support Groups Don't Work

While I was getting my legs waxed this morning, I read of a report that ranks South Dakota as the happiest state in America. Apparently, the state has the lowest depression level and suicide level in the country.

I am not surprised. South Dakota is happy because only seven people live there. As for suicide rates, this can't be a surprise since it's nearly impossible to kill yourself in South Dakota. Have you ever tried to fling yourself off a tent?

Meanwhile, in the humanity-clogged centers of California and New York, the pursuit of happiness makes it impossible to be happy. As long as someone is doing better, you're feeling rotten. If someone is doing worse, they're asking you for money or to sleep on your couch. Hence, on both coasts you're overloaded with therapists. Meanwhile, you have deliriously happy people in South Dakota, where there's nothing to do, and no one to do it with. The most you can really hope for is a knowing glance from an elk—and even those beasts are fickle.

And this brings me to the weirdest study I've heard of in the last fourteen minutes. Researchers at the University of Haifa in Israel report that if you're going to experience helplessness, it's best to do it alone. They figured this out by giving electric shocks to rats— some in pairs, and some alone. The rats shocked in pairs coped less well than rats shocked in isolation. By "coping," I think they mean how well the rats adapted to life after the trauma. The rats that were made to feel hopeless—by being isolated—actually got on better. They resumed their life of leisure—eating cheese and watching rodent TV. I hear they love *Frasier*.

Anyway, I love experiments with rats because they remind me of my fellow man. Think of the scrappy solo rats as the greatest generation, and the whiny loser rats as the Age of Aquarius. Or think of it as John Wayne versus Woody Allen. Or Ronald Reagan versus Barack Obama. It comes down to this: Faced with adversity, do you (a) toughen up and get back on that wedge of cheese, or (b) roll over and urinate on your wood shavings? If the former, you tend to accomplish more in the long run, like, say, winning world wars; if the latter, you usually end up saying things like, "Why do they hate us?"

Of course, when mice say it, it just sounds like a bunch of squeaking.

"Bum" Is a Better Word Than "Homeless"

If I were homeless, I'd like to be called a bum, or at the very least, a hobo. I don't know—it just sounds cooler, and more fun. "Hobo" at least evokes the 1930s, Woody Guthrie, riding the rails...the in-vogue description "indigent" just sounds like you're constipated.

For what it's worth, back in the seventies, kids like me were "bums" for Halloween. We'd have a dirty face, with a burnt-cork beard shadow, a cigar nub, a soiled derby hat, short baggy overlarge trousers with holes, beat-up brown shoes, a plaid flannel shirt that was buttoned incorrectly, and a red bandanna bundle tied to the end of a stick. If you were really into it, a melted Baby Ruth added the authenticity of smeared poop.

In England, people don't use the word "homeless." They call them "tramps," which is a great word, in my humble opinion—"tramp" is like "hobo" with a banjo. I think it makes our unhoused brethren sound more interesting, more exciting, and possibly even entertaining. Remember the funk band, the Trammps? With two Ms! They were great! Which brings up my next question: Do you think the homeless would enjoy house music? Or would they find it insulting?

I don't know. All this thinking is making me hungry. Off to the park!

Astronauts Were Once Astronauts; Now They're Handymen

You ever notice how, lately anyway, astronauts are doing far less floating around doing cool astronaut stuff, and much more "fixing"?

I don't know why they don't bother fixing this stuff before they blast off into outer space. I remember a few years back astronauts on the *Endeavour* space shuttle spent hours tinkering with the machine that's designed to turn their piss and sweat into drinking water. Apparently this device, which costs over a hundred million dollars, is vibrating more than it should—which is a problem if you don't want urine all over your shiny space suit. Here in New York City, there are people who pay a great deal of money for exactly this experience. But that's Elton John's business.

Now, imagine if this toilet problem was occurring at the restrooms where you work. Generally speaking, as an accountant or graphic designer or whatever you do, you would not be called in to fix a plumbing issue. Your office manager would call in Roto Rooter, and a real man with real skills would come to unclog the mess.

So why is it that astronauts are expected to fix a faulty piss machine—I mean, they're astronauts! Not piss machine fixers.

The answer to this question is simple: If it wasn't for "tasks" like this, the astronauts would have absolutely nothing to do. It's true—their occupation consists of less activity than giving the watching world a thumbs-up. They fix crap that allows them to go into space to fix crap that allows them to go into space to...oh, crap. Toll booth operators have more responsibility—and their uniforms suck.

Note to NASA: If you want us to give a flying poop about the astronauts then why not show us something interesting? Why not film the astronauts:

- Trying to eat soup.
- Dropping large objects outside and watching them float off? (Would be cool to see Barney Frank drift off into the black space; don't worry, we'd have him attached to fishing line.)
- Disposing of reality TV stars.
- Holding their breath in outer space for forty-five seconds (I hear it's impossible, according to my friend Ron, who owns a full-body cutout of Captain Picard).

Or why not play pranks on them?

- Tell them they're on an unstoppable course toward the sun.
- Put laxatives in their Tang.
- Have a wife call in to say she's found the hidden porn at home.
- Order them to attack Belgium.
- An oldie but a goodie: Tell them there was a sudden thermo-nuclear war, earth's population is dead, you can never return.

These are just my thoughts, and like I always say, my thoughts are your thoughts. If you have any suggestions for what the astronauts should be doing, please write them down on some tissue paper, then swallow them. Repeat process until you require hospitalization.

Fireworks Are Supposed to Be Dangerous

Every year around the end of June, you find the same mundane article within the pages of *USA Today*, reporting the harm fireworks cause during the Fourth of July celebrations. "Fireworks killed eight people and injured another 9,600 in 2004," etc.

To which I always add: You call that dangerous? And speaking of danger—isn't that the point of fireworks? They aren't called "sugary fun pillows," are they? They are called "fireworks." Put "fire" before any word, and it better be a little harmful.

Which brings me to fireworks stands, which, sadly, no longer exist anywhere in California. When I was a kid, it was different. They were everywhere. An overstocked fireworks stand smelled dirty and dangerous, like my underwear drawer. I love fireworks. But I always loved stories about people being harmed by dangerous fireworks more.

"Billy Fargate lost his eye on a bottle rocket last summer."

"Andy Clarkson blew his hand off with a pack of firecrackers."

"Billy Fargate lost his other eye on a bottle rocket last summer."

And so on.

Now, wherever you go, fireworks are illegal, and in a sense the active (read: dangerous) life that a young boy used to lead is also illegal. It's getting so bad that you can't even throw cats out of moving cars anymore. Frankly, the dangers of fireworks are small compared to the dangers of boredom. Take away fireworks, and boys will find other things to make their parents really nervous: chemistry sets, switchblades, cooking classes. We need to bring back fireworks. We need to do it not for us, but for the children. Because for every child who doesn't lose a finger to fireworks, there is a child who has lost a precious memory of losing that finger. And what about the memories of all the other children who saw that child lose that finger? Those are gone, too. Do you really want to be the person who will deprive the children of that?

What kind of monster are you?

The Fact That Reclining Your Seat in Economy Class Annoys the Person Behind You Only Makes It That Much More Satisfying

I'm not entirely sure why this is true. I only know that it is true. I'm sure there's some greater truth to be had here, but frankly I can't find it. Let's move on.

You're 48 Percent Less Attractive Than You Think You Are

I hate digital cameras, because they show you exactly what you look like right when the picture is taken. This means, unlike the old ways of taking photographs, you can't say, "Wow, I looked really tired when you took this," or, "I must have been sick that night." Nope, right then and there, posing at the Carnival Cruise salad bar, a digital camera captures exactly how fat and swollen you are, and you see immediately how much less attractive you are than you think you are. A digital photo informs you that no matter how great you thought you looked when you left the house an hour ago, your assessment is not only undependable, but overwhelmingly exaggerated. Which leads me to an even more disturbing conclusion: that legitimately hot people like Megan Fox actually think they're hotter than they are. That can't be good for you (call me, Megan, and we'll discuss).

Unless You're a Biker or in the Service, You Don't Deserve a Tattoo

I used to hate tattoos. Almost as much as I used to hate people who had tattoos. But now I realize that tattoos are really helpful, for they act as an identifiable marker for people you wish to avoid. When someone gets a tribal tattoo, or something with Asian lettering, what they're really saying to you is: "Stay away from me, I am a tool, for I have never possessed an original thought in my life."

You have to admit, any tattoo that says all that is pretty impressive.

However, there are exceptions to this "all people with tattoos are idiots" rule. If you're in the military, joined a biker gang, worked as a longshoreman or a seaman and you're over fifty-four—then you've earned your tattoos. My spite is directed only at the boys and girls who work in bookstores, coffeeshops, or bookstore/coffeeshops and are covered with more ink than a pissed-off jellyfish. I hate those people. And, I might add, I also hate jelly. And fish.

Music Is Just Melodic Porn

I spend about a hundred bucks a week buying songs off iTunes—and with the exception of nude calisthenics, it might be the most enjoyable part of my day.

But, sadly, I rarely listen to any of the songs through to the end. Instead, I listen to about forty-five seconds and then jump to something else. I now listen to music the way I used to surf porn—searching for novelty, absorbing it quickly, then moving on to more novelty. I no longer listen to songs, just fragments, and I barely even listen to those anymore. It's sad.

It's strange how a delivery system that is supposed to enhance your enjoyment by making something more accessible actually has the opposite effect.

But it's true. When I was in my teens, if I wanted to listen to new music, I had to jump on my bike and ride fifteen minutes down San Mateo's El Camino to the Wherehouse and finger through the bins till I found a reasonably priced Cheap Trick record. Then I would stare at the cover for twenty minutes and wonder to myself if this record would truly change my life or just disappoint my adolescent hunger for excitement. The disappointment verged on hopelessness.

But the ritual of putting the vinyl album on the turntable and laying the needle down added a bit of effort and gravity to the whole deal, and jumping to the next song was a pain in the ass. So you listened.

Back then, with five hundred or so records in my collection, I knew every groove—even in awful records by the Knack and Mi-Sex. I devoured the music, never lifting the needle off the vinyl until a song, or a side, was finished.

Now, as a person who truly thinks he's a "music lover," I own thousands of "recordings" (a pretentious, stupid word), and I can barely listen to them. Unless, of course, I'm housecleaning or doing laundry—which is almost never. Somehow, like books and manners, music doesn't require your attention anymore.

Compare that transformation of music to the transformation of porn. Getting porn was a monumental struggle that usually negated the act of getting it. I mean, you had to vanquish the embarrassment of buying it, then you had to find a place that would sell it to you. On El Camino in San Mateo, I was thrown out of three places before I could buy an actual *Playboy*. But when you finally did get the porn, you really enjoyed that moment of self-pleasure. Five, maybe even six times, that afternoon. Hell, you earned it.

Purchasing porn wasn't even the hardest part, because then you had to hide it (you'd always put it between the mattress and the box spring—which was the first place any halfway intelligent parent would look). And then there was the guilt you experienced from indulging in it. The guilt had to be there to make all this be fun.

And so, porn in the 1970s was just like music: a commitment whose hard work made you appreciate it all the more. Now music and porn both arrive as soon as your synapses decide you require it. And you have no use for either, after a few minutes. It's the death of our attention span: a thing so depressing it makes oh look at that waterbug! There's a waterbug running across my kitchen!

But Then Again: Nostalgia Sucks

Whenever I return to sunny San Mateo, I find myself in an orgy of nostalgia, rummaging through my mind and finding all the things I suddenly loved about growing up in the Bay Area that in reality I probably hated during that time.

That's the trick of nostalgia—making you think you liked the crap that you actually hated growing up.

The fact is: None of the stuff in the past was any good. It all sucked. Stuff is better now.

Living in the past while you're alive in the present is knowingly sacrificing time from your life. You're essentially just killing yourself.

Thing is: When you're a kid you just aren't paying attention to the very things that you think you're missing now. Just like adults: When I'm eighty, I'm going to get wistful remembering T.G.I. Friday's—a place I never liked, ever. But as you get older, you look back, and you apply some misdirected charm to something that really was nothing more than a more primitive, crappier version of all the great stuff you have now.

And for what it's worth, one theory holds that you remember past events more positively than reality as a form of functional amnesia—so if you're faced with the prospect of repeating a horrid experience, you won't kill yourself.

Which is probably true. It explains why so many people remarry.

Attractive Stalkers Are Called Groupies

Pity the stalker. Powerless, anonymous, and often unattractive, fate has dealt them an unfortunate hand. I'm always troubled by the cruel, thoughtless humor directed at these poor souls, mainly because stalking is something everyone does, to varying degrees. And the only reason some people get away with it, while others don't, comes down to looks. If you're a hot woman, you're never a stalker—you're an "avid fan." If you're someone who likes to venture "backstage," and you've got big tits, then that's not stalking—that's the band's dinner.

And if you're a successful man, stalking is actually called "courting." Or used to be, back when Henry Fonda was president.

I only bring this crap up after reading that Joan Cusack's older sister, John, has filed a restraining order against a homeless woman who he claims thinks she lives with him. Her awesome name is Emily Leatherman, and she's made more than a few visits to his home, causing a lot of pain and suffering for Cusack—who, if you remember from the movie *Say Anything*, stood outside Ione Skye's bedroom window while holding a boom box over his head. If that's not stalking, then I'm torching the voodoo doll I made of Anderson Cooper out of discarded toenails. (Besides, these days, Cusack can use all the stalkers he can get.)

It's horribly unfair, the line that's drawn between "admirers" and "stalkers," a line that distinguishes between the peacock trickery of a glamorous groupie and the disarming honesty of a soiled psychopath. This intolerance makes me sick to my stomach. If anything, people who are fat or unattractive have to try harder to gain the affections of the world's most alluring celebrities, and hindering them with pesky restraining orders seems a targeted act of bigotry. I believe that these so-called "stalkers" should be encouraged to pursue their romantic quest for acceptance and love. And they should also be armed with tasers and duct tape in case the object of their affection resists.

But this is just my opinion, and it doesn't reflect the beliefs of anyone else, except possibly my stalkers, which, as it stands, is just me.

Identical Twins Aren't Really Two People

First let's examine the science (which required me surfing Wikipedia on the toilet): Identical twins happen when a single egg is fertilized to create one zygote, which then splits into two separate embryos. Clearly this means that twins were originally one person, split into two half-people.

This explains a number of interesting commonalities among twins:

- There is usually a good twin and a bad twin, just as every single human individual has a good side and a bad side. But twins are like hopscotch ice cream—one is made of good, happy chocolate, the other is evil, evil vanilla. This theory has been validated in every movie featuring twins. Which is why the bad twin always has to die, usually at a party featuring large amounts of ice cream.
- Twins often pretend to be each other, especially in situations involving double dates, where one has to hide in a closet or behind a tree, while the other assumes that hiding twin's identity. If I had a dollar for every twin that has switched with the other twin in order to have sex with me, I would be a very rich man (if by "rich," you mean "poor").
- Twins dress the same. Parents start this practice young, often forcing these nonpeople to wear the same striped shirts and shorts to picnics, church, and church picnics. This is the parents' way of saying: GOD, I WISH YOU WERE ONE PERSON.
- Twins are creepy as hell. They prove that we're no miracle; instead we're a product of a software program that spits out duplicates at will. Weren't twins punished way back when for being twins? If not, perhaps we should consider a constitutional amendment, which I believe is almost like a law or something.

- When a twin is not with the other twin, she likes to tell you that she has a twin. The appropriate answer, always, is, "Well I hope she's the cute one."

While we're on the topic of twins, can we please stop photographing conjoined twins? Frankly it only encourages them. I apologize if I'm offending my loyal conjoined twin readership (my apologies, Chang and Eng), but they all freak me out. Whenever I look at them, I get that weird tingly feeling inside me. Does anyone know the medical name for that creepy tingling you get when you think about something that makes you squeamish? (Please don't tell me it's polio.)

Other things that make me feel squeamish:

- Sticking my finger in my belly button.
- Rubbing two balloons together.
- That soft part of a baby's head, the name of which I cannot remember.
- When someone tells me about a skin condition he has, and it is something I don't already have.
- Old people sitting down slowly (I always wait to hear cracking noises).
- Preoperative transgendered sex workers pretending they don't have a deep voice, when it's clear they do.
- Preoperative transgendered sex workers pretending they didn't steal your wallet, when you know they did—but you can't confront them, because you're afraid you'll be wrong, or that possibly he/she will beat the crap out of you.
- Small children with melted ice cream on their hands.
- Anyone from King of Prussia, Pennsylvania.
- Anywhere Rosie experiences chafing.

Hobbies Were Invented to Keep Your Mind off Drinking

Right now one of my good friends is at a museum. And get this, he's a guy. It's hard to believe that when a man has a full day with nothing to do, he'd go to a place to look at objects that aren't in orange shorts serving you hot wings.

But the reason he's at the museum—and the reason he's going to an art exhibit tomorrow—is that he quit drinking. And he doesn't know what to do with himself.

And that brings up a fundamental point about our civilization that no one seems to recognize. Hobbies, diversions, and anything else you do to make you feel civilized were invented only to put off drinking. The ultimate example: anyone who spends hours trying to construct ships in a bottle. There's a man who's dying to have a scotch on the rocks—but can't. He's simply exchanged one bottle for another. Without hobbies, when they weren't working, men would be drunk all the time.

The only exception to this "hobby puts off drinking" truth is go-karts. If men were allowed to drive go-karts all day without the accusation of looking silly, we would gladly trade that in for drinking. I, for one, would never have another drop if I knew I could take a go-kart wherever I pleased. Until that happens, I will remain at all times drunk.

No One Sees UFOs in Big Cities

Here's how it works. Those who see UFOs will always tell you about them. And when they tell you about them, they might also reveal that they have chronic fatigue syndrome, think 9/11 was an inside job, and believe Elton John is a manatee (I'm with them on the last point). The fact is, people obsessed with UFOs will believe in just about anything. They embrace conspiracy theories as easily as they advocate amino acids or astrology (FYI: I am a Virgo, but you could already tell by my emotional intelligence and anal qualities). These people are not harmless. They are intellectual terrorists, here to erase intelligent thought and replace it with things that masquerade as thinking but aren't.

I only bring this up because recently in Stephenville, Texas (note: Never trust anyone from a town that adds "ville" to a man's first name), a dozen or so people reported seeing a large silent object with bright lights flying low and fast in their neighborhood. They're calling it a UFO, while others might call it a plane.

The alarming fact of the matter: No one ever sees alien space-craft in big cities or places where there's fine dining, good shopping, and at least four decent gay bars. Sightings of strange flying objects only occur in small towns, where there is little else to do but hope and pray for an anal probing. There are worse things to pray for, by the by.

This is not an insult.

Small towns are great because it's quiet and the beer is cheap—two factors that allow for wishful thinking. See, to me UFOs are the small-city version of big-city recycling. Because although I'm sure recycling exists, I've never seen it. Seems like it all goes into one bin.

It's not that I don't believe in UFOs. It's just that I have enough problems with things I *can* identify. I don't need the unknown to complicate matters. I see things every day that are all too real, and horrifying. But, then again, I do live with a large clan of black bears, so go figure.

Stephen Hawking Isn't That Smart

Sorry, folks—I love the guy, but if he wasn't disabled, no one would give a labradoodle about the dude. Recently, for example, the so-called genius claimed that the survival of the human race depends on its ability to find new homes elsewhere in the universe. That's because, the genius claims, there's an increasing risk that a disaster will destroy earth. We should probably move to the moon, he adds.

This kind of pronouncement is what you call the "ominous genius pronouncement," something intellectuals are obliged to say every three years in order to stay relevant. But, in terms of common sense, it does not mean jack. There's nothing we can do about it, and no way that we can prove it's true—so the statement only exists to remind us how important and untouchable Stephen Hawking is. My guess is, he likes making these pronouncements about the same time his book sales start flagging (A *Brief History of Time* remains the most bought book that's never been read).

FYI, here are some other facts about Stephen Hawking that I bet you didn't know:

- He ranks third in the world in telling people mindblowing shit.
- He can cook an entire seven-course meal using nothing but the tools in his wheelchair. It takes him two days.
- In 1987 the scientist was accused of shoplifting an entire canned ham from an Albertson's in San Mateo, California. The matter is now closed in a sealed court document.
- Was secretly cured of his affliction back in 1972, but has been faking it ever since.
- Predicted the exact date and time of Dom DeLuise's death, based on a mathematical formula derived from the *Match Game* theme.

Toilet Paper Doesn't Do the Job

That's all I'm saying on that front.

Never Trust a Bongo Player

Recently I read about a so-called musician who got very sick from anthrax—because the bongo drums he owned were made from imported animal skins that may have harbored the disease. I am sure, somewhere on the planet, this was seen as a tragedy. But I see it differently. Of all the percussive instruments, the bongos are the least appealing and most annoying. The fact is, you do not have to know how to play bongos in order to play bongos. It's not a musical instrument: Rather, it's a device designed to get girls to stare at you. They are slightly below the tambourine or maracas on the "I'm untalented but onstage" scale.

Want to impress me? Bang on some animal skins while the animal's still in them. Let's see you accompany your poetry slam while whacking a live rhino. Now *that's* talent!

Worse, bongos always make me think of Maynard G. Krebs, the beatnik played by Bob Denver in *Dobie Gillis*. And, sadly, whenever I think of Bob Denver, I think of Cindy Sheehan.

And when I think of Cindy Sheehan, I think of Paul Hogan.

And when I think of Paul Hogan, I think of Bob Denver.

And then it starts all over again.

This is why I hate bongos.

Chinese Music Sounds Chinese

I have no idea if it's true or not, but according to some very strange farmers, cows tend to "moo" in regional accents. It's very interesting that these lumbering, lazy beasts only say one word, but even that word is affected by where the fat beast says it. According to one article, "herds in the west country" moo with a "distinctive Somerset twang," which means they sound a lot like Gwyneth Paltrow in *Emma*.

"Actually, people say I sound more like Kevin Costner in *Robin Hood: Prince of Thieves*," says one cow.

Shut up, cow!

Ugh. Very distracting.

But this brings me to a far more important point: I never understood the concept of accents. I just don't get how where you live affects the way you speak. I also don't understand how the variations in music across different cultures can so accurately reflect the culture the music is from. For example, when I hear music in an Indian restaurant, somehow, in my brain, I know it's from India. It just sounds Indian. The same thing occurs when I hear Chinese music in a Chinese restaurant. I just know it's Chinese. This, however, never happens when I dine at Bennigan's. Perhaps because at Bennigan's, they only play Three Doors Down.

I hate Three Doors Down.

And I know what you're going to say in response to my musical meanderings: "Well, it's because from an early age, you've been trained to link specific types of music to its cultural origins."

I don't buy that. I didn't start eating out until I was fifteen. And yet, when I hear the Mexican Hat Dance, I can't help but think of tacos.

And Erik Estrada.

But I find myself thinking of Erik Estrada often—with or without music.

Outrage Lasts As Long As It Takes You to Think About Something Else

Here's how the cycle of outrage begins:

- A horrific crime is reported in the papers. It involves an innocent victim attacked by thugs.

- The papers spend a few weeks on the story, sparking legitimate outrage—often citing earlier examples of bad deeds gone unpunished.
- The thugs are captured. The police are applauded. Tabloid editorials will scream for mandatory life sentences.
- A new season of 24 begins. It's fantastic.
- Spring training gets under way. Apparently this is some kind of sports tournament.
- Some starlet announces she wants to have twins. But only for a week.
- A politician announces that the nation's youth are too fat. This sparks debate on the problems of teenage obesity, which only makes everyone bored...and hungry. Four months later, the thugs are sentenced. They are light sentences, but we've moved on.
- Six months later, one of the thugs gets out and bludgeons a granny with a log.
- And the cycle begins again—just in time for a new season of 24!

In the end, a criminal act may leave a lasting impression on the victim (especially if that victim is DOA), but it has a short shelf life in the public brain. This is why it's so easy for criminals to continue to be released, and then repeat their crimes.

It makes you wonder: If there was only a way to keep an actual record of people who do bad things, and then put them in a secure place where they couldn't harm anyone!

I can dream.

A Tragedy That's Mistaken As "Part of the Act" Means You Shouldn't Be Performing Said Act

In front of about a hundred people in a village in western Ireland, a clown acrobat with the Royal Russian Circus was somehow crushed to death after a circus stunt went awry. More important, people in the audience initially thought the accident—involving a falling cage—was part of the act.

This reminds me of a book idea I had while I was drunk. It was called *Part of the Act*, the contents being a catalogue of tragedies that had occurred during a performance that were initially mistaken as "part of the act."

I came up with a long list, including:

- The time William Burroughs shot his wife in the head. That was not part of the act.
- When the helicoptor blade sheared off Vic Morrow's head. That was also not part of the act.
- When I was nine and Santa made me sit on his lap and try to find the candy cane in his pocket. I don't think that was part of the act.

But I did it anyway.

And I got two candy canes!

Anyway, if you are involved in any kind of work in which your death could be seen as part of the act, you should get out of that line of work immediately. Find something else where grievous injury would look very out of place. That eliminates any or all circus acts, stunts involving explosives or jumping cars, weird shows involving animals, and being me.

Concluding Thoughts About This and That

This is the part of the book where I wrap everything up into a tidy package, one that summarizes my intended goal, and bid you adieu (a French, or possibly Italian word) armed with cozy feelings and a newfound respect for your own gut instinct. And that's the only purpose for this book, really (besides paying for my medical treatments—I won't get into this here, but they're experimental and I'm hoping they work better than the apparatus I bought in China-town): to validate your own awesome assumptions about the world and make you confident that you instinctively know what's best. Because you do!

I thank you for reading, and I also hope that you continue reading my rants, wherever they turn up!